"This is a very well-written, erudite and thought-provoking book. It addresses one of the most central and least understood aspects of organisational change—time. We know from our own experience that change is iterative, rarely proceeds in a linear fashion and that our perception of time is not constant. Yet we still persist in planning and managing change by the clock and the calendar. By challenging conventional views of time, this book makes a major contribution to our understanding of change."
—Bernard Burnes, University of Stirling, Scotland

"Time and temporality are integral to processes of change, storytelling and sensemaking yet remain surprisingly absent from mainstream studies. This book usefully examines how time is conceptualized in science, social science and philosophy and then through a broad review of the literatures associated with organizational change provides profound insights on their explicit and implicit use in concept development and theorization. In an excellent chapter on narrative time and stories in making sense of change the authors shed some much needed light on an otherwise neglected topic. Patrick Dawson and Christopher Sykes are to be commended for this insightful and valuable addition to the organization studies canon."
—Andrew D. Brown, University of Bath, UK

"This book offers a brilliant analysis of the concept of time in relation to the study of organizational change. Lucid and thought-provoking, it provides much needed insight into the philosophy, psychology and sociology of time and temporality. Most of all, it offers a deep social scientific appreciation of issues of temporal process and multiplicity. Essential reading for those seeking a rich understanding of the nature of time in contemporary society."
—John Hassard, University of Manchester, UK

Organizational Change and Temporality

Organizational Change and Temporality: Bending the Arrow of Time looks to address the important area of time and temporality, especially as it relates to frameworks and studies for explaining change processes in organizations. It commences with a selective history on the science and philosophy of time before examining the place of time in work and employment and the presence and absence of theorized time in explanations of organizational change. The intention is to bring to the fore concepts and debates that have largely remained hidden, furthering our knowledge and understanding of time and temporality in changing organizations.

The authors provide a more informed theoretical explanation of the temporal dimensions of organizational change. They examine the concepts and debates behind change theories, philosophical positions and scientific concerns on time and material existence, drawing connections that have previously remained unexplored. This book is key reading for researchers within the organizational change world and will further the academic debate of time and temporality in organization studies.

Patrick Dawson is an emeritus professor at the University of Aberdeen, Scotland, and an honorary professorial fellow at Wollongong University, Australia.

Christopher Sykes is a senior lecturer in the School of Management Operations and Marketing at the University of Wollongong, Australia.

Routledge Studies in Organizational Change & Development

Series Editor:
Bernard Burnes

For a full list of titles in this series, please visit www.routledge.com

Organizational Change and Temporality

Bending the Arrow of Time

Patrick Dawson and Christopher Sykes

Routledge
Taylor & Francis Group

LONDON AND NEW YORK

First published 2016 by Routledge

2 Park Square, Milton Park, Abingdon, Oxfordshire OX14 4RN
52 Vanderbilt Avenue, New York, NY 10017

Routledge is an imprint of the Taylor & Francis Group, an informa business

First issued in paperback 2018

Library of Congress Cataloging-in-Publication Data
Names: Dawson, Patrick, author. | Sykes, Christopher S., author.
Title: Organizational change and temporality : bending the arrow
    of time / by Patrick Dawson and Christopher Sykes.
Description: New York : Routledge, 2016. | Series: Routledge
    studies in organizational change & development ; 15 | Includes
    bibliographical references and index.
Identifiers: LCCN 2015050446 | ISBN 9781138801226 (cloth)
    | ISBN 9781315755076 (ebook)
Subjects: LCSH: Organizational change. | Organizational behavior. |
    Time—Sociological aspects. | Time—Psychological aspects.
Classification: LCC HD58.8 .D3925 2016 | DDC 658.4/06—dc23
LC record available at http://lccn.loc.gov/2015050446

ISBN: 978-1-138-80122-6 (hbk)
ISBN: 978-1-138-62406-1 (pbk)

Typeset in Sabon
by Apex CoVantage, LLC

To Stephen Massey
and
Stanley and Margaret Sykes

Contents

About the Authors

Patrick Dawson is an emeritus professor at the University of Aberdeen, Scotland. He holds a PhD in industrial sociology from the University of Southampton and during his early career worked at the University of Surrey and the University of Edinburgh. He moved to Australia in the 1980s and took up a position at the University of Adelaide before returning to Scotland in 1997.

In studying change in UK, Australian, and New Zealand-based organizations, Patrick has worked on a number of Australian Research Council (ARC) and Economic and Social Research Council (ESRC)-funded projects in collaboration with scholars at other universities. He has examined change in a number of organizations including: Pirelli Cables, BHP Billiton, Royal Dutch Shell, British Rail, Aberdeen Asset Management, British Aerospace, Laubman and Pank, General Motors, Hewlett Packard, Central Linen Services, State Bank of South Australia, Illawarra Retirement Trust, TNT, and the CSIRO.

Patrick has held visiting professorships at Roskilde University and the Danish Technical University in Denmark, an adjunct professorship at Monash University, and a professorial fellowship at the University of Wollongong in Australia. He is currently researching time, affect, storytelling, and change through engagement in a number of collaborative projects in the UK and Australia.

Christopher Sykes is a senior lecturer at the University of Wollongong, Australia. He has a PhD in business and economics from the University of Sydney and has worked as an academic at the Universities of Sydney, Western Sydney, and over the last seven years, Wollongong. Prior to his academic career, Chris worked in the not-for-profit sector in various managerial roles. His research is informed by practice and process theories in examining areas of change and learning in organizations. He is experienced in the use of a range of qualitative methodologies, including collaborative and participative action research and ethnography, that require use of ethnographic methods such as various forms of interviewing and observation. His research has appeared in journals such as: *Organization Studies*; *Journal of Organizational Change Management*; *Studies in Higher Education*; and *Continuing Studies in Higher Education*.

Acknowledgments

We would like to acknowledge the dialogue and conversations we have had with fellow academics at a range of conferences including: Seventh International Symposium of Process Organization Studies, 'The Temporal Experience of Organizing' at the 31st EGOS Colloquium, British Academy of Management 29th Annual Conference, and 29th Australian and New Zealand Academy of Management Conference. There has been a wide range of discussions with alas more people than we could ever possibly remember to list here, but we would like to thank: Michael Zanko, Peter McLean, Lorna McKee, Julian Randall, Ian McLoughlin, David Preece, Mats Alvesson, Tor Hernes, Barbara Simpson, Kristian Wasen, Robin Dawson, Stephen Vorley, Lynne Keevers, Jinqi Xu, Heather Marciano, Richard Owens, Elden Wiebe, and Alexandre Schwob.

We would like to give special acknowledgment and appreciation for the feedback and comments made on specific chapters of the book by the following: David Buchanan, Bernard Burnes, Stuart Clegg, John Hassard, Karolina Kazimierczak, David Knights, Paul Luff, Darren McCabe, Ian McLoughlin, Zoe Morrison, Özgü Karakulak, Andrew Brown, Yannis Gabriel, David Boje, Simon Ville, Ian Buchanan, Mark Dibben, and Melissa Errey.

We would also like to thank our publisher, Routledge, especially Briana Ascher, David Varley, and Manjula Raman for steering the manuscript along the road to publication, Nabi Zaher for his comments and work on compiling the index, and the anonymous reviewers for their useful thoughts and feedback on how to further improve the manuscript.

Part I

Laying the Foundations

Time and Temporality

1 Introduction

Our sensory perception of space and time is often viewed as changeable in being relative to our frame of reference, and yet, we cannot see, touch, feel, or hear time. Perhaps our sense of time is illusory, and time does not exist as anything other than a social construction. But time may also be understood as all pervasive, immovable, and absolute, existing outside our external observations of movement. Questions abound on the existence of time; for example, if time is relational to matter, how can time exist within a vacuum, where distances between objects or events cannot be measured? Is time temporal with a past, present, and future, or is it a continually reconstituted 'now'? Do the past and future exist in the same way that the present is said to? Is the arrow of time bendable? There are a host of questions, but for people in society, concerns are generally more grounded in life experiences where perceptions of temporality are, and always will be, integral to understanding and making sense of their existence within the world whether or not time exists.

Time is a concept with which we are all familiar; a term that we use every day, it shadows life experiences and acts as a calendar for marking intervals and events as well as a lens for recalling memories and projecting futures, and yet, it is also something apart, untouchable, and unseen. The scientific arrow of time is a powerful concept for explaining the place of the world in the universe, entropy, and the nature of human existence. It captures the compelling idea of progressive movement as the universe expands towards some distant event and as people move ever forward on their life's journeys from cradle to grave. It promotes notions of time in which the past is determinant (it has happened and cannot be changed), where the future is full of indeterminate potentialities (it has not yet happened so has not yet come into being), and in which the present is simply a series of now moments (which at one time was a future possibility and soon will be a past moment that cannot be changed). The arrow of time does not however usefully explain human temporal engagement, feelings of timelessness, and the way our experiences of the present are shaped by our expectations of the future and our interpretations of the past (that change over time). The more conventional distinctions and conceptions of time, such as the arrow of time, are increasingly being questioned both in the scientific world of quantum mechanics and among social scientists, including organizational scholars, especially those who draw on the philosophical world of process theorists. For example, Hernes (2014) argues that there has been considerable complacency with regard to time and little if any attention given to the implications of time for the experience of organizing, whereas Dawson (2015) claims that research on time in organizational studies has been rather sporadic, thinly spread, and dominated by considerations of clock time, asking the rhetorical question: 'Does it matter if clocks can tell us the time but not what time is?'

In addressing this situation we set out to embark on a broad yet selective journey into a variety of time perspectives from branches of science and disciplines in social science. Science in the study of inanimate and animate objects, social science in the study of meaning and human consciousness, and philosophy in the study of reality, knowledge, and existence, all need to be considered in our examination of time for organization studies. In this book we advocate a view of time and temporality that embraces multidirectional non-linear temporal flows whilst also recognising the importance of more traditional conceptions of time in shaping human behaviour. We identify and address a number of emerging issues and pertinent debates that increasingly take centre stage as scholars seek to make sense of the world in which we live. Our principal focus is on organizational change and temporality, which provide both a structure and a lens through which to selectively examine contributions on time to our understanding of change processes in organizations.

Whereas there has been some interest in time and organizations, these have been rather sporadic and thinly spread, and for these reasons, we would support the claim by Hernes (2014) that time and temporality in organization studies are areas that warrant further conceptual and theoretical exploration. As a dimension of organizational change, it is often assumed to be self-evident; it is rarely explained and often underplayed. Simple progressive notions of time pervade research in this area, but these ideas are never fully articulated and often act as implicit notions underpinning models and frameworks that seek to explain the nature of organizational change. Those who view change as emergent or represent change as a punctuated shift in an otherwise stable equilibrium all draw on elements of time as an unfolding tapestry or as noticeable episodes of disruption to an otherwise orderly balance of forces. Time is a vital, an ineluctable component to understanding change, and yet it is rarely unmasked, examined, and theorized. When attention is turned to the paradox of time, long-standing problems of how to explain time gain intellectual momentum, making what appears as common sense complicated and difficult to explicate through language. On this count, the German sociologist Norbert Elias (1897–1990) conceived time as the supreme puzzle that stimulates the inevitable search for solutions, arguing that such hunts ultimately prove to be a 'wild-goose chase' for something that we are unable to touch, taste, see, or hear (Elias, 1993: 123). Perhaps this goes some way to explaining the relatively small number of studies and commentaries on time in organization studies, but it does not negate the need for a more thorough investigation, and this is what our book sets out to accomplish.

Dualism: Objective and Subjective Time

There are a range of time perspectives that arise and are discussed throughout this book, but at this early stage, it is worth making some initial comments on the distinction that is often made between objective forms of time and subjective experiences of time. Objective time is often characterized by the clock, either as a stand-alone material object (a wall clock or watch) or as embedded in a raft of electronic and mobile devices most of us use on a regular basis. It is this image of clock time then tends to predominate within the modern industrial world. At any moment the clock provides us with a specific and understandable 'time' that we can also use to separate and differentiate from the time that has elapsed and the time that the clock is progressing towards. People use this clock time as a measure of time to schedule and regulate their work tasks, social events, and home activities. Atomic clocks enable the synchronization of precise intervals in the coordination of local sporting activities through to world events and the scheduling and monitoring of, for example, international flights as people travel across the International Date Line (IDL). Different time zones are all controlled by a world clock based on Greenwich Mean Time (GMT), which provides an absolute time reference for human activities on earth. The standardization and formulation of time through the development of early measurement systems through to the atomic clock have enabled interval mapping of geological developments and chronologies of human history as well as providing practical support in space project initiatives, interplanetary travel, and scientific investigations. Yet whilst we can register the life cycle of our existence from birth to death in measured intervals, objective (clock) time ultimately fails to tell us about the meaning of time for our own existence. There is often a misalignment, for example, in the way that we experience time duration with time scientifically measured. In other words, the more existential and subjective elements of time are not fully captured or even usefully explained by precisely measured intervals.

If the clock represents and characterizes time as standard measurable intervals (objective time), then what should we use to capture our subjective experiences of time where, for example, our engagement in an activity can affect our sense of time's passage? In this we need to turn our attention to consciousness and being, to the introspective realm of our individual existence, as well as to those experiences grounded in social practices that are interactively and intersubjectively constituted. Our intimate encounters with time are marked by tangible moments, by extended, physical, time-pressured activities in, for example, a team sporting competition, and in forms of time-less immersion that provide a disconnect from external reality.

Time can be viewed as both real and ephemeral. It is on the one hand easily recognised and understood and, on the other, untouchable and mysterious, tending to slip away from the edge of understanding as we try to explain what time is. It is a paradox: known in being unknown, an abstract concept, a subjective experience, an objective interval that is made scientifically useful through the Gregorian calendar and the atomic clock. The way time is differentially experienced does not prevent the collective social acceptance and use of reified time in the planning and coordination of work and leisure activities. Nor does this render time as an abstraction any more real, rather it creates a divide in which we can, through language, compare and contrast objective and subjective forms of time, whilst in life we move seamlessly between multiple temporal worlds.

Although the dualism represented by objective and subjective time is a boundary construct, the division is important for three main reasons. First, the concept of objective time is useful in examining the growth of commerce and industrial organization and the importance of clock time to the development of organizations and innovations in management. Second, the construct has been used extensively to inform the development of theories for organizational change and acts to shape organizational discourse and formal rational narratives that are in turn used to prescribe best practice stage models for managing organizational change. Third, the mismatch between objective and subjective time is often used to explain change phenomena associated with, for example, polyvocality, sensemaking, resistance, and politics. But this artificial division can also misdirect in moving beyond a useful explanatory category to a characterization of the way life 'really' is.

In developing our own perspective on organizational change and temporality, we highlight the importance of multiple temporalities in the way that individuals and groups accommodate different conceptions of time in giving and making senses of their experiences of change in organizations and the interplay and interpenetration of objective and subjective time. Although the divisional construct seeks to reinforce a more clearly delineated, separatist world, we contend that the two coexist in relation to each other and as such are mutually constituted in everyday life. We also advocate that too much attention has been placed on the objective dimensions of time in theoretical explanations and especially on models and concepts that attempt to master, control, and predict change. We contend that even within frameworks that have been less prescriptive, these elements have crept in with a tendency to overemphasise objective forms of time and to downplay the more subjective experiential dimensions. We aim to counter this tendency in a more thorough examination of time and organizational change especially: as it relates to subjective time; in examining the use of objective time in change models; through considering the relationship of objective and subjective time as separate, identifiable elements (divisional construct) and as mutually constituting (relational); and more generally, in exploring the concept of temporality in relation to the complex processes of organizational change.

Main Aims of the Book

As process researchers we are interested in the history of cultural practices and the way that they unfold and are shaped and shape how we live and experience time as part of our physical and existential existence. Although our main concern is with organization studies and models of change, we also intend to step outside of our mainstream discipline to draw on concepts and ideas from major philosophical and scientific thinkers and then to bring these back in to our critique and analyses of the use of time in formulating explanations of organizational change. Two aspects about time and temporality that we have already discussed and that we find particularly striking are: first, the way that individuals and groups appear to move seamlessly between time as experienced and time as measured, and yet as scholars, we find it immensely difficult to explain this complex interplay of time; and second, how theories of organizational change often take a simple progressive view of time (linear temporality) in which many aspects of time are ignored or simply taken for granted. This once again points to the need for further research, conceptual refinement, and theoretical discussion, as Roe and colleagues note (Roe, Waller, & Clegg, 2009: 1):

> One might think that the temporal aspects of everyday human life would saturate the field of management and organization theory but, instead, one is more likely to find that it is relatively timeless knowledge which fills our textbooks and journals.

Our book sets out to address these gaps in our knowledge and understanding with a particular focus on the way they relate to frameworks and studies for explaining change processes in organizations. Our five key aims can be summarized as follows:

1. To cover an important gap that we have identified in the field of organization studies, namely, how time and dimensions of temporality relate to explanations (models and frameworks) of organizational change. Our intention is to unpack the implicit concepts of time that underpin the main theories of organizational change and then to critically evaluate and comment upon these perspectives to provide a more informed theoretical explanation of the temporal dimensions of organizational change.
2. To explore how time has become institutionalized, objectified, and taken for granted in the way that work is managed and controlled in

organizations whilst also providing a more explicit and thorough under-standing of subjective notions of time and how subjective temporalities relate to the way that people experience and make sense of change in organizations.

3. To investigate and provide a more robust explanation of the appar-ently seamless movement between objective and subjective forms of time exhibited in workplace behaviours and to uncover the ways that power shapes structures and meaning making as these are played out in the social and political exigencies evident in everyday prac-tices (that are paradoxically very difficult to capture and explain in language).

4. To examine the relationship between objective time and conventional views of change as a naturally occurring (forward) progression (as captured in the concept of the arrow of time) and subjective tempo-ral experience. We seek to clarify this relationship both as separate categories of time that provides analytical support and informs theo-rization (yet in presenting this division encounters the predicament of dualism) and as interpenetrating mutually constituting facets of time (a relational view in which the multiplicities of time exist in relation to each other).

5. To clarify and refine process perspectives to enable greater insight across the field in broadening our understanding of time, temporality, and change and, in so doing, contribute to further conceptualization, theori-zation, and practice.

In approaching these aims we cover a range of perspectives, themes, and debates in and around organization studies. In our focus on organizational change and temporality, the objective/subjective divide is useful, but as already indicated, this boundary construction does not fully explain time and can, if used as a time map, inadvertently constrain and limit discus-sion and investigation into time, temporality, and organizational change. Whereas we use notions of objective clock time and subjectively experienced time to examine and evaluate different approaches to organizational change, we are also interested in the interplay and interweaving of time dimensions and the broader ideas, concepts, and debates that have arisen as scientists, philosophers, and informed commentators grapple with notions of time, temporality, and the nature of existence.

Structure of the Book

The three chapters that follow provide a brief history of concepts and debates on time in the sciences and the social sciences. From the early work of Aris-totle, who argued that there is an intimate connection between time and space in which material objects exist (i.e., all objects simultaneously exist in both space and time), to the philosophy of Bergson (1913), McTaggart

(1993), and Whitehead (1929) and the science of Barbour (2000) and Hawking (2011). In Chapters 2 and 3 we selectively explore theories and perspectives on time from branches of science, philosophy, psychology, sociology, and organization studies. We show how these debates have often played out around an objective/subjective dualism, and in Chapter 2, the distinction between material place and movement and our conscious understanding of time (using internal and external notions of time) are explored. Questions about temporality and the very existence of time (tensed and untensed conceptions of time) from the absolutist argument of Newton (2014) through to the relativity of Einstein (Lorentz, 2008) and notions of the multiverse (see Frank, 2012: 287–293) are summarized, and their contribution to our understanding of time is appraised. Individual time perspectives and time as an essentially social phenomenon are examined in Chapter 3, and the general absence of broader time awareness in models and theories developed in organization studies is called into question. The paradox of time, dualism, and the problem of theorization are then revisited in considering aspects of social and material time (an issue that resurfaces on many occasions in our exposition of time and temporality) and their implications for knowledge development. The main intention of these two chapters is to provide the reader with an easily accessible account of some of the main theories and concepts of time in science and social science that are drawn upon and used in organization studies and continue to stimulate critical discussions that can inform theorization in the field of organizational change.

Chapter 4 turns attention towards industrial forms of organizations and charts how developments in the organization and control of work have reified and institutionalized time in organizations. Time is often accepted as something that 'is' without conscious thought; it is ever present, intuitively understood, yet missing in action through the use of conventional assumptions that are rooted to the time discipline of industrial capitalism captured in the clock and the calendar and so well illustrated by Charlie Chaplin in *Modern Times* (Chaplin, 1936) and the classic article by E. P. Thompson (1967). This reification of time into something that can be measured and categorized (quantitative temporality) is pervasive in organizations where linear notions of clock time have become embedded and deeply sedimented in the way workdays are measured, divided, and planned through to the strong associations between time and money. In this chapter, the development of the modern conception of work time is discussed through an examination of work and employment from ancient times to the present day.

Chapter 5 examines episodic time in sequencing organizational change. It covers n-step models of change including the two well-known change models associated with Lewin's (1947, 2009) three-phase model comprising unfreeze, change, and refreeze and the punctuated equilibrium model of change (see Romanelli & Tushman, 1994; Tushman & Romanelli, 2012). Key to these models is the notion of inertia and the consequent forces that are needed to stimulate movement and change. For Lewin, it is about breaking out of a quasi-stationary equilibrium through changing the set of dynamic forces that maintain stasis. These models hold onto very linear conceptions of time in moving from position T1 (that represents a present state that requires fixing), through a transition state (implementation of change that represents movement over time), to position T2 (that represents the new, desired state). Once the organization has achieved the planned change through a prescribed sequence of events and activities, then, attention is given to ensuring that the new system of operation is 'frozen' into place to prevent further changes occurring. This is seen to be particularly important in preventing the system reverting to a pre-change stage. In this example, the temporality of change is characterized as a progression from a redundant system to a new superior system that needs to be firmly anchored within a different set of behavioural norms. Time is compartmentalized into a series of episodes that can be structured and managed in an orderly fashion.

Sociomaterial time in networks and technologies, and as characterized by the concept of entanglement in the continual reconstitution of being and matter, is discussed in Chapter 6. This interesting turn in organization studies and, in particular, studies of technology and information systems (IS) has arisen from an interest in quantum mechanics following the work of Karen Barad (2003, 2007) and the publication of *Meeting the Universe Halfway: Quantum Physics and the Entanglement of Matter and Meaning* (Barad, 2007). In this perspective—that rejects technological determinism, questions conceptualizations that separate the social and the technical, and acts as a corrective to social determinism (i.e., those studies that advocate that everything is socially constructed)—ideas presented in Actor Network Theory (ANT) are built upon in forwarding the notion that the social and the material are 'entangled' and continually reconstituted in practice. The essential argument is that there is a need to observe things as they happen or in 'performance'. Although there is considerable debate within this approach, many scholars advocate the use of a practice lens in studying work practices as they occur (see Orlikowski, 2007, 2010). However, 'problems' have been identified with Barad's broader positioning (promotion of agential realism) in which she argues that the entanglement of ideas and materials cannot be understood by reflexive representational methodologies but, rather, require a diffractive methodology that enables a more performative account. Some of the 'practice' problems for studying sociomateriality that arise from this have been highlighted by Leonardi (2013: 66) and Mutch (2013). On the question of time, Mutch (2013: 32) notes how the role of time is ignored in 'producing particular constellations of position-practices that emerge from the activity of persons'. Both Leonardi (2013) and Mutch (2013) argue for the replacement of agential realism with critical realism in accommodating agency and structure and recognising the importance of time in the study of sociomateriality. This chapter examines how time is present, hidden, or absent in sociomaterial studies that attempt to provide an alternative lens for examining change.

Chapter 7 then examines political time as an instrument of dominance and power. This chapter extends some of the concepts and ideas presented in Chapter 4 in looking more closely at the use of time as a way of controlling and regulating the behaviour of people in organizations. Writers in critical management studies (see Alvesson, Bridgman, & Willmott, 2011), such as McCabe (2007), Knights and Willmott (2000), Alvesson and Spicer (2012), as well as those concerned with power in organizations, including Hardy (1996) and Clegg and Haugaard (2013), and writers who have developed political models for explaining change processes in organizations, for example, Buchanan and Badham (2008), Pettigrew (1973), are all examined. The way time is used to structure and regulate routines (forms of continuity) and to introduce new methods of monitoring performance and ways of working (change) whilst reaffirming authority and power relations (e.g., in reinforcing the managerial prerogative of managers to manage which entails using their power to get workers to change in ways that they would rather not) are all discussed.

From the narrative turn in the social sciences (see, e.g., Butler, 1997; Czarniawska & Gagliardi, 2003; Fraser, 2004; Pentland, 1999; Sims, 2003), an extensive body of literature has arisen. Chapter 8 examines the temporal dimension to narrative time and the way stories and story making may enable or constrain temporal sensemaking during times of change. For example, Czarniawska (1998) notes that narrative plots rely on human intentionality and context and are based on a chronology of events. In this narrative story form, there is a linear conception of time that links antecedent(s) with agency (a sequence of actions or events) that leads to outcomes (a consequent state of affairs). The narrative provides causal links that offer an explanation (this happened because we did this, which resulted in this), and as such, these types of stories can be viewed as theory laden (see Czarniawska's (1998) concept of petrified stories). They provide meaning and a sense of coherence to complex sets of events in enabling temporal connection and in reducing what Brown and Kreps (1993: 48) refer to as the 'equivocality (complexity, ambiguity, unpredictability) of organizational life'. Our examination of this literature takes us on a journey, which begins with an examination of the more conventional storytelling work of Gabriel (2000), where stories are seen to have a plot and characters with a beginning, middle, and end, to the unfinalized storying and antenarratives of Boje (2011) and Buchanan and Dawson's (2007) depiction of change as a multi-story process. In examining a range of studies on time, temporality, narrative, sensemaking, and organizational change, we move through structured forms of time in long-established stories to temporal work and prospective sensemaking and to the polyvocality and relativity of temporal sensemaking during times of uncertainty and change.

Processual time, non-linear change and the concept of temporal merging are considered in Chapter 9. From this perspective, the timetabling and scheduling of activities and tasks through the use of conventional clock time (objective time) in the planning of events and the implementation of change are seen as an integral part of not only managements' change strategies but also fieldwork studies (Dawson, 2013). Whilst the use of calendars and clock time is integral to organizing fieldwork, ethnographic engagement places the researcher among those being studied (the recipients of change), who differentially experience processes of change in drawing on their past interpretations of events as well as their expectations of the future in making sense of the changing present. These subjective experiences (that include elements of subjective time) interplay with their understanding of conventional time (e.g., as represented through the calendar and the clock) in their various interpretations of change. In this regard, objective and subjective time intertwine both, for example, in the way that recorded and calendared events mix with recollections and memories of past activities shaping our understanding of the present and in the way, as researchers, we seek polyphony and multiple subjectivities of change yet must schedule our time in the field. A facilitating temporal frame is forwarded comprising the concepts of: temporal awareness, which is about bringing to the foreground awareness of multiple conceptions of time that we often ignore or implicitly assume; temporal practices that refer to the process by which the researcher builds and refines his or her own knowledge and experience in applying and using different conceptions of time throughout the research process; and finally, temporal merging, in the interweaving of objective and subjective concepts of time accommodating the way that the past and prospective futures shape human experience of the ongoing present. The chapter highlights how research engagement attends to the non-linearity of change through drawing on the subjective experiences of change agents and recipients whilst also accounting for the importance of conventional time, especially in the way that existing plans, implementation schedules, and regularised activities influence action and behaviour and in our research designs and fieldwork studies (see Dawson, 2013, 2014).

A discussion of time and temporality as it relates to emergent approaches to change is presented in Chapter 10. Developments in our understanding of emergent change are evident in the use and refinement of concepts that emphasise change through adaptation and innovation at the micro level of routines and practices (Feldman, 2000; Orlikowski, 1996, 2002; Tsoukas & Chia, 2002; Weick & Quinn, 1999). The contributions of practice approaches (Feldman & Orlikowski, 2011; Gherardi, 2001; Nicolini, 2012; Reckwitz, 2002; Schatzki, 1996, 2001, 2002) and their application in temporal work are examined (Kaplan & Orlikowski, 2013; Orlikowski & Yates, 2002) and an elaboration of the different dimensions of temporal work, for example, as temporal orientation, awareness, and accommodation, are examined. (Dawson, 2014). We illustrate how this turn away from a process approach that maintains some representational allegiance towards process as a relational ontology has been informed by elements of Eastern philosophical thought (Chia, 2003, 2010, 2014; Jullien, 2011; Marshak, 1993) as well as recent approaches in organizational studies that draw on Western process philosophers (Helin,

Hernes, Hjorth, & Holt, 2014; Hernes, 2008, 2014; Hernes & Schultz, 2015; Hernes, Simpson, & Soderland, 2013; Langley, Smallman, Tsoukas, & Van de Ven, 2013; Langley & Tsoukas, 2010; Tsoukas & Chia, 2002). Change occurs in the improvised performance of practices over time and as the scholarly work discussed here makes clear, there is a move from time as a reification that sits implicitly in the background exhibiting limited temporal awareness in earlier processual approaches, towards stronger views of process based on the works of process philosophers that emphasise change and becoming as an ontology in which temporal awareness is raised and made explicit.

Chapter 11 seeks to extend existing concepts of time and temporality in developing processual approaches for understanding organizational change. Recent works by process scholars in organization studies have increasingly turned to the ideas of Western process thinkers such as Whitehead, Mead, Bergson, and Schutz in attempting to more adequately conceptualize process approaches to organizational theory and practice (Helin, Hernes, Hjorth, & Holt, 2014). These approaches have engaged more deeply with the concepts of time and temporality as illustrated by the recent work of Hernes (2014) in his book *A Process Theory of Organizations*, which as the title suggests, attempts to build a comprehensive theory of process. Hernes' (2014) conceptual framework based on the concepts of the living present, events, and clusters of events and meaning structures and their articulations are first examined. Then, in seeking to extend the discussion we turn to some key concepts from Deleuze's work (1994) and his ontology of difference and the implications for time drawing on insightful commentaries provided by Buchanan (2000, 2008), Grosz (2004), and Williams (2012: 13). Deleuze puts forward three temporal modalities which are required for us to experience time, namely, habitual time (the way repetition draws out something new), memorial time (in which memory does not just describe the past but creates the past), and future time (which is used to refer to the external return of difference) that together affirm the contingent nature of things.

A short concluding chapter is provided in Chapter 12 in which we give heed to the subtitle of the book in a playful discussion of bending the arrow of time. Our argument that threads throughout the book that there can be no one time, but rather, there are multiple times and temporalities, is reasserted as well as the apparent contradiction that different representations of time—that are necessarily partial—can and do provide useful insights for understanding time and temporality. We delineate a number of different arrows of time that draw on branches of science, philosophy, psychology, sociology, and management studies that provide some purchase on the paradox of time and the implications of views on temporality for theory development. We conclude not with a bringing together, a closure, or a final word but with a continuing process in providing some ideas for further openings.

Our central aim, as with the book as a whole, has been to bring to the fore concepts and debates that have largely remained hidden or unexplored in the change management literature in furthering our knowledge and understanding of time and temporality in changing organizations. Time remains a paradox, and whilst many issues remain unresolved, we hope that the insights presented in this book provide readers and our academic audience with useful material that stimulates further dialogue and engaging conversations as well as provides a firm foundation from which to embark on further investigations (empirically and theoretically) in building new conceptual knowledge on the complex dynamic processes of organizational change.

References

Alvesson, M., Bridgman, T., & Willmott, H. (Eds.). (2011). *The Oxford Handbook of Critical Management Studies*. Oxford: Oxford University Press.

Alvesson, M., & Spicer, A. (2012). Critical leadership studies: The case for critical performativity. *Human Relations, 65*(3), 367–390.

Barad, K. (2003). Posthumanist performativity: Toward an understanding of how matter comes to matter. *Signs, 28*(3), 801–831.

Barad, K. (2007). *Meeting the Universe Halfway: Quantum Physics and the Entanglement of Matter and Meaning*. London: Duke University Press.

Barbour, J. (2000). *The End of Time: The Next Revolution in Our Understanding of the Universe*. London: Phoenix, Orion Books.

Bergson, H. (1913). *Time and Free Will: An Essay on the Immediate Data of Consciousness*. London: George Allen & Company.

Boje, D. M. (Ed.). (2011). *Storytelling and the Future of Organizations: An Antenarrative Handbook*. London: Routledge.

Brown, M., & Kreps, G. L. (1993). Narrative analysis and organizational development. In S. L. Herndon & G. L. Kreps (Eds.), *Qualitative Research: Applications in Organizational Communication* (pp. 47–62). Creskill, NJ: Hampton Press.

Buchanan, D. A., & Badham, R. J. (2008). *Power, Politics, and Organizational Change: Winning the Turf Game* (2nd ed.). London: Sage.

Buchanan, D. A., & Dawson, P. (2007). Discourse and audience: Organizational change as multi-story process. *Journal of Management Studies, 44*(5), 669–686.

Buchanan, I. (2000). *Deleuzism: A Metacommentary*. Durham: Duke University Press.

Buchanan, I. (2008). *Deleuze and Guattari's Anti-Oedipus*. London: Continuum International Publishing Group.

Butler, R. (1997). Stories and experiments in social inquiry. *Organization Studies, 18*(6), 927–948.

Chaplin, C. (Writer). (1936). *Modern Times*. California: United Artists.

Chia, R. (2003). From knowledge creation to the perfection of action: Tao, Basho and pure experience as the ultimate ground of knowing. *Human Relations, 56*(3), 953–981.

Chia, R. (2010). Rediscovering becoming: Insights from an oriental perspective of process organization studies. In T. Hernes & S. Maitlis (Eds.), *Process, Sensemaking and Organizing* (pp. 112–139). London: Sage.

Chia, R. (2014). Reflections: In praise of silent transformation—allowing change through letting happen. *Journal of Change Management, 14*(1), 8–27.

Clegg, S. R., & Haugaard, M. (Eds.). (2013). *The SAGE Handbook of Power*. London: Sage.

Czarniawska, B. (1998). *A Narrative Approach to Organization Studies*. Thousand Oaks, CA: Sage.

Czarniawska, B., & Gagliardi, P. (2003). *Narratives We Organize By*. Philadelphia: Imprint Amsterdam.

Dawson, P. (2013). The use of time in the design, conduct and write-up of longitudinal processual case study research. In M. E. Hassett & E. Paavilainen-Mäntymäki (Eds.), *Handbook of Longitudinal Research Methods: Studying Organizations* (pp. 249–268). Cheltenham: Edward Elgar.

Dawson, P. (2014). Reflections: On time, temporality and change in organizations. *Journal of Change Management, 14*(3), 285–308.

Dawson, P. (2015). *Time in Organizational Studies: Does It Matter If Clocks Can Tell Us the Time But Not What Time Is?* Paper presented at the British Academy of Management 29th Annual Conference, University of Portsmouth, Portsmouth, England.

Deleuze, G. (1994). *Difference and Repetition*. New York: Columbia University Press.

Elias, N. (1993). *Time: An Essay*. Oxford: Blackwell Publishing.

Feldman, M. (2000). Organizational routines as a source of continuous change. *Organization Science, 11*(6), 611–629.

Feldman, M., & Orlikowski, W. J. (2011). Theorizing practice and practicing theory. *Organization Science, 22*(5), 1240–1253.

Frank, A. (2012). *About Time*. Oxford: Oneworld Publications.

Fraser, H. (2004). Doing narrative research. *Qualitative Social Work, 3*, 179–201. Retrieved from http://qsw.sagepub.com.ezproxy.uow.edu.au/cgi/reprint/3/2/179, accessed July 2015.

Gabriel, Y. (2000). *Storytelling in Organizations: Facts, Fictions, and Fantasies*. Oxford: Oxford University Press.

Gherardi, S. (2001). From organizational learning to practice-based knowing. *Human Relations, 54*(1), 131–139.

Grosz, E. (2004). *The Nick of Time: Politics, Evolution and the Untimely*. Durham and London: Duke University Press.

Hardy, C. (1996). Understanding power: Bringing about strategic change. *British Academy of Management, 7*(Special Issue), S3–S16.

Hawking, S. (2011). *A Brief History of Time: From the Big Bang to Black Holes*. London: Bantam Books.

Helin, J., Hernes, T., Hjorth, D., & Holt, R. (Eds.) (2014). *The Oxford Handbook of Process Philosophy and Organization Studies*. Oxford: Oxford University Press.

Hernes, T. (2008). *Understanding Organization as Process: Theory for a Tangled World*. London and New York: Routledge.

Hernes, T. (2014). *A Process Theory of Organization*. Oxford: Oxford University Press.

Hernes, T., & Schultz, M. (2015). *Organizational Time*. Paper presented at the Seventh International Process Symposium, Kos, Greece.

Hernes, T., Simpson, B., & Soderland, J. (2013). Managing and temporality. *Scandinavian Journal of Management, 29*(1), 1–6.

Jullien, F. (2011). *The Silent Transformation*. Calcutta: Seagull.

Kaplan, S., & Orlikowski, W. (2013). Temporal work in strategy making. *Organization Science, 24*(44), 965–995.

Knights, D., & Willmott, H. (2000). *The Reengineering Revolution: Critical Studies of Corporate Change*. London: Sage.

Langley, A., Smallman, C., Tsoukas, H., & Van de Ven, A. (2013). Process studies of change in organization and management: Unveiling temporality, activity and flow. *Academy of Management Journal, 56*(1), 1–13.

Langley, A., & Tsoukas, H. (2010). Introducing 'Perspectives on process organization studies'. In T. Hernes & S. Maitlis (Eds.), *Process, Sensemaking, and Organization* (pp. 1–26). Oxford: Oxford University Press.

Leonardi, P. M. (2013). Theoretical foundations for the study of sociomateriality. *Information and Organization, 23*(1), 59–76.

Lewin, K. (1947). Frontiers in group dynamics: Concepts, method and reality in social science, social equilibria and social change. *Human Relations, 1*(1), 5–41.

Lewin, K. (2009). Quasi-stationary social equilibria and the problem of permanent change. In W. W. Burke, Lake, D. G., & J. W. Paine (Eds.), *Organization Change: A Comprehensive Reader* (pp. 73–77). San Francisco: Jossey-Bass.

Lorentz, H. A. (2008). *The Einstein Theory of Relativity*. Retrieved from http://www.amazon.co.uk, doi: 9488783-1561908, accessed July 2015.

Marshak, R. (1993). Lewin meets Confucius: A review of the OD model of change. *Journal of Applied Behavioral Science, 29*(4), 393–415.

McCabe, D. (2007). *Power at Work: How Employees Reproduce the Corporate Machine*. London: Routledge.

McTaggart, J. M. E. (1993). The unreality of time. In R. Le Poidevin & M. MacBeath (Eds.), *The Philosophy of Time* (pp. 23–34). Oxford: Oxford University Press.

Mutch, A. (2013). Sociomateriality—taking the wrong turning? *Information and Organization, 23*(1), 28–40.

Newton, I. (2014). *The Mathematical Principles of Natural Philosophy*. Retrieved from http://www.amazon.co.uk, accessed July 2015.

Nicolini, D. (2012). *Practice Theory, Work, and Organization: An Introduction*. Oxford: Oxford University Press.

Orlikowski, W. J. (1996). Improvising organizational transformation over time: A situated change perspective. *Information Systems Research, 7*(1), 63–92.

Orlikowski, W. J. (2002). Knowing in practice: Enacting a collective capability in distributed organizing. *Organization Science, 13*(3), 249–273.

Orlikowski, W. J. (2007). Sociomaterial practices: Exploring technology at work. *Organization Studies, 28*(9), 1435–1448.

Orlikowski, W. J. (2010). The sociomateriality of organisational life: Considering technology in management research. *Cambridge Journal of Economics, 34*(1), 125–141.

Orlikowski, W. J., & Yates, J. (2002). It's about time: Temporal structuring in organizations. *Organization Science, 13*(6), 684–700.

Pentland, B. T. (1999). Building process theory with narrative: From description to explanation. *Academy of Management Review, 24*(4), 711–724.

Pettigrew, A. (1973). *The Politics of Organizational Decision-Making*. London: Tavistock.

Reckwitz, A. (2002). Toward a theory of social practices. *European Journal of Social Theory, 5*(2), 243–263.

Roe, R. A., Waller, M. J., & Clegg, S. R. (Eds.). (2009). *Time in Organizational Research*. Abingdon, Oxon: Routledge.

Romanelli, E., & Tushman, M. (1994). Organizational transformation as punctuated equilibrium: An empirical test. *Academy of Management Journal, 37*(5), 1141–1166.

Schatzki, T. (1996). *Social Practices: A Wittgensteinian Approach to Human Activity and the Social*. New York: Cambridge University Press.

Schatzki, T. (2001). Introduction: Practice theory. In T. Schatzki, K. Knorr Cetina, & E. Von Savigny (Eds.), *The Practice Turn in Contemporary Theory* (pp. 1–14). Oxon: Routledge.

Schatzki, T. (2002). *The Site of the Social: A Philosophical Account of Social Life and Change*. Pennsylvania: Pennsylvania State University Press.

Sims, D. (2003). Between the millstones: A narrative account of the vulnerability of middle managers' storying. *Human Relations, 56*(10), 1195–1211.

Thompson, E. P. (1967). Time, work discipline and industrial capitalism. *Past and Present, 38*, 56–97.

Tsoukas, H., & Chia, R. (2002). On organizational becoming: Rethinking organizational change. *Organization Science, 13*(5), 567–582.

Tushman, M. L., & Romanelli, E. (2012). Organizational evolution: A metamorphosis model of convergence and reorientation. In J. Child (Ed.), *The Evolution of Organizations* (pp. 508–559). Cheltenham: Edward Elgar.

Weick, K., & Quinn, R. (1999). Organizational change and development. *Annual Review of Psychology, 50*(1), 361–386.

Whitehead, A. N. (1929). *Process and Reality: An Essay in Cosmology*. New York: Free Press.

Williams, J. (2012). *Gilles Deleuze's Philosophy of Time*. Edinburgh: Edinburgh University Press.

Williams, J. (2013). *Gilles Deleuze's Difference and Repetition: A Critical Introduction and Guide*. Edinburgh: Edinburgh University Press.

2 Understanding Time and Temporality
History, Science, and Philosophy

> In our conversation, no word is more familiarly used or more easily recognized than 'time'. We certainly understand what is meant by the word both when we use it ourselves and when we hear it used by others. What, then, is time? I know well enough what it is, provided that nobody asks me; but if I am asked what it is and try to explain, I am baffled. All the same I can confidently say that I know that if nothing passed there would be no past time; if nothing were going to happen, there would be no future time; and if nothing *were*, there would be no present time. Of these three divisions of time, then, how can two, the past and the future, *be*, when the past no longer is and the future is not yet? As for the present, if it were always present and never moved on to become the past, it would not be time but eternity. If, therefore, the present is time only by reason of the fact that it moves on to become the past, how can we say that even the present *is*, when the reason why it *is* is that it is *not to be*? In other words, we cannot rightly say that time *is*, except by reason of its impending state of *not being*.
>
> (Augustine, 2002: 262)

This opening quotation from Saint Augustine's confessions is one of the most well-used reflections on time taken up and referred to by scientists, philosophers, and organization theorists. It usefully captures the paradox of time in steering us to our own common-sense assumption of time as something that exists, pervades our lives, and is both easily recognised and understood, and yet, it also turns our gaze inwards to thoughts about the nature and composition of time and, in particular, about our present as it relates to both our past and anticipated future. We move from notions of time as something represented by the ticking of a clock or the digital flashing of LED displays to time in motion, as movement with duration and history. This flow and positioning of time beyond the present is often what people refer to when they talk about temporality. For Augustine, time is never still and gains its duration from ongoing movement, for example, in the way that the present continually becomes the past, whereas with eternity there is no movement into the past as all is present (Saint Augustine, 2002: 261–262). Temporality is a concept that captures these three divisions of time, and he refers to these as: past time, present time, and future time. Perhaps more so than time, temporality is where the debates, controversies, and theories arise, especially as they relate to attempted explanations of the unresolvable paradox of time and theory development in organization studies. As we shall see, the Scottish philosopher John McTaggart usefully captures the two dominant ways in which these divisions have been used and understood in explanations of time, whereas he himself maintains that time is simply an ideal and that our perceptions of time are illusory.

The centrality of time to the way we attempt to understand and relate our experiences of the past, present, and future and our existence within the wider cosmos has remained a central concern generating science-based theories of time and space, philosophical discussions on the existence and non-existence of time, and a range of other social science approaches on temporality and the importance of culture and context to our perspective(s) on time. In a selective review of these literatures, key debates within philosophy, science, and the social sciences of psychology and sociology are summarized and critically evaluated. Although space dictates selectivity, the intention is to provide an accessible précis that engages with some of the main debates, philosophies, and theories that have emerged around our concepts of time and temporality in, for example: the distinction between material place and movement and our conscious understanding of time; questions on temporality and the very existence of time (tensed and untensed conceptions of time); consideration of multiple times and universes coexisting and of psychological time perspectives and social time; as well as the classic scientific debates that range from the absolutist argument of Newton (2014) through to the relativity of Einstein (Lorentz, 2008). These and many others are outlined and discussed. The intention is not to provide an exhaustive treatise on time but to provide a selective, accessible review of the key concepts, controversies, and debates, some of which are taken up and drawn upon in later chapters by scholars, such as Deleuze, Grosz, Julien, Mead, Schütz, and Whitehead.

Time as Lived and Measured

There have been a number of historical accounts and social and scientific overviews of time as well as a range of popular books that provide useful summaries (see, e.g., Adam, 2004; Bluedorn, 2002; Carroll, 2010; Frank, 2012; Greene, 2005; Hall, 1983; Hammond, 2012; Hawking, 2011; Hoffman, 2009; Levine, 2006; Peake, 2012; Penrose, 2011). Considerable interest and controversy continues to surround questions on the nature of time and temporality and how they relate to our own existence and the nature of the universe. For example, Frank (2012), in an historical account of time from sundials to quantum clocks, argues that there has been a long-standing link between personal (human) time and cosmic time arising from our engagement with the material needs of the cultural context (space) in which we are located.

In his focus on Western developments from Mesopotamia, Greece, the Dark Ages (the term used by Frank), and the Industrial Revolution through to the modern Western world, Frank charts how our Palaeolithic (old Stone Age) ancestors were integrated within the world of nature and the life of other animals. The world of hunter-gatherers is entwined with the environment in the gathering of ripened food and in the following of herds throughout the seasons (Frank, 2012: 14–18). With the warming of the planet and the receding of glacial activity a new Stone Age (Neolithic) evolved in which there was less movement as people were able to set up more permanent abodes, developing tools for grinding plants and domesticating animals, which necessitated new ways of organizing and a redefinition of time (Frank, 2012: 18–26). Monuments, such as Stonehenge, were built to accommodate the regular patterns of cosmic time in making links to astronomical events, such as the solstices, whilst also acting as burial sites for tribal elders. As Frank (2012: 24) states: 'Where the hunter-gatherer lived through time as an unbroken whole, the farmer lived within a time marked by the daily rounds of animal husbandry, home maintenance and village life. Thus time and the cosmos had to change because the ways in which people encountered the material world had changed'. Following the Dark Ages, dominant religious beliefs and the centrality of God to existence and creation held back the presentation of new scientific theories on the place and movement of the earth. For example, the forthright proclamations of Galileo (1564–1642) that the planets and the earth revolved around the sun, which contributed to the scientific revolution and promoted the heliocentric theory of Copernicus (1473–1543), sharply contrasted with the Aristotelian (384–322 BCE) geocentric view that all heavenly bodies revolved around the earth. Galileo's controversial position brought him into conflict with the Inquisition that resulted in him being placed under house arrest for the last nine years of his life after being found suspect of heresy by the Holy Office (Brecht, 2008). This example highlights how fundamental the concept of time is to our understanding and ordering of our world and our place in the universe.

Methods for measuring time have a long history, and for the most part they were accepted provided they did not call into question the normative religious ordering of time, space, and existence. A site dating back to the eighth millennium BCE discovered in Aberdeenshire (Scotland) may provide the earliest evidence of the use of a time-reckoning system (Gaffney et al., 2013). Other time interval measurement devices have been traced back to sundials (evidence goes back to 2000 BCE, with the first authentic record of a sundial dating back to 742 BCE), water clocks (Egyptians), sand glasses (Persians and Sumerians), the wind (Chinese), bells (monastic scheduled prayers), and candles (used in ancient Asia). Early versions of the mechanical clock began to appear in public areas during the 14th and 15th centuries, originating in the towers of some large Italian cities (beginning with Orvieto in Italy in 1307). These clock towers soon spread to other major cities across Europe (e.g., Windsor Castle gained a clock in 1353) and during this period changed from the clockwork regulation of the ringing of bells at set intervals (audible time) through to the introduction of the more visual representation of time through the placement of clock dials on the tower (Frank, 2012: 72–73). Greater accuracy and reliability was achieved through the development of the pendulum clock by Christian Huygens in 1656, with the invention of the first quartz clocks in the 1920s and atomic clocks in the 1950s. Clocks have become increasingly smaller, with the Chip Scale Atomic Clock (CSAC) made commercially available during the 2010s (Coxworth, 2011).

Within the Western world, the common-sense concept of time that is used for everyday purposes is institutionalized in clock time and embedded within the rhythms of our work-life activities. Mobile phones, computers, and iPads all provide instant access to clock time, allowing people to keep track of time, offering reminders for scheduled events, and enabling individuals and groups to coordinate movements and activities. Time is readily available and unproblematic in daily life as people coordinate different world times across the globe in arranging phone calls or Skype communication with colleagues and friends in local or distant locations. Duration of time is marked by the intervals between two points measured with the use of clocks and calendars in, for example, marking out the beginning and end of a trip overseas or a visit to the local shop. Without difficulty, we are able to measure movement over distance, such as monitoring the speed (time taken) to cover a five-kilometre lunchtime run. The past (what happened in a meeting last week), the present (the here and now), and the future (a conference presentation planned ahead of time), as well as concepts of things occurring after each other (succession) and occurring at the same time (simultaneity), are easily grasped and understood. They do not present challenges to the way we live or think about the world, nor do they present conceptual obstacles to the way we make sense of things as they happen in our daily lives. Time, duration, movement, succession, simultaneity, and temporality are all unproblematic in our conscious existence and through their common usage by us and others in our everyday interactions and conversations (although we may use different calendars, this common understanding of time acts as a unifying force, a point of global consensus—the agreement is real even if time as a concept is not). Clock time remains central to understanding organizations, especially in making sense of business operations and the way processes and activities are measured, regulated, and controlled, regardless of whether clocks provide a measure of time more broadly conceived or are simply devices for measuring intervals (standardized through the adoption of Greenwich Mean Time and Coordinated Universal Time) and commonly referred to as time.

However, long before the arrival of the clock, the search for answers to cosmological questions was vibrant and early developments in geometry, mathematics, and philosophy were used to reflect and debate on the nature of time as something 'real' or 'illusory'. A comparison is often made between an ancient Greek philosopher Parmenides, who argued that there was no change and hence that time was an illusion, and Heraclitus, who saw the world as being in a continuous state of flux and forwarded the well-used dictum that one cannot step into the same river twice (Peake, 2012). These different views of time have persisted in various forms to the present day, and echoes of these debates will be evident in the discussions that follow.

Time and Philosophy

There has been a long-standing philosophical debate around time, being, and existence from the metaphysics tradition of early Greek philosophers through to the present day. A key question that arises from these debates is whether time exists or is merely an illusion. This conundrum has attracted the attention of many philosophers who have displayed an array of complex, nuanced ideas and abstract concepts. Returning to our opening quote from St Augustine, we would concur with his reflections that whereas we all seem to have an intuitive sense of what time is and to understand our place in a world with a past, present, and future, when we look deeper and try to explain what time is, we often come unstuck. This inability to fully explain time has led to an ongoing philosophical debate about the 'reality' of time.

In addressing this concern the ontological and epistemological perspective of scholars is important; for example, ontologically we may view the external world as being separate from our inner consciousness, or we may adopt a more relational ontology where everything exists in relation to everything else (Slife, 2004); epistemologically, we may differ in our views on the methods and ways we can build up knowledge and understanding of time. For example, Aristotle saw an intimate connection between time and space in which material objects exist (all objects simultaneously exist in both space and time). He thereby contrasts physical objects with thoughts (whether conscious or otherwise) existing in time but not space. This distinction between material place and movement (simultaneity) and our conscious understanding of time (extra-spatial) has been referred to in a number of different ways, including the distinction between objective and subjective time—a dualism that continually resurfaces in discussions on time. Our focus here however rests on two central issues arising from these philosophical concerns about the existence or unreality of time—first, whether temporality in terms of a past, present, and future is essential to time or whether time is tenseless and only exists in the moment of being (a present now) and, second, whether time is seen as something essentially external and connected with space or whether time can only be truly understood in terms of consciousness and internal, extra-spatial experiences of being. These ontological and epistemological concerns overlap and inform each other and are evident in a broad range of philosophical work, but here, we turn our attention to these two central issues before examining the main focus and concerns about time in the world of science.

The Illusion of Temporality: Tensed and Untensed Time

The notion of time as an illusion stems from the early Greek Eleatic School and is encapsulated in the views of Parmenides, who states that change is impossible because something cannot become what it is not, and consequently what is 'real' is permanent. He can be credited as the first philosopher to suggest that time is unreal—insofar as we live in a timeless present in which the past and future do not exist. This issue of temporality was made prominent again by the Scottish philosopher McTaggart (1993) through the notion of tensed (past, present, and future) and untensed time (e.g., dates, such as, July 4, 1776). McTaggart argues that the temporality of tensed time is essential for time and, through a series of logical progressions, uses this to eventually show why he regards time as unreal. On this count he notes:

> In philosophy, time is treated as unreal by Spinoza, by Kant, and by Hegel. . . . Such a concurrence of opinion is highly significant, and is not the less significant because the doctrine takes such different forms, and is supported by such different arguments. I believe that nothing that exists can be temporal and that therefore time is unreal. But I believe it for reasons which are not put forward by any of the philosophers I have just mentioned.
>
> (McTaggart, 1993: 24)

McTaggart (1993) labels the series of positions from past to present to future as the A series (tensed view). From this perspective, an event (moving from future to present to past) has a series of temporal positions that continually transform (change). The past is viewed as determinant, for example, on August 6, 1945, an American B-29 bomber dropped the world's first deployed atomic bomb over the Japanese city of Hiroshima. This event happened on this date in this particular place and cannot be changed (although it was only on this date in this particular place as in other parts of the world this event happened at a different time and date—e.g., the day before or day after—in this sense the date is a combination of when and where an event took place). Under this perspective, whereas the past is determinant and unchangeable, the future is indeterminate and hence changeable as there remains a range of possibilities yet to come. The past has happened, and the present is now (real), whereas the future is not yet real as it has yet to be (it will only be real as a present or past event). This contrasts with the views of the untensed theorists (also known as B-theorists) who maintain all time is equally real; we just know less about what we call the future than we do the past. In this relational approach (that refers to 'later to earlier' or 'earlier to later'), there is no sequence from past (that no longer exists), to present (present real), to future (potentialities of becoming) and thereby no temporal becoming—rather the difference between past, present, and future is merely an illusion of human consciousness as all are equally real. As authors writing this book, 2016 is present, but for the people in 2026, 2026 is present, and we are in the past. Nobody is wrong as things do not come into and go out of being (and belief that they do is an illusion); all is just there; existence is an irreducible feature of time. His argument unfolds thus:

> We perceive events in time as being present, and those are the only events which we actually perceive. And all other events which, by memory or by inference, we believe to be real, we regard as present, past, or future. Thus the events of time as observed by us form an A series.
>
> (McTaggart, 1993: 25)

From this explanation of tensed and untensed views of time, McTaggart posits that if the real nature of time is more related to the B series (the earlier and later distinctions), we would not be able to perceive of time as it really is. He views the B series (which is tenseless) as essentially untenable, claiming that the A series (the view that time involves change) is integral to time, arguing, 'the events of time as observed by us form an A series' (McTaggart, 1993: 25). However, he recognises that our view of time is subjective and therefore may be simply an illusion, a trick of the mind. He develops his argument on the unreality of time from an A series perspective, stating that first, if an event can only be past, present, or future and yet all events have at one time to be a future moving into present and past (or they have characteristics of being past, present, and future), then this is inconsistent and sets up an unresolvable contradiction. In other words, if time requires A series properties and yet these properties are incompatible determinations (contradictions), then ultimately this undermines time as anything 'real' (pointing to the unreality of time) and suggesting time does not exist as anything other than a social construct.

Becoming and Being Time: Process Philosophy

McTaggart's position contrasts with process philosophers who argue that being and existence can only be fully understood in relation to other occasions and not as some isolated, tenseless, now moment. One early Greek philosopher who has influenced process philosophy is Heraclitus, who argued reality is change, and everything is in a state of flux. His conception of the world is usefully captured by his illustrative notion that you can never step into the same river twice because even though the river may appear the same, there is continual flow—time is an ongoing process of becoming. In viewing reality as a process, temporality and change is seen as fundamental to understanding the world. As Hernes (2014: ix) states at the outset of his process theory of organization:

> Until now organization studies has been somewhat complacent about the effects of time on the experience of organizing. Writers have been inclined to seek refuge in spatial representations of reality, while tending to relegate time and temporality to static representations against which space has been understood. Process philosophers, however, invite us to afford time and temporality an active role in organizational life. Bluntly speaking, they invite us to explore the 'work' performed by time and temporality on spatial representations of organizational life. What tends to be forgotten in organizational theorizing is that actors act upon a future state of affairs based on their histories, even if those same histories may be fakes, forgotten, or rejected by those actors.

These processual ideas were later taken up by a range of philosophers, including those discussed in other chapters of this work, such as Spinoza, Leibniz, Heidegger, Bergson, Mead, James, Pierce, Deleuze, and Whitehead (see, e.g, Cobb, 2008c; Griffin, 1988; Helin, Hernes, Hjorth, & Holt, 2014). To focus particularly on Whitehead at this point, he rejects Cartesian dualism, Kantian idealism, and Einstein's idea that space-time has physical properties such as curvature (Lorentz, 2008). In regard particularly to his understanding of the universe, his thinking was based on geometry, in which he was an expert (Lowe, 1990). The closest Whitehead comes to 'space-time' is what he calls 'the extensive continuum', but this is construed as potential rather than actual (Cobb, 2008b). Much current work using aspects of his thought in management tends to hold to Cooper's (1976) original notion of the 'open field'. That is, at best, there is a focus on the minutiae of process in terms of the relations *between* things.

A more complete rendering, however, entails an understanding that experience is always active, not passive (Griffin, 2008). This is immediately counter-intuitive, but put simply, it is not what happens to us that counts (what in process thought is termed the 'external relation') but rather what we make of what happens to us for ourselves and others (the internal relation) (Cobb, 2008a; Wood & Dibben, 2015). In this view, our common understandings of past, present, and future are not aspects of Whitehead's extensive continuum but rather are better understood in a relational sense as extensively *connected*. In addition, this relationality is made manifest in 'serially ordered societies of occasions of experience' (Whitehead, 1929), such that two occasions occurring at the same moment cannot be directly causally related. In this, Whitehead is perhaps the ultimate sociologist of the individual (Halewood, 2014; Wood & Dibben, 2015).

For Whitehead, 'duration' just precisely is that facet of reality in which contiguous occasions are contemporaneous (Cobb, 2008b). The present occasion always takes *past* occasions into account and, in its becoming, turns them to its own use. In this sense, the present is 'perpetually perishing' but is 'immortal in the past', such that 'the many become one, and are increased by one,' ad infinitum (Sherburne, 1981; Whitehead, 1929). Thus the past is all around us, but it is not quite the past because there is a novel aspect to it, which just precisely makes it the present—which then in the next moment is *past*. For Whitehead, the future is undecided because creativity is the ultimate feature of reality; even God has a 'primordial' (passively ever-the-same) *and* a 'consequent' (actively changing-in-response) nature (Cobb, 2007; Hartshorne, 1984; Whitehead, 1929). Crucially for social science in general and management in particular, this means all occasions are inherently active subjects in their experience of becoming; they are only passive objects once they have perished to the past for subsequent occasions to appreciate (Dibben, 2015; Neesham & Dibben, 2012; Whitehead, 1929). The full complexities of Whitehead's pan-experientialist process metaphysics are beyond the scope of this book. Suffice to say, however, that in some respects it bears comparison with that of Bergson (1913), and *aspects* of it have formed the basis of a great deal of work, notably by Deleuze (1994) and Deleuze and Guattari (1987) and a range of management writers in recent times relying largely on him, such as Chia (2002), Hernes (2014) and Tsoukas and Chia (2002).

Nonetheless, the foregoing is sufficient to appreciate that for process philosophers, when fully worked through, Whitehead's contribution is to reveal an inherently active, intra-connected, fully relational, and ever-evolving, open (i.e., not externally predetermined) universe (Jungreman, 2000; Phipps, 2009). Using this understanding, 'organization' can be rendered in process terms not just as verb or adverb but as noun (Dibben, 2009). In sum, for Whitehead, reality is founded on momentary events (see Weik, 2004: 306); although, finally, we should note that unlike Deleuze, Whitehead never used the term 'event' in any *technical* sense. A wedding is an event for Whitehead just as it is for us. That is, technically speaking, what we tend to understand as an event would for Whitehead consist of a multiplicity of 'durations', which we retrospectively or prospectively artificially delineate into a unit of analysis for descriptive, explanatory, or analytical purposes (Wood & Dibben, 2015).

Whitehead's understanding of *becoming* stands in close comparison with Heidegger's understanding of *being* (Cooper, 1993). In his book *Being and Time*, Heidegger (Heidegger, 1996, published in 1927) emphasises temporality and posits how through an awareness of our own mortality that we are able to come to understand time and, by immersion in everyday life, comprehend our own being. He uses the term 'da-sein', which literally means 'being-there' to conceptualize our embedded existence in a world that is everywhere around us. We experience the world through what we are doing, and we are always in a place, participating in something, influencing others, and immersed in the everyday, and in this sense, everything we do comes out of our ways of existing in the world. In refuting Kant's sceptical view of human ability, in which he develops a priori categories including time and space, Heidegger turns to ontology and da-sein as the only possible way of knowing the realities of time and space (Blattner, 2006).

Central to being in time is the temporality of human existence or da-sein as Heidegger is critical of any linear notion of time or of there being a series of 'now' moments that he views as having dominated philosophical thinking from Aristotle to Hegel. This prioritizing of the present he refers to as 'vulgar' time, whereas 'primordial' time (a recognition that our time comes to an end at our death) is seen to capture being in the world and the movement of human finitude. We have a primordial past where our former ways of being can come back to face us, a primordial future in which we project the trends coming towards us and may face our existential death, and a primordial present in which the past may be experienced with difference in facing our projected future. Thus for Heidegger people are not caught within a series of present moments but experience temporal being with a past, present, and projected future. Although there are sections of the book that were never finished, especially those that relate to time, he argued that the connections in life between birth and death consist of a succession of experiences 'in time' (for a further discussion of McTaggart and Heidegger in management practice, see Bakken, Holt, & Zundel, 2013). As Heidegger explains:

> In this succession of experiences only the experience that is objectively present 'in the actual now' is 'really' 'real.' The experiences past and just coming, on the other hand, are no longer or not yet 'real.' Da-sein traverses the timespan allotted to it between the two boundaries in such a way that it is 'real' only in the now and hops, so to speak, through the succession of nows of its 'time.' For this reason one says that Da-sein is 'temporal.' The self maintains itself in a certain sameness throughout this constant change of experiences.
>
> (Heidegger, 2010: 356)

The Illusion of Time: The External and Internal Debate

Immanuel Kant (2006) in *Critique of Pure Reason* (1781/2006) argues that time is unreal and that we can never truly know what time is. Contrary to Newton's absolute realist view of time, Kant saw time as a category, not a substance; it is uncaused and created by God. He views space and time as dependent on the mind, an intuitive creation to organize our experiences. For Kant, space is not an empirical concept as we cannot represent to ourselves the absence of space. This inability to conceptualize the absence of space is accommodated through inner intuition in which time is constructed. In other words, time is a part of our perception—we intuitively sense time—and then we apply this sense of time to the world around us, including objects. This framework of space and time limits and constrains our mind in the way we construct our experiences of reality; we connect and represent all things to our intuitive understanding of time. As Kant (1781/2006: 54) states:

> Time is a necessary representation, lying at the foundation of all our intuitions. With regard to appearances in general, we cannot think away time from them and represent them to ourselves as out of and unconnected with time, but we can quite well represent to ourselves time void of appearances.

Time, like space, is viewed as a homogenous medium (something that is indifferent to how it is filled) and is represented in terms of its spatial characteristics. Humans (unlike animals) are able to identify objects and conceptualize their relationship to one another and, through language, describe an objective, external world. This type of symbolic representation is seen to mirror conscious life where psychic states that recur and relate to each other can be identified. Whereas other philosophers, such as Hegel (Hegel, 1979; Singer, 2001), also claim time is unreal (through a different reasoning), Heidegger (1996)—as we have already shown—offers a view of time as 'real' and as knowable (Hoy, 1994: 573). But it is Bergson (2001), in *Time and Free Will*, who directly contests what he views as a Kantian determinism and challenges the symbolic representation of Kant's perspective which does not take into account the way human consciousness experiences time. His attention turns to the inner, subjective, extra-spatial experience of time (in contrast to spatial time external to the mind) and the different ways in which we experience time's duration (or *durée*), for example, from the slowing of time's duration often associated with waiting for a kettle to boil to the quickening of time during times of high engagement in the pursuit of enjoyable activities. For Bergson: 'past states cannot be adequately expressed in words or artificially reconstructed by a juxtaposition of simpler states, it is because in their dynamic unity and wholly qualitative multiplicity they are phases of our real and concrete durations, a heterogeneous duration and a living one' (Bergson, 1913, 2001: 239).

Identification of the nature of differences, in particular difference of degree or difference of kind, is a central concept in Bergson's work and method, which he terms 'intuition'. Intuition, outlined in *Matter and Memory* (Bergson, 2010), aims to ensure that the right or properly formulated questions are developed and asked. For Bergson, this is the central exercise in philosophy. That is, philosophical questions must be clear to differentiate differences of kind and differences of degree, so they are not conflated or confused (Deleuze, 1994). He maintains that such changes are qualitative and of a different order or kind to quantitative effects. Space is quantitative, objective actual, and multiple. Time/duration is qualitative, subjective, virtual, and a multiplicity, as Deleuze says, not the one and the many but the one in the many. Deleuze comments that for Bergson, duration is ongoing change, succession 'becoming and change that is substance itself' (Deleuze, 1994: 37). Bergson says, 'The truth is we change without ceasing and that the state itself is nothing but change' (Bergson, 2001: 2). This radical conception of change locates it substantively.

Bergson (1913/2001) thereby refutes Kant's external view of time (the intuition of a homogenous medium peculiar to humans) that characterizes time as symbolic duration rather than what Bergson refers to as 'pure duration' (unique, unrepeatable moments) that cannot be adequately captured by words or symbols. In his examination of our inner experiences of time, Bergson shows how there has been a general tendency among philosophers to conflate space with time (which he considered differences of kind), and this has resulted in time being wrongly defined as the measurement of movement through space, whereas time is neither an easily understandable nor a scientifically resolvable phenomena:

> Kant's great mistake was to take time as a homogenous medium. He did not notice that real duration is made up of moments inside one another, and that when it seems to assume the form of a homogeneous whole, it is because it gets expressed in space. Thus the very distinction which he makes between space and time amounts at bottom to confusing time with space. . . . Though we generally live and act outside our own person, in space rather than in duration, and though by this means we give a handle to the law of causality, which binds the same effects to the same causes, we can nevertheless always get back into pure duration, of which the moments are internal and heterogeneous to one another, and in which a cause cannot repeat its effect since it will never repeat itself.
>   (Bergson, 2001: 232–233)

This quotation from Bergson provides a useful orientation to his ideas and his refutation of a Kantian perspective in which time is seen to be wrongly treated like space. The link between space and time common to science is seen to simplify and externalize time, presenting the idea of necessary determination without due regard for the heterogeneity of time as immediate consciousness perceives it and the free choices arising from pure duration. In short, 'If time, as immediate consciousness perceives it, were, like space, a homogeneous medium, science would be able to deal with it, as it can with space' (Bergson, 1913: 234).

Time and Science

Within the world of science, time also stands out as a long-standing conundrum. Three main debates focus our attention: first, the notion of absolute and relative time; second, time as a macro or micro explanation; and third, the notion of a single or multiple universes.

Absolute and Relative Time

Isaac Newton advocated the notion of absolute time and was a highly influential figure during the scientific revolution of the 17th century as an English physicist and mathematician (he was also a philosopher and astronomer). In his most acclaimed work, *Philosophiae, Naturalis, Principia Mathematica (Mathematical Principles of Natural Philosophy)*, Newton questions the geocentric view of the universe embedded in Aristotelian philosophy and moves away from more qualitative views of nature in building on quantitative mathematical insight and understanding. Through a series of mathematical calculations he develops three basic laws governing quantitative description of bodies in motion. These state:

1. Stationary bodies remain stationary unless an external force is applied.
2. Force = mass × acceleration, and as such, a change in motion is proportional to the force applied.
3. For every action, there is an equal and opposite reaction.

These laws and universal principles of gravity were revolutionary in explaining movements within the universe (planetary orbits, how the moon revolves around the earth, gravitational pull of the sun, etc.). For Newton, absolute (mathematical) time continues regardless of what is happening within the universe. He argues that this is not simply the measures of intervals between cycles of changes, for example, the interval between an hour and a day, which Newton saw as relative duration. Time is an independent fourth dimension of the universe in which events occur in sequence. In this way, Newton had a realist view of absolute time that he argued could be separated from notions of relative time.

The relative notions of time were evident pre-Newton but took on another level of meaning following the work of Albert Einstein, who studied the effects of relative motion on time. Einstein set out to show how space, distance, and motion were not absolute but relative; life is not fixed but rather comprises a network of relations. As such, speed occurs in relation to other movements, and time is thereby seen as a measure of relationships. Einstein is famous for his general theory of relativity and the equation: $E = mc^2$ (also known as the mass energy equivalent equation) in which E is the energy, m is the mass of the object, and c represents the speed of light. In this equation, energy of a physical system is numerically equal to the product of its mass and the speed of light squared. Speed is calculated by the distance covered by light divided by the time taken to move in space from position A to position B. A key insight is the notion that energy can become matter and matter can become energy (small amounts of matter can produce large amounts of energy). In his special theory of relativity, published in 1905 (predating his general theory), Einstein sidestepped the issue of gravity which, he later incorporated into his general theory.

When younger, Einstein liked to imagine what it would be like to ride on a beam of light. One day when looking back at a clock tower, he imagined how if moving away from the clock at the speed of light the hands would seem to stop; noting that, the faster one moves through space then the slower one moves through time. For Einstein, this revelation suggested that time and movement in space are related (the fabric of space-time). This was radical to the thinking of the day and challenged the established scientific position on time. Initially, there was no response to his work until Max Plank (a renowned European physicist) looked over Einstein's material and recognised the importance of the work. Plank was instrumental in getting his paper published in the leading physics journal *Annalen Der Physic* in June 1905. Einstein's theory highlighted the connection between space and time and how they are both relative to the observer, overturning the view that what is happening in the here and now is the same as what is observed happening from elsewhere in the universe.

Einstein used his theory of relativity to show how if you reach the speed of light, distortions start to occur, space contracts, objects get heavier the faster they move, and time slows (the concept of gravitational time dilation). This theory of special relativity introduces the fourth dimension (the three normal dimensions of space being length, width, and height) not of time per se but of space-time (combining space and time into a single continuum). Under this theory, time is no longer independent of motion (progressing in an orderly sequence) but is relative and can vary according to events. The example of synchronizing two atomic clocks and then sending one up in a space shuttle is often used to illustrate how time is relative; for example, when the clock returns, it is no longer synchronized with the clocks that have remained on earth. In this way, if there are two twins, and one left the earth moving at an incredible speed, then when this person returned, time would have passed differently for the travelling twin; the trip would be relatively brief compared to the longer period of time experienced by the twin remaining on earth. Consequently, the twin who had remained on earth would be chronologically older than his returning twin. Another illustration often used is how people observing the same event from points distant to each other will see the event as occurring at different times (due to the constant speed of light), even though the event is actually occurring at the same moment in time. In other words, whilst an event occurs at a certain moment, our observation of the event is influenced by distance and the speed of light.

However, Einstein's special theory of relativity only dealt with an object moving in one direction at a constant speed, and therefore, it was not able to accommodate real-world situations with speed variation. In attempting to accommodate this, Einstein realised that he would have to include gravity into his theory to make it a general theory that explains not only time but also the influence of gravity on the working of the universe. Einstein imagined the situation of a person in a windowless capsule floating in space and asked the question of how, as the occupant, you would know whether or not you were moving. From this thought experiment Einstein concluded that the occupant would not know. However, if the capsule was propelled forward by a rocket, the floor of the capsule could rush towards the occupant, weighing him down. This feeling of being weighed down in an accelerating rocket produces the same effects as the experience of gravity on the earth. This led Einstein to question conventional notions of gravitational pull and to argue that space can be curved (matter, e.g., a planet, will cause space to curve), and this curvature resultant of the presence of mass explains gravitational influence and the malleability of the fabric of space-time. Under this new theory, the gravitational force of the sun curves space, and if you shine a light towards the sun, rather than the beam moving in a straight line (as one would expect under existing theories), Einstein argued that it will follow the curvature of space created by the sun (the light will bend). He finalized a new theory of gravity in November 1915, which he presented to the Prussian Academy; however it was not until evidence was gained by William Campbell in 1922 (in his eclipse expedition to Australia) that data were made available proving space-time curves around the sun (Isaacson, 2008). In summary, his special theory of relativity highlights how speed, distance, and gravitational dilation can change our perception of time, whilst the flow of time remains in a forward direction and is constant.

Macro and Micro Explanations of Time

Einstein's theory continues to provide an accurate explanation for how the universe operates, but at the micro level of electrons and protons, a new science has emerged contradicting the broader theories and scientific conceptions of time. Quantum mechanics (also referred to as 'quantum theory' and 'quantum physics') seeks to explain the atomic and subatomic dual wave and particle interaction of matter and energy. These theories have questioned whether time is continual or whether it should be quantized in little chunks and judders with, for example, a jiffy identified as the smallest amount of time (measured by the time taken for light to cross the smallest of atomic particles). There are a number of institutes (mainly in Germany) building on the original work of Max Planck (1858–1947), a German theoretical physicist who originated quantum theory. Operated through the Max Planck Society, these institutes cover a range of fields. For example, the Max Planck Institute for Gravitational Physics at Potsdam-Golm was established in 1995 and is composed of scientists who study the complete spectrum of Einstein's theories, whereas the Max Planck Institute for Radio Astronomy in Bonn recently investigated a pulsar, an extreme object confirming Einstein's *General Theory of Relativity*. The pulsar example is far more extreme than those previously studied. The surface of the pulsar has a gravitational strength 300 billion times stronger than the earth, and in the centre of the pulsar, 1 billion tons of matter is squeezed into a volume equivalent to a sugar cube (Antoniadis, Freire, & Wex, 2013).

Although support remains for Einstein's *General Theory of Relativity* as an explanation of the wider universe, at the microscopic level, a disjunction arises with theories that draw attention to photons of light, atoms, and electrons. For example, particle wave duality highlights indeterminacy and the strange occurrences where observation alone can change what one is observing (a particle may change to a wave, but the change is indeterminate). There is an entanglement of electrons in which all the things that could happen are happening at the same time. At this microscopic level, time takes on another form outside of our understanding of space-time as it relates to broader theories of the universe. Time is created by photons and electrons as new photons of light within their own time-space combine with electrons in wave-particle duality. In contrast to relativity that works at the larger scale, this theory starts to break down when used to predict how things will behave at the atomic and subatomic levels. In quantum mechanics the future is not determined; the atom has an infinite number of choice possibilities, and yet when observed and measured, it is 'forced' into making a choice between these multiple options. From this perspective, there are no certainties but only probabilities, and as such, there is an innate unpredictability. This raises the question of whether we can really predict what happens within the world and the universe if evidence suggests that we cannot even accurately predict the behaviour of a single particle. In this, there is an incompatibility between the indeterminacy of quantum mechanics and Einstein's theory of relativity.

Multiverse or Universe

Whereas most of us are familiar with the notion of a universe, there has been increasing interest, scientific research, and some speculation on the notion of a multiverse. For example, Barbour (2000) in his book *The End of Time* argues for the existence of multiple now moments, multiple beings in time, viewed as snapshots of a multiverse in which time does not exist. This leads him to ask the question: why do we experience instant now moments that are timeless and static as something temporal and dynamic (Barbour, 2000: 11)? He uses the example of 100 million, million human molecules being destroyed and replaced every split second to highlight how we are never the same person from one moment to the next. There is no continuity of sameness over time, only multiple snapshots of existence. Drawing on the work of Ernst Mach (for a discussion on Mach and Einstein, see Greene, 2005: 33–38, 416–418), Barbour suggests that any coherence is accidental, and time is simply a convenient way (an abstraction) for making sense and ordering our experiences in the world. As he argues,

> A radical alternative put forwards by Newton's rival Leibniz provides my central idea. The world is to be understood, not in the dualistic terms of atoms (things of one kind) that move in the framework and container of space and time (another quite different kind of thing), but in terms of more fundamental entities that fuse space and matter into the single notion of a possible arrangement, or configuration, of the entire universe. Such configurations, which would be fabulously richly structured, are the ultimate things. There are infinitely many of them; they are all different instances of a common principle of construction; and they are all, in my view, the different *instants of time*. In fact, many people who have written about time have conceived of instants of time in a somewhat similar way, and have called them 'nows'. Since I made the concept more precise and put it at the heart of my theory of time, I shall call them *Nows*. The world is made of Nows.
>
> (Barbour, 2000: 16)

Under this view, space and time are dependent on the mind for existence, returning us again to our earlier discussion of philosophical debates. Interestingly, there are some similarities and overlaps in the debates among philosophers and scientists when it comes to questions about time and temporality; for example, quantum microtheories spotlight indeterminacy and, in a sense, rescue or reassert the notion of free will as advocated by Henri Bergson's philosophical work. As we shall also see in the chapter that follows, the divide between concepts, such as spatial and extra-spatial time, objective and subjective time, and microscopic and macroscopic time takes us back to the persistent issue of dualism and the paradox of time. Before closing, the next section briefly discusses this pervasive issue in a brief return to the debate between Einstein's theory of relativity and quantum mechanics.

Dualism and the Paradox of Time

Within science, a main focus has been on objective notions of time in explaining the movement of objects and planets and the relationship between space and time. However, between Einstein's theory of relativity and quantum mechanics, there remains a puzzle, a disparity of explanation between the macroscopic and the microscopic that centres around the wave-particle dualism of light in which light has both a wave and particle state but not at the same time. The laws of science that are able to explain planetary movements and cause-and-effect relationships for objects on gravitational earth are not generalizable to the quantum world. The wave-like nature of light and the concept of space-time (a fourth dimension where space and time come together) can be used to provide an explanation of time as movement in space in which differences in time occur relative to where we are and how fast we are moving.[1] The fabric of space-time is curved, and this curving of space-time explains time dilation occurring in high gravitational contexts, such as black holes, where time slows. In this representation motion is smooth with continuous change, which differs at the subatomic level, where there is a 'jumpiness' of action (changes of energy or quanta), where photons (particles of light) from a distant system can influence another particle, even though they are separated by comparatively great distances (what is known as a 'nonlocality issue'). This phenomenon—that Einstein famously referred to as 'spooky action at a distance'—appears to occur outside of space-time and does not align with Einstein's theory of relativity.

An important component of this disparity is the significance of the 'uncertainty principle'—a principle developed in the 1920s by German physicist Heisenberg to account for the odd behaviour of subatomic objects—where there are indeterminacy and uncertainties about quantities, such as position, energy, and time, until a measurement of a particle is made and a momentum observed. Under quantum uncertainty a particle may spin clockwise or counterclockwise, but when it interacts with another particle, it no longer acts independently but becomes entangled; their states become mixed. In relation to space-time these two could be separated by light-years and yet remain interdependent with the spin of one linked to the other and in which the immediacy of the correlation is inexplicable by Einstein's special theory of relativity (Linden, Popoesu, Short, & Winter, 2014). The certainty of the laws of classical physics is thus called into question by the indeterminacy and unpredictability evident in nature in this microscopic world of quantum physics (which in turn has been used to raise issues about the possibilities of multiple universes and the theoretical possibility of time reversal[2]). As Jha (2013) explains,

> The uncertainty principle is one of the most famous (and probably misunderstood) ideas in physics. It tells us that there is a fuzziness in nature, a fundamental limit to what we can know about the behaviour of quantum particles and, therefore, the smallest scales of nature. Of these scales, the most we can hope for is to calculate probabilities for where things are and how they will behave. Unlike Isaac Newton's clockwork universe, where everything follows clear-cut laws on how to move and prediction is easy if you know the starting conditions, the uncertainty principle enshrines a level of fuzziness into quantum theory.

It should be stressed, however, that this uncertainty principle is insignificant for macroscopic objects (the influence is so small, e.g., in working out the trajectory of a tennis ball that the differences would be infinitesimal). Hence, even within the spatial world of science, the ability to explain and represent phenomena with language is strained, and the ordered nature of existence is called into question.

There is a scientific-spatial paradox raised by wave-particle dualism, the uncertainty principle, and 'spooky action'. Time can no longer be explained by Newton's absolute time or Einstein's conceptualization of the curved fabric of space-time as these established laws of physics do no hold for subatomic objects. In attempting to accommodate the uncertainty principle of quantum mechanics and the theory of relativity, Hawking, in working with Penrose (2011), has forwarded the notion of a boundaryless universe (there are no singularities) in which all moments in time simultaneously coexist. The concept of imaginary time is used to capture the nature of time in this completely self-contained universe. Hawking (2011: 158) argues that in using the concept of real time, we come to see the universe as having a beginning and an end that are marked by two points (singularities) from Big Bang to Black Hole. These boundary markers can be used to explain the containment of space-time and temporality in movements from the past to the present and into the future. However, through the concept of imaginary time, Hawking removes the singularity of the Big Bang, arguing that there is no single point (moment in time past) but rather that we should reorient our visualization to more sphere or globe-like conceptualization (he uses the example of the South Pole) that presents a more plausible characterization. From this perspective (visual image), you do not go backwards and forwards in time but, rather, move in terms of spatial positioning—that is, running perpendicular in relation to real time that runs along a horizontal axis from past to future. Once again, the difficulties of language in trying to represent and capture this notion arise, but in this case, we move back to a more spatial understanding of time that does not accommodate the way people differentially experience time. We will return to this issue again at the end of Chapter 3.

Conclusion

This chapter has highlighted the paradox of time as something that appears easily understood and yet continually evades our attempts to define and conceptualize. The simple categories of past, present, and future are seen as self-evident, and yet, the way we variously experience and make sense of time attests to the existence of multiple temporalities within what appear as clearly demarked boundaries of time (Cipriani, 2013: 5–6). Questions on whether space and time exist independently of objects (an absolute notion), whether time exists in relation to objects (a relational view of time), and issues on the relationship between more objective forms of external time with our inner experiences, all provide potential material for building a more critical approach to understanding time and temporality in the field of organization studies. Our sensory perception of space and time is often viewed as changeable and relative to our frame of reference and the way we talk about stretching time—making time go quicker and creating time, and yet, we cannot see, touch, feel, or hear time. Perhaps our sense of time is illusory, and time does not exist as anything other than a social construction. But time may also be understood as all pervasive, immovable, and absolute, existing outside our external observations of movement. Questions abound on the existence of time; for example, if time is relational to matter, how can time exist within a vacuum where distances between objects or events cannot be measured or defined? For people in society, concerns are generally more grounded in life experiences where perceptions of temporality are, and always will be, integral to understanding and making sense of their existence within the world, whether or not time 'actually' exists. We argue here that a fuller understanding of temporality is critical to further research in organization studies, especially in building theory and analysing empirical data, and that time should not be left hidden or implicitly assumed as being self-evident in the models we develop and the empirical studies that we present.

Notes

1. As a fourth dimension where space and time come together, different (relative) time durations can occur. If we return to the illustration of the twin experiment (we shall call them John and Paul), if John moves away from the earth at very fast speeds, and Paul remains on earth, then time changes between the two. If John continues to move much faster than Paul, then when John returns to earth, Paul will be older than John. However, if they both had atomic measuring devices recording the time that passed in the interval between John leaving earth and arriving back, then for Paul the interval would be longer. In other words, the intervals measured by time-metering devices would remain constant for both of them—that is, Paul has not aged quicker than John—however, they have occupied different space-time, and hence time intervals between them returning to the same space-time is different (Einstein's theory of relativity). Whereas the dimension of space-time helps explains the difference in relative time between Paul and John, Newton's notion of absolute time still holds in terms of measured intervals captured by the atomic clock with regard to the speed of time's duration in respect to the chronological ageing process experienced by Paul and John. Thus, whilst the duration of time has been constant (absolute time), their relation to each other on the space-time dimension has changed (relative time). To think of it another way, one can pose the question of whether they have been moving forward along the arrow of time at different speeds and whether the arrow of time is linear or curved.

   If we think back to a three-dimensional plane (and the one to which we our most familiar), then if they were travelling at different speeds, John would simply arrive earlier in time at their agreed destination than Paul. He would then have to wait for Paul to arrive. However, in our example John leaves from a place on earth moving out into space-time in a four-dimensional universe only to return to the place he left at a distant time, at which time the two different atomic clocks would register different durations for John and Paul. In Einstein's thought experiment from which his theory on relative time developed, the fourth dimension of space-time draws attention to the need to move beyond our linear conception of the arrow of time to a more curved understanding of the space-time conception. But in this, we often find it difficult to think beyond our intuitive understanding of time as an arrow (linear progression) and to reconcile theoretical understanding with our actual experience of time.

2. The notion of time reversal would conflict with the second law of thermodynamics, where entropy (randomness) always increases (or remains the same) at a later time. This scientific law supports the irreversibility of time and has been reinforced by the fact that there have been no scientific studies that have proven the practical possibility of people being able to go against the arrow of time and travel back in time (this remains in the realm of science fiction). Although theoretically it is possible, especially if one accepts the notion that every moment of time already exists within a block universe, for example, in the way that satellites are able to photograph back in time capturing events that happened 14 billion years in the past (due to the speed of light, e.g., the sun is eight minutes old by the time we see it through our eyes on earth). In practical terms, travelling back in time remains a theoretical possibility rather than a practical reality.

References

Adam, B. (2004). *Time*. Cambridge: Polity Press.

Antoniadis, J., Freire, P., & Wex, N. (2013). A massive pulsar in a compact relativistic binary. *Science, 340*(6131).

Augustine, A. (2002). *Confessions*. London: Penguin Books.

Bakken, T., Holt, R., & Zundel, M. (2013). Time and play in management practice: An investigation through the philosophies of McTaggart and Heidegger. *Scandinavian Journal of Management, 29*, 13–22.

Barbour, J. (2000). *The End of Time: The Next Revolution in Our Understanding of the Universe*. London: Phoenix, Orion Books.

Bergson, H. (1913). *Time and Free Will: An Essay on the Immediate Data of Consciousness*. London: George Allen & Company.

Bergson, H. (2001). *Time and Free Will: An Essay on the Immediate Data of Consciousness* (F. L. Pogson, Trans.). Mineola, NY: Dover Publications.

Bergson, H. (2010). *Matter and Memory* (N. Paul & W. Palmer, Trans.). Overland Park, Kansas: Digireads.com Publishing.

Blattner, W. (2006). *Heidegger's Being and Time*. London: Coninuum International Publishing Group.

Bluedorn, A. C. (2002). *The Human Organization of Time: Temporal Realities and Experience*. Stanford, CA: Stanford University Press.

Brecht, B. (Ed.). (2008). *Life of Galileo*. London: Penguin.

Carroll, S. (2010). *From Eternity to Here: The Quest for the Ultimate Theory of Time*. Oxford: Oneworld.

Chia, R. (2002). Essai: Time, duration and simultaneity: Rethinking process and change in organizational analysis. *Organization Studies, 23*(6), 863–868.

Cipriani, R. (2013). The many faces of social time: A sociological approach. *Time & Society, 22*(1), 5–30.

Cobb, J. B. (2007). *A Christian Natural Theology* (2nd ed.). London: Westminster John Knox Press.

Cobb, J. B. (2008a). Person-in-community: Whiteheadian insights into community and institution. *Organization Studies, 28*(4), 567–588.

Cobb, J. B. (2008b). *Whitehead Word Book: A Glossary with Alphabetical Index to Technical Terms in Process and Reality*. Claremont, CA: Process and Faith.

Cobb, J. B. (Ed.). (2008c). *Back to Darwin: A Richer Account of Evolution*. Cambridge: Eerdmans.

Cooper, R. (1976). The open field. *Human Relations, 29*(11), 999–1017.

Cooper, R. (1993). Heidegger and Whitehead on lived-time and causality. *The Journal of Speculative Philosophy, 7*(4), 298–312.

Coxworth, B. (2011). The Chip Scale Atomic Clock makes atomic time-keeping portable. *Gizmag*. Retrieved from http://www.gizmag.com/portable-chip-scale-atomic-clock/18580/, accessed February 2015.

Deleuze, G. (1994). *Difference and Repetition*. New York: Columbia University Press.

Deleuze, G., & Guattari, F. (1987). *A Thousand Plateaus: Capitalism and Schizophrenia*. Minneapolis: University of Minnesota Press.

Dibben, M. (2009). Exploring Whitehead's understanding of organizations: Moving beyond the organising experience of individual managers. *Philosophy of Management, 7*(2), 13–24.

Dibben, M. (2015). Management and the care for our common home. In J. B. Cobb & I. Castuera (Eds.), *For Our Common Home: Process-Relational Responses to Laudato Si'* (pp. 274–285). Claremont, CA: Process Century Press.

Frank, A. (2012). *About Time*. Oxford: Oneworld Publications.

Gaffney, V., Fitch, S., Ramsey, E., Yorston, R., Ch'ng, E., Baldwin, E.,... Howard, A. (2013). Time and a place: A luni-solar 'time-reckoner' from 8th millennium BC Scotland. *Internet Archaeology, 34*.

Greene, B. (2005). *The Fabric of the Cosmos: Space, Time and the Texture of Reality*. London: Penguin.

Griffin, D. R. (Ed.). (1988). *The Reenchantment of Science*. Albany: Sate University of New York Press.

Griffin, D. R. (2008). *Unsnarling the World-Knot: Consciousness, Freedom and the Mind-Body Problem*. Berkley, CA: University of California Press.

Halewood, M. (2014). *Rethinking the Social: Durkheim, Marx, Weber and Whitehead*. London: Anthem Press.

Hall, E. T. (1983). *The Dance of Life: The Other Dimension of Time*. New York: Anchor Books and Doubleday.

Hammond, C. (2012). *Time Warpes: Unlocking the Mysteries of Time Perception*. Edinburgh: Canongate Books.

Hartshorne, C. (1984). *Omnipotence and Other Theological Mistakes*. Albany: State University of New York.

Hawking, S. (2011). *A Brief History of Time: From the Big Bang to Black Holes*. London: Bantam Books.

Hegel, G. W. F. (1979). *Phenomonology of Spirit* (A. V. Miller, Trans.). Delhi: Galaxy Books.

Heidegger, M. (1996). *Being and Time* (J. Stambaugh, Trans.). Albany, NY: State University of New York Press.

Heidegger, M. (2010). *Being and Time* (J. Stambaugh, Trans.). Albany: State University of New York Press.

Helin, J., Hernes, T., Hjorth, D., & Holt, R. (Eds.). (2014). *The Oxford Handbook of Process Philosophy and Organization Studies*. Oxford: Oxford University Press.

Hernes, T. (2014). *A Process Theory of Organizations*. Oxford: Oxford University Press.

Hoffman, E. (2009). *Time*. London: Profile Books.

Hoy, R. C. (1994). Parmenides' complete rejection of time. *The Journal of Philosophy, 91*(11), 573–598.

Isaacson, W. (2008). *Einstein: His Life and Universe*. London: Pocket Books.

Jha, A. (2013). What is Heisenberg's uncertainty principle? *The Guardian*. Retrieved from theguardian.com website: https://www.theguardian.com/science/2013/nov/10/what-is-heisenbergs-uncertainty-principle

Jungreman, J. A. (2000). *World in Process: Creativity and Interconnection in the New Physics*. Albany: State University of New York Press.

Kant, I. (1781/2006). *Critique of Pure Reason*. London: Penguin Modern Classics.

Levine, R. V. (2006). *A Geography of Time: The Temporal Misadventures of a Social Psychologist or How Every Culture Keeps Time Just a Little Bit Differently.* Oxford: Oneworld Publications.

Linden, N., Popoesu, S., Short, T., & Winter, A. (April 25, 2014). New quantum theory could explain the arrow of time. *Quantum Magazine.*

Lorentz, H. A. (2008). *The Einstein Theory of Relativity.* Retrieved from http://www.amazon.co.uk, doi: 9488783-1561908, accessed July 2015.

Lowe, V. (1990). *Alfred North Whitehead: The Man and His Work.* Baltimore: John Hopkins University Press.

McTaggart, J. M. E. (1993). The unreality of time. In R. Le Poidevin & M. MacBeath (Eds.), *The Philosophy of Time* (pp. 23–34). Oxford: Oxford University Press.

Neesham, C., & Dibben, M. (2012). The social value of business: Lessons from political economy and process philosophy. *Research in Ethical Issues in Organizations, 8*(1), 63–83.

Newton, I. (2014). *The Mathematical Principles of Natural Philosophy.* Retrieved from http://www.amazon.co.uk, accessed July 2015.

Peake, A. (2012). *The Labyrinth of Time: The Illusion of Past, Present and Future.* London: Arcturus Publishing.

Penrose, R. (2011). *What Came Before the Big Bang? Cycles of Time.* London: Vintage Books.

Phipps, R. (2009). The philosophy of an open, infinite and integrated universe. In M. Dibben & R. Newton (Eds.), *Applied Process Thought, Vol. 2* (pp. 149–203). Frankfurt: Ontos Verlag.

Sherburne, D. (1981). *A Key to Whitehead's Process and Reality.* Chicago: University of Chicago Press.

Singer, P. (2001). *Hegel: A Very Short Introduction.* Oxford: Oxford University Press.

Slife, B. (2004). Taking practice seriously: Toward a relational ontology. *Journal of Theoretical and Philosophical Psychology, 24*(2), 157–178.

Tsoukas, H., & Chia, R. (2002). On organizational becoming: Rethinking organizational change. *Organization Science, 13*(5), 567–582.

Weik, E. (2004). From time to action: The contribution of Whitehead's philosophy to a theory of action. *Time & Society, 13*(2/3), 301–319.

Whitehead, A. N. (1929). *Process and Reality: An Essay in Cosmology.* Cambridge: Cambridge University Press.

Wood, M., & Dibben, M. (2015). Leadership as relational process. *Process Studies, 44*(1), 24–47.

3 Understanding Time and Temporality
Psychology, Sociology, and Organization Studies

Given the pervasiveness and importance of time to understanding management and the world of work, there has been surprising absence of discussion around concepts and theories developed in the field of organization studies (see, e.g., Ancona, Okhuysen, & Perlow, 2001; Glennie & Thrift, 1996; Goodman, Lawrence, Ancona, & Tushman, 2001; Roe, Waller, & Clegg, 2009). There is a sense in which our own intuitive notions of time should not be questioned as this taken-for-granted knowledge underlies our everyday understanding of movement, episodes, sequences of activities, and temporal events (Huy, 2001). Time becomes known yet hidden, a Pandora's box that should remain firmly closed to prevent discombobulation, disorder, and conceptual confusion (Stacey, 2005; Zimbardo & Boyd, 2008). But as Hernes and colleagues describe (Hernes, Simpson, & Söderlund, 2013: 2), there are many types of time, such as 'railway time', 'banana time' (coping with monotonous work time, see Roy, 1959), 'project time', and 'beach time', but most of these remain rooted in clock time and are unable to fully address time and temporality in organization studies. They claim that there has been an absence of temporal vocabulary and that there is a need to go beyond conventional clock time that is so pervasive in studies of management.

In examining time and temporality in organizations, we embark on a selective review of debates in the social sciences that range from individual time perspectives and concepts drawn from psychology to more collective representations of time from social psychological and sociological studies that take culture and context seriously, through to critical management studies in which there has been a tendency to focus on the way clock time is used to control and discipline workplace behaviours. Our central interest in organizational change and temporality guides this exposition in which the long-standing issue of dualism in demarking dichotomies and delineating boundaries between, for example, notions of the past, present, and future, are raised and discussed. These issues of dualism and the paradox of time take us back to earlier discussions on the science and philosophy of time, raising concerns and controversies that remain central to the social sciences and organization studies. Our purpose is not to resolve these contradictions; on the contrary, these tensions purchase insights in enabling us to compare and contrast concepts as well as to engage with the blurring of divisions in a more entangled perspective. As such, we argue that there is value in studying socially constructed boundaries in organizations that separate individuals and groups in, for example, the establishment of formal authority relationships in the development of hierarchical structures and in the organizational use of quantifiable objective time as well as moving beyond a representational view towards a more entwined approach that accommodates the interweaving, fusing, and blurring of boundaries adopting, for example, a diffractive methodology and relational view of organizations. In this, we compare two organization perspectives in which flow and interconnectedness of one approach contrasts with a more fixed and separatist world view of another.

Psychological and Sociological Debates on Time

Within the social sciences—with the exception of philosophy—concerns over the failure to adequately conceptualize temporality and complaints about the reluctance for theorists and researchers to take time seriously are issues that continually resurface (Goodman et al., 2001; Roe et al., 2009; Thrift, 2004). Time is often viewed either as a scientific conundrum best left to the mathematical physicists or as an esoteric and abstract domain best left to the philosophers. Because it is not possible to cover each social science domain in detail, our selective focus here is: first, on the recent upsurge in interest and research on individual psychological time perspectives (Zimbardo & Boyd, 2010); second, on the importance of culture and context in more social psychological and sociological approaches that examine social time (Bergmann, 1992; Levine, 2006); and third, on the general absence of concepts of time and temporality in the field of management studies other than as a tool for management control.

Individual Time Perspectives and the Social Psychology of Time

> The life-space of an individual, far from being limited to what he considers [sic] the present situation, includes the future, the present, and also the past. Actions, emotions, and certainly the morale of an individual at any instant depend upon his total time perspective.
>
> (Lewin, 1942: 103–104)

Moving away from the Cartesian and Kantian conception of time associated with the work of Freud, in which the individual can be separated from the world and his or her temporal existence (the isolated mind as an objective entity that looks out on an external world), more contemporary psychological work (see Jones & Brown, 2005) bring to the fore the temporal and contextual nature of being in the world. Pearl (2013), for example, draws on Heidegger's *Being and Time* (1996) in taking up the view of humans as inseparable from both their world and their lived experience of time, advocating the importance of temporality to psychoanalysis. Essentially, temporal motion is seen as a part of human existence, but this may, through repression of some past event, be temporally fractured, and this in turn can limit not only access to the past but also to the present and future that are shaped by that past (see Pearl, 2013).

Since 2005, there has been a noticeable resurgence in interest in psychological and social psychological approaches to time and temporality following the work of Phillip Zimbardo and John Boyd and their development of the Zimbardo Time Perspective Index (ZTPI). This highly influential work is usefully brought together in their popularized book *The Time Paradox* (Zimbardo & Boyd, 2008). They argue that time is a central yet too quickly ignored aspect of living that influences behaviour and, if managed properly, can lead to well-being and health but, if left to its own devices, may result in deviant and antisocial behaviour. Zimbardo and Boyd (2008) note how most people pay more attention to how they spend their money rather than how they spend their time. This devaluation of time is seen as endemic to modern Western societies (studies have largely focussed on Western society, but an increasing number of followers are extending research into a range of different cultural areas). They argue the need for a reorientation towards time and temporality as this will have an impact on financial decision making, health, relationships, and the ability to deal with stress in working towards a better future. The basic tenet is that our perspective on time governs our lives. It is claimed that we carry around our psychology of time perspective in our minds in which the fluid flow of human experience becomes embedded into temporal time frames. As people, when we are faced with a situation requiring us to make a decision, our temporal perspective shapes this process. Our temporal frame is influenced by our present orientation (like things now), our future orientation (anticipated consequences), and our past orientation (the way memories and past experiences influence our decisions in the present). In addition, there are several biases influencing our time perspective including: class, culture, education, religion, geography, and the political and economic stability of a country or region.

In drawing on Tawney's work, published in 1926 on *Religion and the Rise of Capitalism* (Tawney, 1969), Zimbardo and Boyd point out how Calvinism reinforced our common notion of time is money—which is largely an unassailable driving assumption in the modern Western industrial world—shaping all forms of social, economic, and political behaviour. These cultural influences that emerge from historical developments also influence other aspects of time orientation; for example, they refer to Levine's (2006) *A Geography of Time*, spotlighting how our sense of duration, how much time we feel has expired, will vary in different cultures and geographies and how these contextual influences differentially impact upon individual and collective behaviours. They argue, for example, that people who live close to the equator are more present orientated due to the consistency of climate (that changes very little over the seasons), whereas people living in settings with distinct seasons tend to have a greater sense of change and transition. In forwarding the concept of a time perspective they promote the idea that how we view ourselves and our relationships within these different frames of time affects our well-being. The five different frames are as follows:

1. *Past Positive*: This is when one is positive about the past things that have happened in one's life; there are happy, good memories that build self-esteem and friendliness in the present. It is argued that too much living in the past can have detrimental effects on our capacity to live a full life in the present.
2. *Past Negative*: This occurs when people constantly revisit past nightmares or events and situations they deeply regret or feel embarrassed, ashamed, or angry about. Memories often capture thoughts of all the things that could have been done but were not. Too much past negative can lead to aggressive behaviours, depression, and anxiety. According to this theory, people who suffer from high past negative are generally unhappy, sad individuals with low energy levels.
3. *Present Hedonistic*: These are novelty-seeking individuals who have lots of energy and are often highly creative. There is sensation seeking, some aggression, and a desire to engage in pleasurable activities. The main problem is the tipping point where the pursuit of pleasure becomes addictive, and people make decisions on the spur of moment without thinking about future consequences.
4. *Present Fatalistic*: Under this category people exhibit high aggression, and there is a tendency towards high levels of anxiety and depression; for example, people do not care about the future because in their view nothing works out anyway.
5. *Future Oriented*: Those high on this element tend to resist temptations and get work done (high achievers). They tend to be conscientious, live longer, and are quick to follow advice on healthy living.

Under Zimbardo and Boyd's time perspective, individuals who score a high past negative combined with a high present fatalistic are diagnosed as at risk, possibly requiring remedial therapy. They argue that individuals with a past negative time perspective may suffer from recurrent depression through placing too much significance on past negative or painful events in life. Those with an intensive present orientation tend to be risk takers and are hedonistic. In this case the advice is to moderate the hedonism with 'a dose of the holistic present' (2008: 303). They claim that individuals who are future oriented are often driven to achieve, but if this becomes an endless competitive pursuit, then, individuals may find themselves isolated from family and friends. In summing up ZTPI they conclude:

> Given the research we have done—and acknowledging our inherent bias as residents in the Western world—we believe that the optimal time perspective profile is:
>
> • High in past-positive time perspective
> • Moderately high in future time perspective
> • Moderately high in present-hedonistic time perspective
> • Low in past-negative time perspective
> • Low in present-fatalistic time perspective
>
> This blend offers three critical advantages: A sense of positive past gives you *roots*. . . . With a future perspective, you can envision a future filled with hope, optimism, and power. . . . A hedonistic present gives you *energy* and joy about being alive. That energy drives you to explore people, places, and self.
>
> (Zimbardo & Boyd, 2008: 297–298)

Collective Time Perspectives and the Importance of Context and Culture

The importance of culture and context in shaping time as a social concept is evident in Durkheim's *Elementary Forms of Religious Life*. He shows how time exerts a compulsion on the way people experience and make sense of the world. For Durkheim (1915), time cannot be explained by our psychological makeup, nor should it be seen as simply a derivative of individual consciousness, rather it is social, reflecting the nature of society. Social time is not independent of culture (language, symbols, festivals, traditions, etc.) but is collective in character. For Jones and Brown (2005), there is a distinction that can be made between those cultures that are more present oriented and those that orient towards a future, as they state:

> The basic distinction made about cultures comes down to a contrast between an orientation toward the future (temponomic) and a preference for living in the present (temponostic). Hall (1983) distinguishes these perspectives with the concepts of *monochromic time* (M-time) and *polychromic time* (P-time). M-time is characterized by doing one thing at a time, following schedules, and considering time to be tangible. P-time is characterized by "doing many things at once". Punctuality or even time-based appointments are regarded lightly, and time is intangible. P-time is social and this is based on "transactions". M-time is

arbitrary, imposed, and ultimately learned as a consequence of cultural socialization. But, Hall argues, M- and P-time are not mutually exclusive and often interact.

(Jones & Brown, 2005: 309–310)

A 'temponomic orientation' represents a society in which time is seen as an asset, time has value and is important (time is money), and it can be saved, invested, and wasted. People who use time wisely are praised, and those who squander time are punished—'an idle child is the Devil's playmate'—in these communities, clock time structures activities and behavioural responses. In contrast, a 'temponostic orientation' is a culture, society, or community in which there is a greater indifference to time. Jones and Brown (2005) use the example of Trinidad time as cyclical time that follows the seasons, is linked to the music of the people, and for example, breakfast is not at a set clock time but when people decide to eat. Brislin and Kim (2003) also draw attention to the importance of culture and context in the way groups understand and use time. Some cultures place a greater emphasis on the present, on events and social time, whereas others are more focussed on clock time, tasks, and punctuality. They note how long silences are often difficult for cultures where clock time has become naturalized, whereas in event time cultures this can indicate respect.

In clock-based, work-disciplined cultures, doing things quicker is seen as 'efficient', whereas in event-oriented cultures there is a more relational view of time in the building of trust and working together in a slower pace of life in which leisure time is equally important as 'getting things done on time'. Jones & Brown (2005: 310) point out that in many African cultures, there are no words to capture the notion of working for the future as the collective perspective is on the present (*sasa*) and the past (*zamani*). Bernardi's (1974) research on Swahili culture highlighted how this sasa-to-zamani axis captures a two-dimensional temporality represented by a cyclical view of time with an emphasis on dreams and myths. This contrasts with the more Western, conventional, linear view of time in which the past precedes the present, which precedes the future. Event-time cultures are more cyclical and Einsteinian (relative), whereas the more familiar linear time is more Newtonian (absolute). For Jones and Brown (2005), African cultures are more associated with a present-time perspective that links with together-time, rhythm, improvisation, orality, and spirituality (the TRIOS model). Time in being together through rituals is moved by rhythms connected to ancestors (spirituality) with the traditions, stories, and practices passed on through oral renderings (songs, words, stories, and speeches). As they note,

> Improvisation occurs in time as well, because its essence is the online success of creatively solving unanticipated challenges or the spontaneous expression of a thought, a desire, or means of attaining a goal. It is contrasted with the planning approach, which tries to foresee and even

create the contexts in which a given behaviour will unfold. Improvisation is a value expressed as preference for being-in-the-now, for creating one's life moment by moment in characteristic ways that define one's individuality.

(Jones & Brown, 2005: 315)

These and other studies by anthropologists and cultural social scientists question our conventional temporal division between past, present, and future (see Bohannan, 1967; Evans-Pritchard, 1940; Gell, 2001). For example, the early work by Barden (1973) on Australian Aborigines highlights the importance of 'dream-time' and how this relates to an understanding of the present, which does not align with the conventional past, present, and future temporality. Although general time characteristics may be identified within certain societal forms, such as agrarian or industrial societies, there are also differences in time orientation among individuals and groups within such societies (Cipriani, 2013; Herzfeld, 1991). For example, Bergmann (1992: 95), in summarizing a comparative study of time orientation among various subcultural groups in the U.S., notes:

Americans of Spanish origin were found to be significantly more present-oriented, as were the Navajo and Zuni Indians, for whom however the past took second place; while the Chinese population was significantly more past-oriented. . . . Despite the differences revealed in the USA . . . Coser and Coser (1963: 641) stress that in Western cultures, an active, individualistic orientation towards the future dominates. Other social time orientations can then only be understood as 'divergent' or 'variant' (Kluckhohn & Strodtbeck, 1961: 13), that is, as subcultural deviations.

Just as time orientations can vary within groups and subcultures within different types of society, so individuals can exhibit different time perspectives and temporal orders. However, the predominance of measured time within the Western industrialized world has led Adam (2004) to argue that clock time has become naturalized as a cultural norm in which the linear perspective of time is absorbed, decontextualized, and operationalized in the control and coordination of life activities that quantify and objectify in the name of economic efficiency. Time is depersonalized and commodified ('time is money'); the clock becomes the pendulum of the market economy in an endless linear flow of capital accumulation. Adam suggests that time is becoming increasingly compressed through the use of modern technologies, controlled through the modification of natural processes (e.g., in slowing down the ripening of fruit so that food has a greater shelf life) and in the temporal global colonization of time. As we describe in Chapter 4, globalization of the market economy is seen to herald wider imposition of clock time on newly developing economies, imposing standardization and the naturalization of objective, quantified time as an industrial norm that must be adhered to if one seeks to compete in the global marketplace. Adam (2003) refers to this process—that she sees as endemic to global modernization—as the five Cs of temporalization comprising: the creation of time to human design, the commodification of time, the compression of time, the control of time, and the colonization of time (for a full description of these, see Chapter 4). As she notes when discussing the compression of time (Adam, 2003: 67),

> When time is money, then faster means better. When (clock) time is commodified, time compression becomes identified, equated even, with efficiency and profit: speed is valorized as an unquestioned and unquestionable good. Naturalized, the valorization of speed overshadows other social or environmental considerations. Time compression, as Castells (1996) and Harvey (1989) identified, has been achieved by a number of means: by increasing activity within the same unit of time (introduction of machines and the intensification of labour), re-organizing the sequence and ordering of activities (Taylorism and Fordism), using peaks and troughs more effectively (flexibilization), and by eliminating all unproductive times from the process (just-in-time production).

For Adam (2003), the colonization of clock time is endemic to modernization through developments in a digitalized global economy in which the metrics of quantified time predominates. Foucault (1979: 147–159) captures some of these historical developments in his description of the timetable and the imposition of a new 'disciplinary time' in the organization of serial space to prevent idleness in dividing up the day and ensuring simultaneous work for all through establishing rhythms and regulating cycles of repetition. In these new ways of administering time (and as we shall discuss further in the chapter that follows), new practices of domination and forms of control arise in organizations. Within the global economy, time is closely associated with money, as a commodity to be compressed. Progressive change is linked with faster and more efficient ways of producing through increasing activities within defined time intervals and eradicating unproductive time that serves to reduce costs and increase profits.

Key questions raised by this global trend of clock time colonization are not only whether the different cultural time perspectives identified in places like Trinidad, Portugal, and more remote parts of the world can survive but whether they will continue to offer alternative time orientations. Marshak (1994: 403) has usefully categorized a range of culturally comparative views in his analysis of contrasting cultural approaches to change. He reveals how different assumptions underlay and shape change approaches in countries with East Asian and Confucian traditions when compared to the West, drawing attention to some of the issues and problems associated with an undifferentiated Westernized perspective. Liao and colleagues (2013) also highlight the importance of local structures and culture in their sociological study of temporality among university students, but the focus is on the local context. They examine physical (clock time) and time subjectively experienced, arguing that the relation between the two senses are synchronized within the social collective and embedded in structures and social situations (Liao et al., 2013: 149). Time is social, emerging historically and shaped by culture and context.

Time and Organizational Studies: Presence in Absence

In organizational studies, research on time has been rather sporadic and thinly spread, unlike other areas in the social sciences. Whereas the organizational use of the atomic clock and Gregorian calendar can be seen to underlie established organizational practices and institutional arrangements (Thompson, 1967), this conventional time concept has evaded critical analysis. Czarniawska (2004: 773) highlights the dominance of chronological time to factory-like organizing in which the reification of time into something that can be measured and categorized (quantitative temporality) is pervasive and taken for granted. In organizations, linear notions of clock time have become embedded and deeply sedimented from the way workdays are measured, divided, and planned through to the strong associations with financial budgeting and the commonly held view that time is money. The tendency to reify time and to uncritically accept the institutionalized notions of time also underpins a great deal of management research in the development of models and theories that seek to explain and provide practical advice or best practice guidelines (e.g., how to organize work or manage change). It is perhaps surprising, therefore, that given the history and centrality of clock-based regulation to systems of domination and task regimes that dehumanize work, that this area has generated little interest among critical management scholars (see Alvesson, Bridgman, & Willmott, 2011; Alvesson & Spicer, 2012; Knights & Willmott, 2000; McCabe, 2007). Writers concerned with power in organizations (Clegg & Haugaard, 2013; Hardy, 1996) rarely address time directly, even though these studies often implicitly draw out how time (in the form of clock time) is used to structure and regulate routines (forms of continuity) in the introduction of new methods of monitoring performance (change) that simultaneously reaffirms authority and power relations in reinforcing the managerial prerogative of managers to get workers to change in ways that they would rather not (see Chapter 7 for further discussion). From the early writings of labour process theorists (Braverman, 1974; Littler, 1982; Noble, 1979; Zimbalist, 1979), who highlighted the process of valorization in the transformation of labour power (a worker's capacity to work) into labour (work), the elevation of time as an identifiable, measurable, economic resource central to management in the organization and control of work has been spotlighted (see the chapter that follows for a discussion on the institutionalization of time and critical evaluation of the work of Glennie & Thrift, 1996; Thompson, 1967).

Slawinski and Bansal (2012) illustrate in their research on time and climate change that time perspectives often remain implicit in organization studies. They show how firms tended to exhibit either a linear time perspective, seeking solutions to problems in the present, or a cyclical time perspective, where firms draw on past experiences and consider future possibilities in making decision on how to approach the present. They argue that these two perspectives of linear clock time (*chronos*) in which time progresses forward and is irreversible (a Newtonian view that they claim is all pervasive in Western culture) and cyclical event time (*kairos*), which is non-linear, subjective, and emphasises relationships, are seen to be the two prominent views that have dominated discussions within the social sciences (Slawinski & Bansal, 2012: 1540–1541). They conclude that whilst event time was in evidence in some organizations, this has been largely ignored by researchers who uncritically adopt a linear clock time perspective as their basis for theorization within organization studies (2012: 1557). They are critical of this narrow focus claiming that: 'Viewing time as "scarce" encourages a faster pace of life and a focus on the present, with little thought given to future consequences' (2012: 1561).

Within the mainstream change management literature, where time should be a central component in addressing not only current 'problems' but ways of moving forward to an 'improved' future, one would expect far more consideration would be given to both kairotic and chronological time (in exploiting opportunities in organizing and planning for strategic futures). Ironically, whereas time is integral to theoretical explanations and model development, the tendency has been to view time as self-evident, working with an implicit assumption that time is uncontentious (Dawson, 2014), even though concepts such as time and temporality and the interplay between linear clock time and event time would seem to be essential to understanding change in organizations (for a more detailed discussion, see Chapter 5). However in management research, objective time predominates, generally characterized by the clock, either as a stand-alone material object (a wall clock, watch, mobile phone, computer, etc.) or as embedded in a raft of devices most of us use on a regular basis, whereas subjective time is used to capture our experiences grounded in social practices in which the present is made sense of in relation to memories of the past and expectations of the future (temporality) and in which experiences are also interactively and intersubjectively constituted.

Although the binary divide represented by objective and subjective time is rightly criticized as a boundary construct (that is, not a representation of how time is), the division, nevertheless, remains important for understanding the tools and techniques used for managing change interventions as well as the experiences of those on the receiving end of change. The emergence and institutionalization of clock time is examined in more detail in the chapter that follows, but before we conclude here, it is worth returning briefly to the issue of dualism and the relationship between objective and subjective time that are particularly pertinent to understanding the theoretical positioning and concepts used within the different perspectives we examine in the second part of this book.

Dualism and the Paradox of Social and Material Time

These social science studies not only illustrate the importance of culture and context but also the question of whether differentiating between the time associated with clocks and the Gregorian calendar (Westernized view of objective time) with the way time is experienced (subjective time) is analytically useful for examining time and the relationship between the two or whether this ultimately distorts our understanding of time through an inappropriate conception of time (as metering devices that measure sequenced intervals) or through separating and dividing that which is ultimately inseparable. Caution is needed to ensure that the tendency to develop a type of conceptual dualism between 'natural' or 'physical' time and 'social' or 'organizational' time (among others) does not lead us on what Elias referred to earlier as the wild goose chase of trying to find some immutable framework that can fully explain time (Elias, 1993: 117). For Elias time is neither objective nor subjective but both; it is 'rolled into one', and hence it is important to avoid the trap of using separate and contrasting concepts as explanations of how time is rather than how time is represented.

In *Matter and Memory* Bergson (2010) attempts to tackle the long-standing theoretical issue of dualism in using the illustrative example of matter in his opening introduction. He contrasts the idealist position in which an object exists only in and for the mind (perception) and a realist perspective in which matter exists independently of consciousness, and as a thing is able to produce perceptions (Bergson, 2010: 5). He argues that a common-sense view tends toward realism in viewing an object existing in and of itself; however, Bergson maintains that it is between these two pictorial perceptions that we must look, as he explains:

> Matter, in our view, is an aggregate of 'images'. And by 'image' we mean a certain existence which is more than that which the idealist calls a representation, but less than that which the realist calls a thing;—an existence placed half-way between the 'thing' and the 'representation'.
> (Bergson, 2010: 5)

This division of objective spatial time from more subjective extra-spatial time can produce a problem of dualism that constrains or limits theorization. Put simply, this binary division can in turn produce a separatist ontology in which opposites are used to form the basic building blocks for the development of knowledge and understanding. But what Bergson (2010) refers to as the 'in-betweens' can remain outside of our lens for theorizing, and this can bring about an early closure to debates about meaning (caricatured in the last chapter as the objective time of scientists and the subjective time of philosophers). It can thus direct attention away from the places between, from the rolling together of times, from the interweaving of objective and subjective time, from seeking to explain seamless movements between category types in everyday practices that people engage in (that ultimately questions this binary division), and from accommodating multiple times and temporalities.

For us, this leaves open the question of whether there are more appropriate ways to tackle this issue of dualism through process perspectives (see Chapters 9, 10 and 11). Two approaches that are discussed in greater detail in Chapter 6, namely, Actor Network Theory (ANT) and agential realism, attempt to do this through a process-based relational ontology. In using ANT as an example of a non-dualistic approach, Reed (1997) describes how attention is focussed on process and flow of social interaction at the local level in which 'organizations and actors are viewed as the temporary products or effects of micro-level processes of ordering and patterning that fashion the interactional chains . . . micro-level practices and patterns are to be regarded as the "ontological bedrock" on which organizational analysis is to be conducted' (Reed, 1997: 25). For Reed, the main problem with this approach is that it ignores structure and hence does not engage with hierarchy, authority relationships, power, and hegemony that form an integral part of peoples' experiences in organizations. ANT is thereby seen to present an apolitical world of process, of continual doings and movements in which nouns are subservient to the dominance of verbs. Essentially, Reed is critical of approaches that attempt to overcome dualism by collapsing the opposites into one (such as agency and structure in, e.g., structuration theory) as these significantly reduce both 'explanatory power and political imagination', taking away the power of people to act or to have any form of agency against, for example, the control and surveillance practices imposed by others. As he states,

> Agency and structure are analytically conflated in such a way that the interplay between the two and its vital role in reproducing and/or transforming social structures is denied by an ontological vision and explanatory logic that can only "see" flat social surfaces without the stratified structural relations and mechanisms that give them shape, consistency and continuity over time.
>
> (Reed, 1997: 27)

The relational ontology of agential realism provides another useful illustration of some of the counter issues that arise in non-dualistic perspectives. In this case the problem centres on how to use representational language to communicate concepts and make theorization intelligible. Barad (2007: 31), in building on the work of Bohr—who rejected representationalism in his early work on atomic theory—examines sociomateriality from the perspective of agential realism. Under this perspective, there is no inherent ontological separability other than what is performed through agential cuts on an entangled sociomaterial world of inseparability. She argues that it is the researcher who determines and enacts boundaries through these cuts and through the use of representational language in which dichotomous relations between nature and culture, the human and non-human, are seen to be an actualization of reality whilst really masking the entanglement of existence in which life is a 'cascade experiment' (Barad, 2007: 394). The entangledness of being in a world where everything exists within everything else, the iterative enfolding of phenomena is, according to Barad, misconstrued when language is used to describe boundaries that misrepresent ongoing intra-action (material discursive practices). In this relational ontology, where 'the world *is* intra-activity in its differential mattering' (Barad, 2003: 817), there are openings for the future (indeterminacy), and in this, Barad attempts to counter dualisms by viewing change as part of the world's intra-active dynamism. But this jettisoning of a representational ontology rooted in language leaves a problem of replacement and displacement. For example, words are still used by Barad to describe and explain this entangled perspective (there is no replacement), and whereas the perspective encourages a stepping outside of a representational world, this is the world as experienced by those who work within a framework of institutionalized time within organizations. In studying people and change, there is also the issue that temporality as storied by individuals and groups in the way that they make sense and give sense to the changes they experience is no longer a representable part of this performative world. But perhaps there is a place for accommodating boundaries, for drawing dichotomies, and for studying the interactions between people in the unfolding of complex change processes in organizations? This is not a simple question as answers can often raise more questions than they resolve:

> Another step in advancing the notion of time in management and organization research involves drawing dichotomous distinctions between different types of time, such as kairos and chronos. . . . These are undoubtedly important, and to some extent overlapping distinctions. We believe that they provide good starting points for discussion.
>
> (Hernes et al., 2013: 2)

Conclusion

Time is a paradox; it is a contradiction, for as St Augustine expressed, time has the dual characteristics of being both real and ephemeral. On the one hand, it is easily recognised and understood, on the other hand, time remains untouchable and mysterious, slipping away from conceptualization as we try to explain what time is. In this sense, time is perhaps the ultimate paradox, an unresolvable puzzle enduring time and memorial. In organization studies, time is an abstract concept that has been made manageable, concrete, and scientifically useful through the Gregorian calendar and the atomic clock. But this reification of time does not render the abstract nature of time any more real, rather it creates a divide in which we can, through language, compare and contrast objective and subjective forms of time, whereas in life we move seamlessly between these temporal worlds. In furthering research on organizational change and temporality, it is important to make explicit our use of time and consider the way conventional and unchallenged conceptions act as an obstacle that not only impedes theorization but also creates sterile, time-regulated work environments that prevent the achievement of more participatory and humane systems of management. As argued elsewhere, the frenetic time demands of managerial jobs, the hurriedness of work-life commitments, the obsession with time measurement, regulation, and efficiency controls sour our experience of time. Time as experienced is increasingly collapsed into the clockwork myopia of a precarious existence within an increasingly antisocial and unequal world. There is a time for a rethink and offload the idea of time as money and a linear belief in progress in questioning time commodification in the pursuit of a soulless arrow of economic efficiency:

> Time and work disciplines continue to regulate activities with new procedural and technical controls being developed and used in monitoring and evaluating immediate and remote behaviours in collecting data on the auditable achievements of employees. In an accelerating world where creativity, innovation and change are central to the hyper competition of business, concerns for employees rather than shareholder value should take centre stage but remain unvoiced and constrained by conventional management thinking. Innovation for excellence is witnessed by the stress of open surveillance, the strains of increasing workloads and the expectations (self, peer-group and organisational) to meet these standards of excellence (which are often set above average thresholds) that ultimately dehumanizes and degrades employees' experience of work. It is argued that the rhetoric of autonomy and participation is being increasingly unmasked in a world of tightening budgets and work intensification where employees are required to take on more 'efficient' methods of work that enables organisations to capture quantifiable and transparent performance data. There is a small but growing call for more humane organisations that reduce oppressive controls, enabling space and freedom for self-management in the performance of tasks and activities, for new forms of social business and for replacing the economic with a more social model of work. This represents a major and difficult challenge requiring organisations to off-load the legacies from the tools and techniques of 20th century management (that are

continually modified and repackaged as something new) which simply serve to stifle creativity, inhibit innovation and limit human initiative that are all critical to developments, not only to more human-oriented organisations, but also to developing more flexible and innovative business organisations for the future.

(Dawson, 2015: 4)

Concepts of time and the theorization of change management models have consequences that go beyond the model to their influence on management practice and their effects on change interventions and the work of employees. There is a need for the production of relevant but critical knowledge in order to further our understanding of organizational change and temporality as well as the value of time beyond the simple commodification of 'time is money'. A more differentiated understanding and recognition of the broader value of time may enable people to engage in emancipatory projects that not only improve experiences of employment but also the place of work and organizations in their lives in constructing a society in which we can all play an active part (Dawson, 2015). In the chapter that follows, we chart the rise and embedding of a particular time that has come to dominate management, namely, digitalized clock time under an increasingly networked global economy.

References

Adam, B. (2003). Reflexive modernization temporalized. *Theory, Culture and Society, 20*(2), 59–78.

Adam, B. (2004). *Time*. Cambridge: Polity Press.

Alvesson, M., Bridgman, T., & Willmott, H. (Eds.). (2011). *The Oxford Handbook of Critical Management Studies*. Oxford: Oxford University Press.

Alvesson, M., & Spicer, A. (2012). Critical leadership studies: The case for critical performativity. *Human Relations, 65*(3), 367–390. doi: 10.1177/0018726711430555

Ancona, D. G., Okhuysen, G. A., & Perlow, L. A. (2001). Taking time to integrate temporal research. *Academy of Management Review, 26*(4), 512–529.

Barad, K. (2003). Posthumanist performativity: Toward an understanding of how matter comes to matter. *Signs, 28*(3), 801–831.

Barad, K. (2007). *Meeting the Universe Halfway: Quantum Physics and the Entanglement of Matter and Meaning*. London: Duke University Press.

Barden, G. (1973). Reflections of time. *The Human Context, 5*(1), 331–343.

Bergmann, W. (1992). The problem of time in sociology: An overview of the literature on the state of theory and research on the 'sociology of time', 1900–82. *Time & Society, 1*(1), 81–134.

Bergson, H. (2010). *Matter and Memory* (N. Paul & W. Palmer, Trans.). Overland Park, Kansas: Digireads.com Publishing.

Bernardi, B. (1974). *Uomo, Cultura, Società*. Milan: Angeli.

Bohannan, P. (1967). Concepts of time among the Tiv of Nigeria. In J. Middleton (Ed.), *Myth and Cosmos* (pp. 315–338). New York: Natural History Press.

Braverman, H. (1974). *Labor and Monopoly Capital: The Degradation of Work in the Twentieth Century*. New York: Monthly Review Press.

Brislin, R. W., & Kim, E. S. (2003). Cultural diversity in people's understanding and uses of time. *Applied Psychology: An International Review, 52*(3), 363–382.

Castells, M. (1996). *The Rise of the Network Society*. Oxford: Blackwell.

Cipriani, R. (2013). The many faces of social time: A sociological approach. *Time & Society, 22*(1), 5–30.

Clegg, S. R., & Haugaard, M. (Eds.). (2013). *The SAGE Handbook of Power*. London: Sage.

Coser, L. A., & Coser, R. L. (1963). Time perspectives and social structure. In A. W. Gouldner & H. P. Gouldner (Eds.), *Modern Sociology: An Introduction to the Science of Human Interaction* (pp. 638–647). New York: Harcourt, Brace & World.

Czarniawska, B. (2004). On time, space, and action nets. *Organization, 11*(6), 773–791.

Dawson, P. (2014). Reflections: On time, temporality and change in organizations. *Journal of Change Management, 14*(3), 285–308.

Dawson, P. (2015). In search of freedom: Legacies of management innovations for the experience of work and employment. *Employment Relations Record, 15*(1), 4–26.

Durkheim, E. (1915). *Elementary Forms of Religious Life*. London: George Allen & Unwin.

Elias, N. (1993). *Time: An Essay*. Oxford: Blackwell Publishing.

Evans-Pritchard, E. E. (1940). *The Neur*. Oxford: Oxford University Press.

Foucault, M. (1979). *Discipline and Punish: The Birth of the Prison*. Harmondsworth: Penguin.

Gell, A. (2001). *The Anthropology of Time: Cultural Constructions of Temporal Maps and Images*. Oxford: Berg Publishers.

Glennie, P., & Thrift, N. (1996). Reworking E. P. Thompson's 'Time, work-discipline and industrial capitalism'. *Time & Society, 5*(3), 275–299.

Goodman, P. S., Lawrence, B. S., Ancona, D. G., & Tushman, M. L. (2001). Introduction: Special topic forum on time and organizational research. *Academy of Management Review, 26*(4), 507–511.

Hall, E. T. (1983). *The Dance of Life: The Other Dimension of Time*. New York: Anchor Books/Doubleday.

Hardy, C. (1996). Understanding power: Bringing about strategic change. *British Academy of Management, 7*(Special Issue), S3–S16.

Harvey, D. (1989). *The Condition of Postmodernity*. Oxford: Blackwell.

Heidegger, M. (1996). *Being and Time* (J. Stambaugh, Trans.). Albany, NY: State University of New York Press.

Hernes, T., Simpson, B., & Söderlund, J. (2013). Managing and temporality. *Scandinavian Journal of Management, 29*(1), 1–6.

Herzfeld, M. (1991). *A Place in History: Social and Monumental Time in a Cretan Town*. Princeton, NJ: Princeton University Press.

Huy, Q. N. (2001). Time, temporal capability, and planned change. *Academy of Management Review, 26*(4), 601–623.

Jones, J. M., & Brown, W. T. (2005). Any time is Trinidad time! Cultural variations in the value and function of time. In A. Strathman & J. Joireman (Eds.), *Understanding Behavior in the Context of Time: Theory, Research and Application* (pp. 305–323). Hillsdale, NJ: Lawrence Erlbaum.

Kluckhohn, F. R., & Strodtbeck, F. L. (1961). *Variations in Value Orientation*. IL: Evanston.

Knights, D., & Willmott, H. (2000). *The Reengineering Revolution: Critical Studies of Corporate Change*. London: Sage.

Levine, R. V. (2006). *A Geography of Time: The Temporal Misadventures of a Social Psychologist or How Every Culture Keeps Time Just a Little Bit Differently*. Oxford: Oneworld Publications.

Lewin, K. (1942). Time perspective and morale. In G. W. Lewin (Ed.), *Resolving Social Conflicts* (pp. 103–124). New York: Harper & Row.

Liao, T. F., Beckman, J., Marzolph, E., Riederer, C., Sayler, J., & Schmelkin, L. (2013). The social definition of time for university students. *Time & Society, 22*(1), 119–151.

Littler, C. (1982). *The Development of the Labour Process in Capitalist Societies.* London: Heinemann.

Marshak, R. J. (1994). Lewin meets Confucius: A review of the OD model of change. *Journal of Applied Behavioral Science, 29*(4), 393–415.

McCabe, B. J. (2007). Spinning a Good Yarn. *HR Professional, 24*(4), 30–30. Retrieved from http://search.ebscohost.com/login.aspx?direct=true&db=buh&AN=26002416&site=bsi-live

Noble, D. (1979). Social choice in machine design: The case of automatically controlled machine tools. In A. Zimbalist (Ed.), *Case Studies in the Labor Process.* New York: Monthly Review Press.

Pearl, J. (2013). *A Question of Time: Freud in the Light of Heidegger's Temporality.* Amsterdam: Rodopi.

Reed, M. (1997). In praise of duality and dualism: Rethinking agency and structure in organizational analysis. *Organization Studies, 18*(1), 21–42.

Roe, R. A., Waller, M. J., & Clegg, S. R. (Eds.). (2009). *Time in Organizational Research.* Abingdon, Oxon: Routledge.

Roy, D. (1959). Banana time: Job satisfaction and informal organization. *Human Organization, 18*(4), 158–168.

Slawinski, N., & Bansal, P. (2012). A matter of time: The temporal perspectives of organizational responses to climate change. *Organization Studies, 33*(11), 1537–1563.

Stacey, R. (2005). Organizational identity: The paradox of continuity and potential transformation at the same time. *Group Analysis, 38,* 477–494.

Tawney, R. H. (1969). *Religion and the Rise of Capitalism.* London: Pelican.

Thompson, E. P. (1967). Time, work discipline and industrial capitalism. *Past and Present, 38,* 56–97.

Thrift, N. (2004). Thick time. *Organization, 11*(6), 873–880.

Zimbalist, A. (Ed.). (1979). *Case Studies in the Labor Process.* New York: Monthly Review Press.

Zimbardo, P., & Boyd, J. (2008). *The Time Paradox: The New Psychology of Time That Will Change Your Life.* New York: Simon and Schuster.

Zimbardo, P., & Boyd, J. (2010). *The Time Paradox: Using the New Psychology of Time to your Advantage.* London: Rider, Ebury Publishing.

4 Institutional Time in the Organization and Control of Work

In this chapter, we outline how time and temporality have become institutionalized in and through shared human work practices and the different forms that these institutions and practices have taken from ancient to contemporary times. We focus on how time has become naturalized in common-sense ways of thinking and embedded in everyday practices and social institutions. Discussions of social institutions and their development are a contested space, and here we adopt the view that they can best be understood as part of the ongoing processes and practices shaping social life more generally (Berger & Luckmann, 1984). Following Hernes (2014: 14), we also emphasise that institutions are 'perpetually in the making'. We therefore focus on the social and historical development of timekeeping practices and their enactment in changing work contexts. A key question then relates to how time becomes what it is or its 'ontogenesis' in relation to work practices (Thrift, 2004).

As the scope of the work is too large to provide a comprehensive analysis of all the institutional forms that have been shaped by time, we limit our study to tracing some of the major forms of time's institutionalization in Western cultures. More specifically, we examine early accounts evident in the pre-industrial period showing the ways time and its rhythms were central to the organization of work practices in the areas of agriculture, trade, and commerce. We trace how many of these rhythms were transformed or made redundant by the increased attention paid to the measurement of time in calendars, clocks, and timepieces within the Middle Ages and Renaissance periods. Any examination of aspects of these developments over the last 50 years of contemporary forms of industrialization shows how time measurement practices are inseparable from these forms. In other words, we suggest time and temporal relations are mutually constitutive of work and its practices. A central concern in examination of work in contemporary times is the pervasiveness of clock time(s) and its overlap and embeddedness in our everyday lives outside so-called work hours in sociomaterial practices associated with commonplace technologies, such as laptops and smartphones.

Clock time(s) are shown to be the ultimate measurement device of global capitalism and the digital network society that can be designed and used to produce structures and authority relations reflecting the locus of power not only in business and society but also in our forms of subjectivity. Thus, the institutionalization of clock time in contemporary work and social life does not come without significant social and human costs, and some of these challenges include: the paradox of simultaneous, instantaneous digital communication resulting in feelings of time poverty; acute sensitivity to clock time as governing work activities but lack of temporal awareness in relation to temporal rhythms, resulting in stress-related individual illness; and burnout and adverse impacts on collective well-being in environmental destruction (Wajcman, 2015).

Several factors have influenced our approach in this analysis: first, examinations of time and work do not fit into discrete disciplinary boundaries, and therefore in this chapter we draw on a wide range of disciplines, such as history, sociology, and anthropology as well as studies of work and organization. As Clark suggests, any history of ancient work necessarily becomes an interdisciplinary enterprise, 'an intricately adjusted web of relationships involving social, religious, psychological and material culture nexus' (Clark, 1989: 4). A corollary then of the interdisciplinary orientation is evident when, at times in our discussion, it is necessary for us to move between constructivist and realist ontologies attached to the sources of the various accounts. Second, whereas some well-known and accepted studies of the history of work and time (Clarke, 1989; Whitrow, 1989) record the history of temporal practices and expressions of time as homogeneous, and their development narratives are presented as comprehensive, linear, and progressive, our focus emphasises the differences associated with contexts. In contrast, Adam (1998: 55) suggests viewing time as timescapes 'emphasising inclusiveness, connectivity and implication' that exceed simple dualisms of time and space and the limits imposed by adherence to one perspective of time; she proposes: 'that we think about temporal relations with reference to a cluster of temporal features, each implicated in all the others but not necessarily of equal importance in each instance. . . . The notion of 'scape' is important here as it indicates, first, how time is inseparable from space and matter, and second, that context matters' (Adam, 2006: 143).

She goes on, 'Where other scapes such as landscapes, cityscapes and seascapes mark the spatial features of past and present activities and interactions of organisms and matter, timescapes emphasize their rhymicities, their timings and tempos, their changes and contingencies. A timescape perspective stresses the temporal features of living' (1998: 11). In our examination, we discuss how multiple timescapes produce different temporal practices and times. Therefore, our purpose in this chapter is not to retrofit work practices into a contemporary historiography by subsuming them into homogeneous categories or by analysing them retrospectively on the basis of contemporary notions of effectiveness and efficiency. For as we have discussed, we are interested in the contexts and history of the cultural practices of timekeeping, their multiplicity, and the ways they unfold or become over time—how they have shaped and continue to shape what it is to do work.

Three main sections are developed in the chapter: first, we discuss early human understandings and uses of time aligned with seasonal, diurnal, and circadian rhythms inscribed in nature and in human bodies and how this notion of time dominated early work practices. Second, we examine how during the Middle Ages and Industrial Revolution, work practices moved away from time hidden in nature's rhythms with the creation of cultural and social times linked to explicit clock times embedded in industrialization and ultimately to the emptying of time and its commodification. Third, we examine how in recent conceptions and uses of time in work, practices are reshaped in networked global capitalism that dominates contemporary institutions and forms of work.

The 'Creation' of Time in Early Cultures

It is evident from the early accounts of human development that people have adapted their ways of living and organizing to temporal rhythms within nature (Clarke, 1989). The passage of time was evident in the spatial changes that occurred in nature, and the pattern of these changes was recognised as occurring in cycles. However, as social and institutional ordering developed, more sophisticated ways of understanding time and its patterns became necessary both for survival and as attempts at making sense of the changing world for cultic and cultural reasons. In this section, we trace some of these developments in the move from cyclical notions of time associated with agrarian cultures through to the later development of linear time in the West.

Cycles of Time in Nature, Bodies, and Culture

Evidence of early human work practices available from archaeology show work to be tied to a number of naturally occurring rhythms: human diurnal rhythms led to the increment of work becoming the period of daylight hours—sunrise to sunset; seasonal rhythms and variations controlled food availability, growth of crops, and animal migrations, whereas cycles in the planets and stars were related to cosmological myths that supported cultic and spiritual practices (Clarke, 1989; Whitrow, 1989). Thus it can be seen how cultural and social embedding of temporal orders not only supported the control of time but imbued the world with meaning (Hassan & Purser, 2007). As Hassan and Purser (2007: 38) posit, 'From the earliest periods of human development as cultural beings, people and societies *created* time by giving duration, growth, decay, and change intrinsic meaning'.

In the development of human communities, work has always been a shared social practice embedded in the development and maintenance of institutions, such as families, clans, and tribes, that link to social, cultural, and religious activities. The needs of survival require the establishment of social orderings structured around shared understandings that support a sense of collective cohesion in the carrying out of everyday routines and work practices. As Darwin demonstrated, physical evolution supporting human survival was linked to the evolution of social organizing in response to changing environments synchronized with nature's rhythms (Grosz, 2004). Human survival was not only an individual, subjective affair but, as social theorists such as Berger and Luckmann (1984) show, was sustained in the ability to share language-based understandings through the 'objectification of subjective processes' (1984: 20). Thus the development of collective memory and social institutions through temporal practices sustained human flourishing.

The expansion and elaboration of these shared temporal understandings became enshrined in myth and ritual (Gell, 1996). An example from Whitrow's (1989) detailed discussion of the historical development of the awareness of time is the balance of early Egyptian society around the cycles of the Nile. The cycles were linked to the pharaoh, who as king-god maintained the earthly balance of the cosmic order. This link is evident for example in timing the coronation of a new pharaoh with 'either the rising of the Nile in early summer . . . or the recession of water in autumn when the fertilized fields were ready to be sown' (1989: 24). Similarly, in Gell's (1996) account of the *ida* ritual of the Umeda people, a glimpse is afforded of the temporal practices of a culture apparently unchanged for thousands of years that has remained separate from mainstream developments. According to Gell (1996), the Umeda have developed the complex and comprehensive *ida* ritual, an elaborate dance performed over two days, that 'enacts a process of bio-social regeneration' (Gell, 1996: 46) and creates and sustains order and structure in their society. The ritual links seasonal time in the cycles of wet and dry seasons to the timing of agrarian work practices; the times for hunting, planting, tending, and harvesting sago, yam, taro coconuts, tobacco, and bamboo shoots.

For early human societies, the temporal connections within myth and religion provided them with capacity to transcend nature's cycles of life and death. For, as Heidegger stressed, human living and conceptions of life are and have always been oriented by 'being unto death' (Heidegger, 1962). Not only did humans seek ultimate meaning and answers to the deep questions relating to the mystery of existence and human purpose, but in the timelessness of religious myths and rituals associated with creation and eternity, they sought to transcend the limitations imposed by temporal existence, for example, in constructing artefacts, such as temples, shrines, and images; in the performance of creation and burial rituals; and in the stories and elaborate mythologies passed from generation to generation. As Birth (2012) reminds us, citing Stonehenge, the Aztec calendar, and the Antikythera mechanism, some of the most famous archaeological objects are related to time.

However, the oldest time measurement device found to date, as discussed in Chapter 2, is the recent discovery in Aberdeenshire (coincidentally close to the home of one of the authors of this work) of an eighth millenium BCE monument that is described by Gaffney et al. (2013) as follows:

> A pit alignment recently excavated in Aberdeenshire . . . provide the earliest evidence currently available for 'time reckoning' as the pit group appears to mimic the phases of the Moon and is structured to track lunar months. It also aligns on the south east horizon and a prominent topographic point associated with sunrise on the midwinter solstice. In doing so the monument anticipates problems associated with simple lunar calendars by providing an annual astronomic correction in order to maintain the link between the passage of time. . . . The evidence suggests that hunter-gatherer societies in Scotland had both the need and ability to track time across the year . . . and that this occurred at a period nearly five thousand years before the first formal calendars were created in Mesopotamia.

According to Whitrow (1989), ancient work practices, in the more well-known ancient cultures such as Sumeria, Egypt, China, and India, diversified as agrarian practices developed in conjunction with trading and technological developments and the increasing sophistication of time measurement technologies. China led the way in many aspects of time measurement in their early water clocks (circa 500–600 BCE) (Whitrow, 1989). However, the influence of the early Egyptian practices of time measurement on the development of clock and calendar time and its measurement is enormous in that we owe much of our present temporal structuring to the early work of the Egyptians. Their time-measuring practices were much more precise than in other dominant early cultures, such as Sumeria and Babylonia. Based on the averaging of time cycles of the rise and fall of the Nile, they used a calendar based on 12 months of 30 days and added 5 extra days to make up 365 days (1989: 26). Similarly their lunar calendar linked to phases of the moon was used to regulate agrarian and religious festivals (1989: 16). The use of water clocks, such as those found in China in similar periods, provided a finer calibration of daily uses of time dividing the day into 24 hours. Interestingly, Whitrow (1989) suggests that the reason for the effectiveness of the Egyptian time measurement practices was their geographical and meteorological location in an area noted for clear sky for most of the year, which enabled time measurement based on accurate astronomical observations and their connections with work rhythms based on the regularity of the Nile flood cycle (1989). In contrast, Sumeria and Babylon civilisations tied to the variation and extremes of the flooding of the Tigris and Euphrates rivers had to contend with greater unpredictability of flood and drought over which they were powerless (Whitrow, 1989: 29). Work was thus regulated by the rhythms of the Nile and linked to temporal practices and social, religious institutions. Following Adam (1990), we conclude that mythical or religious time and epochal time, relating to cosmological cycles and seasonal rhythms, dominated early institutionalized work practices not just in Egypt but also in cultures in this period more generally. 'For agricultural societies, the rhythms of nature became synchronized both with the rhythms of culture' and religious tradition (Hassan, 2007: 39). Thus it can be seen that prior to the advent and explicit dominance of the arrow of time associated with clock time, cyclical time was not entirely separable from the onward movement of time associated with the arrow of time but the movement around a cycle, for example, in the changing seasons, is also a movement forward in clock and calendar time.

The Development and Recording of Linear Notions of Time

A significant contrast to the dominant cyclical views of time was the linear view of time developed in Judaism as a response to Babylonian and Persian invasions. The cycles of time were transformed into a linear notion of time through prophetic predictions of a glorious future emancipation, as eschatological thought from Persian Zoroastrianism and Mithraism seeped into Jewish religious practices. Most evident in apocryphal writings like the book of Daniel, in which the remnant of the once-powerful kingdom sought to make sense of their captivity, time was oriented to a glorious future liberation of the Diaspora. Early Christianity maintained aspects of Jewish eschatology and strengthened the idea of the progression of time. For the early Christians, the story of the supernatural birth and death of Jesus Christ was considered to be a unique event providing a clear division of history encapsulated in the notions adopted later in the Gregorian calendar of before Christ (BC) and *anno dominai* (AD). For Christians, the narrative of the birth and death of Christ thus divided the line of time; Jesus was born on earth, and although his life as a human had passed, his eschatological return in glory pointed to the future for believers as consummation with God. The domination of linear views of time became enshrined in early church dogma and ritual. Although church ritual, embedded in religious calendars, followed annual cycles around Christmas and Easter, temporal orientation of remembering the past in the teachings of Christ, supported the present living of a godly life that in turn prepared the believer for the future and ultimately eternity.

Notwithstanding the importance of early Christian notions of the linearity of time, Whitrow (1989: 64) suggests: 'if it is to Christianity that we owe our modern temporal orientation, it is to the Romans that we are mainly indebted for measurement of time in the form of our calendar and conventions of time recording' (the earliest forms of the recording of time are discussed in more detail in Chapter 2). Our present Gregorian calendar dates to the time of Julius Caesar, and the seven-day week is also an inheritance from the Romans. Constantine decreed that work by magistrates, citizens, and artisans was to cease on Sunday, the Lord's Day, while permitting farm labour to continue (Whitrow, 1989). It was not until late in the fourth century that Theodosius, the last great emperor, abolished the Roman calendar with its many pagan festivals and united Europe with a common calendar (1989: 70).

Early Time Measurement: Calendars and Bells

During the Middle Ages life and working practices in Europe were domi-nated by the church and religious views. Accounts of time and temporality in Europe in the Middle Ages commonly identify two central factors that impelled developing notions of linear time and its measurement, including first, the influence of dominant Christian beliefs within culture and work, and second, the fall of Rome and the Vandal and Barbarian invasions lead-ing to a mass exodus of the population from towns and cities and increased ruralisation (according to Whitrow, 1989, these factors supported the spa-tial and temporal organization of work for 800 years). Time in this period resting under the watchful eye of church surveillance was dominated by the church calendar and the cycle of ecclesiastical rituals and festivals. Zerubavel (1981) identifies the calendar developed by the church as the central institu-tion for the development of temporal regularity saying,

> The first major institution that man invented in order to establish and maintain temporal regularity was the calendar. The calendar is respon-sible for the creation of most of the temporally regular patterns through which all societies, social institutions, and social groups manage to introduce some orderliness into their lives.
>
> (1981: 31)

Zerubavel (1981) shows that the most explicit example of time measure-ment linked to work practices in the Middle Ages is found in the Benedictine monastic tradition, a group devoted to prayer regulated by the Order of Benedict. For Benedictine monks, work and prayer was highly integrated in exacting daily (and nightly) practices. His detailed analysis of the Bene-dictine hours illustrates the micro-level regulation of everyday activities. He discusses the use of the Benedictine horarium and how days, from sunup to sundown, were divided into 12 'hours'. As the length of the period of daylight time varied with the seasons, the length of the hour also varied; in summer, the number of daytime hours was longer than those in winter. He shows how focussed attention on the rigorous structure of the mundane activities of monastic life as a godly discipline led to detailed refinements of the institutions of the calendar and the schedule. Monastic life for the Bene-dictine order was structured around an intense routine related to the 'hours' of prayer and marked by the ringing of bells. Timekeeping was an auditory activity, with different sequences of bell ringing indicating the various activ-ities or 'hours'. Strict adherence to punctuality was considered an act of devotion, whereas lateness at collective prayer times was punishable as a sin. Here, not only do we have institutions that embed temporal practices of calendar and schedule but also elements of what Foucault (1977) would later identify as disciplining practices associated with social control. As Zerubavel explains (1981: 45): 'Gaining control of the calendar has always been essential for attaining social control in general'. Time measurement is institutionalized by the church in the calendar both in cyclical and linear conceptions of time that serve to regulate everyday life. If church institutions dominated time and its use in the early Middle Ages, later in this period, strengthened secular contenders contested its dominance.

The development of work and work times in the late Middle Ages is related to the rationalization and secularisation of time in domains, such as the military, food production, crafts and guilds, trade, and leisure (Le Goff, 1980). As trade developed in the late 12th and early 13th centuries, a period of crisis occurred in which the times of the church came into conflict with the times of merchants and owners of industry. Whereas the merchants' time was also dominated by seasons and climate as commercial networks became more organized, 'time became an object of measurement' (1980: 35). For the merchants and early cloth manufacturers, time was increasingly related to production times and therefore money. Merchant time included the notion that interest accumulated in accounts over time. In contrast for powerful theologians in the church, time was considered like knowledge to belong to God and was given to humans as a gift (Le Goff, 1980). People were not at liberty to do what they wanted with their time and certainly not to sell time for a profit by charging interest on the time taken to repay debts. For the church, usury was a sin ranked with immorality and therefore illegal and condemned.

Le Goff suggests that the technological developments that occurred during the transition from medieval to modern times are inseparable from changing social and cultural practices. He argues that a transition occurred during this time that marked the beginnings of the move from an ecclesiastical to secular society and was linked to changes in time measurement practices (1980: 44). The accepted unit of time was the day—how much land could be ploughed between sunrise and sunset—and was related to seasonal cycles and weather conditions. Merchants required increasingly calibrated measures of time to control work and contested the inexact measures of ecclesiastical time expressed in the use of bells. The changing temporal framework occurred predominantly in an urban context driven by the increasing technological development of machinery in areas like the cloth trade, which required workers to follow regular, routine temporal rhythms that divided the work day into smaller increments around production.

While the view espoused by Le Goff (1980) has become popular in accounts of temporal practices in providing strong separation between the temporal practices in the Middle Ages and those that followed with the development of industrialization, Glennie and Thrift (2009) take strong exception, arguing that this separation was never so complete and the ordering of daily life according to detailed measurement of time was clearly evident by the time of the early Middle Ages (Glennie & Thrift, 2009).

The Emergence and Growing Dominance of Clock Time(s) in Work Practices

> Clock time, we might say is the reckoning of the time or day/night in hours, minutes, and seconds, which we see on clock faces in our homes or cars or computer screens, or on our wristwatches, or on a host of other locations nowadays, shown either by hands on a dial, or digitally. Hours are counted in two sets of twelve, from twelve noon and twelve midnight, and all the hours are of the same length.
>
> (Glennie & Thrift, 2009: 23)

In contrast to the time embedded in nature, clock time is based on the measurement and representation of the passing of time in material objects. As discussed in Chapter 2, the human practice of measuring time in material objects developed for that purpose began at least 10,000 years ago and has taken many forms. The increasing quality and pervasiveness of time measurement devices means our lives today are imbued with time measurement in one form or another to the point that it is difficult to gain sufficient distance to comprehend its effect. Clock time has been described as a cultural equivalent of breathing in that it is so ordinary that it usually goes unnoticed (Glennie & Thrift, 2009). In this section, we examine how this state of affairs occurred or, in other words, how clock time came to dominate social and organizational life.

Clock time reckoning is widely viewed as an answer to the question: What is time? However, whereas clocks can tell us what time it is, they are unable to tell us what time is. As Birth (2012: 2) articulates, 'The artefactual determination of time does not represent a coherent, consistent cultural system, however, but represents instead the sedimentation of generations of solutions to different temporal problems'. He draws on Glennie and Thrift's (2009) seminal work on the history of clock time in England in which they contest the widely accepted view of the use of clock time as a form of work discipline and control as inseparable from the industrialization processes that occurred in England during the Industrial Revolution. They suggest a richer and more finely textured and contextually dependent view. Our discussion focuses on two key aspects: First, based on Glennie and Thrift's (2009) work, and in contrast with Thompson (1967) and others who see clock time either as socially or technologically determined, we present the view that clock time is heterogeneous and inseparable from the work practices of specific communities of practice and their related timescapes. We discuss how with the development of the increased precision and widespread adoption of clock time as the 'combination of the measure of duration and the determination of moments' (Birth, 2012: 68), this 'created' time soon became the accepted industrial form of time shaping work practices (Adam, 2003). Second, we explore the 'commodification' of time as part of the political economy of labour leading to what has been termed 'the emptying of time' (Adam, 2003).

Heterogeneous Clock Times

Clock time has been examined from a number of different perspectives including horological (Birth, 2012), sociological (Adam, 1995), chronographic (Parkes & Thrift, 1980), and historical geographic (Glennie & Thrift, 2009) accounts. Common to many of these accounts is the positioning of clock time as a unitary, homogeneous phenomenon. In this view, modern clocks are assumed to measure accurately the passing of nature's time related to diurnal rhythms in that they are both the measure of time and devices for its measurement. Clocks, watches, and other timepieces may come in different sizes and forms, but the time they measure and their use as timekeeping devices is homogeneous.

In their comprehensive analysis of the development of clock time in the UK, Glennie and Thrift (2009) take exception to this common view aiming to dispel what they see as the myth of the homogeneity of clock time. They argue: 'Neither current practices nor changes in clock time over time can be considered to be "natural"' (Glennie & Thrift, 2009: 23). Based on detailed historical accounts taken from diaries, almanacs, legal records, and church documents, they argue that there is no such thing as a single, homogeneous clock time, but what is termed 'clock time' is a complex of practices. Unlike many accounts of the history of time measurement, their history

> is not a triumphal narrative of the relentless development of time. . . . [Their] history is much more tentative and comprises the stories of many different types of practices . . . Certain practices that were originally highly specialized have spread to become much more general, while the incidences of some other practices have shrunk.
>
> (Glennie & Thrift, 2009: 9)

A key aim of their work is to demonstrate how in England, temporal awareness, through the widespread uptake of clock time, became institutionalized across all social strata, including the workforce, much earlier than is commonly recognised. Taking accounts from everyday life that were not necessarily focusing on aspects of time, they show the growing awareness of time in the period preceding the horological revolution of the late 17th century. They draw on historical accounts from multiple, non-specialist communities of practice such as farming, market, urban labour, and the navy as well as more specialized practices such as the legal system, business, and industry. They argue that the history of clock time has been written according to two main trajectories. First, are the accounts driven by narratives of the technological improvements in clock and timekeeping devices that tell the story of continual improvements in the measurement of time. In this view, the mechanical development of the clock over centuries is central to the timekeeping innovation and its dispersion and infusion within social realities. The horological revolution in the late 17th century was preceded by 500 years of technological development. Birth (2012), for example, examines the technological development of clocks or 'objects of time', showing 'the intersections between mind, culture and objects of time' (Birth, 2012: 2). In his anthropological analysis he suggests that clocks are 'cognitive artefacts', by which he means that objects have cognition embedded or inscribed within them that not only determines their use but provides traces of the sedimented concepts used in their development. For example, 'the current ideas of millennia, centuries, decades, years, months, weeks, days, hours, minutes, seconds and so on, are examples of such sedimented ideas—they are ideas useful in measuring durations of what happens in our world, but their relationship to our world is hardly straightforward' (2012: 2). These concepts have become embedded in the objects of time such as clocks. The history of the technologies associated with clock times is shown to have been gradual and incremental and located in different communities of practice where clocks were used in different ways.

A second group or accounts of the history of clock time presents time measurement as a social invention (Glennie & Thrift, 2009). In contrast to the first view, proponents argue that the normative use of time within social and cultural practices was responsible for the increasing temporal orientation of life and work and how this drove the development of time measurement. A seminal work supporting the view of time measurement as a social invention is found in the work of E. P. Thompson (1967). Thompson discusses the effects of changing understandings of time that occurred in the institutionalization of work in the early developments of industrial capitalism. He sets out to discuss the changes in: 'time-sense that affect labour discipline . . . and influence the inward apprehension of time of working people' (1967: 57). He was interested not only in the external imposition of the disciplinary processes but also in how changes in working habits became internalized within the workforce. He, like Foucault, saw the power of the discipline process when temporality becomes internalized as a self-control mechanism.

Thompson (1967) traces the development of the dominance of new forms of time associated with industrial capitalism. He argues that prior to this, time and temporal practices were inseparable from the rhythms of nature, whether the seasonal fluctuations of weather, the tides, or length of daylight hours. Such links were associated with timing labour according to what he termed 'task-orientation' rather than to 'timed-labour' in fixed hourly or daily rates of pay. In task-orientation, harvesting needed to be undertaken before storms, fishing to occur with the right tides, and farming to align with animals' circadian rhythms. He suggests that the task-orientation view of early work practices is the distinctive difference between early pre-industrial ways of understanding temporal orientations of work and later industrialized conceptions of timed-labour and clock time. He argues that the task-orientation view of time was more supportive of the humanity of the workforce including the intensity and pace of work and the boundaries of work and life (Thompson, 1967: 60). By the mid-17th century, the shift from task orientation to timed-labour was intensifying, but still the unit of time was the day, not the hour. Of course, the move from task orientation to timed-labour was to change this and move the increment of time to the hour, as timed-labour took over due to increasing industrialization: 'Time is now currency: it is not passed but spent' (Thompson, 1967: 61). At first, the move to timed-labour occurred through the use of bells to signal starting and finishing work. The change to increasing industrialization of mills and workplaces was inseparable with the development of more accurate clocks, culminating in the use of the pendulum in 1658. Soon clocks were not only in the hands and houses of the gentry controlling their times but were also in workplaces controlling and measuring labour and work time. This spread became a general diffusion of clocks within England by the time of the Industrial Revolution (1967: 69).

Thompson argues that the Industrial Revolution with the attendant growth in the mechanization of factories meant that not only did labour have to be punctual and reliable, but it also needed to be synchronized both with machinery and other workers (Thompson, 1967). Drawing on Weber, he shows how at the same time as the growth of industrialization, the social influence of the Protestant work ethic was also gaining momentum, especially in northern European countries where the idea of the godly 'redeeming the time' led to the widely accepted principle that 'thrift was related to godliness'. Thompson (1967) shows that the Protestant gentry railing against the lower classes as the disciplining discourse took hold of social society. The idleness and laziness of the poor are highlighted and castigated using the language of morality that is linked to godlessness. Of course, what is overlooked in such broad-brush statements are social groups, such as farm servants and women, that were socially and economically marginalized. Thompson (1967) charts the momentum of industrialization as growing apace, producing: 'the familiar landscape of disciplined industrial capitalism, with the timesheet, the timekeeper, the informers and the fines' (Thompson, 1967: 82), in which the changes in time discipline were not just the result or by-products of new manufacturing techniques but also cultural changes.

However, Glennie and Thrift (2009) refute Thompson's view that the work discipline introduced as a result of the Industrial Revolution precipitated the 'restructuring of industrial work habits and changes in people's inward notations of time' (Glennie & Thrift, 2009: 44). They strongly contest the account of time discipline developed by Thompson (1967) along several lines. First, they suggest that Thompson (1967) proposes time discipline to involve three interrelated dimensions; standardization, regularity, and coordination.

> By *standardization* we mean the degree to which people's time-space paths are disciplined to be the same as one another's. By *regularity* we mean the degree to which peoples' time-space paths involve repetitive routine. By *coordination* we mean the degree to which peoples' time-space paths are disciplined to smoothly connect with one another's.
>
> (Glennie & Thrift, 2009: 45)

Glennie and Thrift argue that Thompson configures these three dimensions as a unity in time discipline occurring in 18th-century Industrial Revolution processes in the move from task orientation to timed-labour. They deem this problematic, arguing that multiple variations and permutations are possible, whereas 'Thompson's approach requires all three to be part of a single disciplinary approach' (Glennie & Thrift, 2009: 46). They show how the factory in which the three may be combined is an unusual and distinctive case but not typical or widespread in early modern England. The unitary position is contested based on demonstrations of how each of the three dimensions are shown to be in operation independently or partially over several centuries preceding the Industrial Revolution.

Second, Glennie and Thrift (2009: 47) suggest Thompson's approach 'is too narrow and too contextually specific' arguing that Thompson's approach

> assumes connections between the way people work and the way they think and that workers may act only minimally towards provided scripts, taking some on board but not others thus giving themselves room to manoeuvre.
>
> (Glennie & Thrift, 2009: 47)

Glennie and Thrift (2009) provide detailed research of specific common practices to more clearly demonstrate the gradual development of contextualized, temporal work practices over several centuries rather than assuming a generalized disciplining process based on the generalization of factory experience occurring only during the Industrial Revolution. They take this up in their fine-grained analysis in several contexts, detailing that specific examples of clock time practices occurred much earlier than previously documented and showing how they were heterogeneous and inseparable from their contexts. For example, they present records showing the early time-keeping practices involving clocks and timed-labour in: business in 1481; the law courts from 1514; urban labour in 1567; the postal system by 1585; farming and market practices by 1642; and sea-faring practices were in regular use before 1300 (Glennie & Thrift, 2009).

Glennie and Thrift (2009) go on to suggest time telling was a simpler practice in these times as the signalling of public and private time occurred through the use of bells and was an auditory process rather than a visual one. Ringing of bells was coded with the number of chimes and peals indicating a range of diverse times. Public timekeeping is shown to be widespread and commonplace through multiple sources and accounts taken from the Middle Ages. Similarly, the private use of clocks is shown to exceed what was commonly considered to be the case. Such extensive evidence pointing to the general population ordering work practices according to public and private use of clocks and watches supports their view of time discipline as much more complex and occurring centuries earlier than Thompson (1967) indicates.

Third, Glennie and Thrift (2009) point out that precision was not a prerequisite for temporal orientation of work practices. Bells and clocks, even though relatively inaccurate by today's standards, were still effective in orienting the general timing, coordination, synchronization, and calculation of time to support temporal ordering of work practices. They also refute Thompson's (1967) claim that the disciplining of the population in relation to temporal ordering occurred through education and schools, showing through their examination of school records how time telling was a product of socialization and practices occurring both at home and in public and not just through students' education at school. In short, Glennie and Thrift (2009) provide a more nuanced and contextually differentiated view emphasising the heterogeneous use of clocks in the development of clock time practices.

In tracing the early developments of time measurement and the institutionalization of time measurement in temporal practices preceding clock time, we have shown how the widespread use of bells and the auditory signalling of time have gradually been usurped by visual representations associated with the manufacture and use of sophisticated clocks and timekeeping devices.

Modern Conceptions of Time

In this section, we discuss what Thrift suggests is the process that occurred in the modern period in which 'the cultural is gradually incorporated in the economic' (1990: 105). This shift in modern industrial societies is said to have resulted mainly as follows: 'the clock became the dominant machine of productive organization; it provides the signal for labour to commence or halt activity' (Hassard, 1989: 19). As such, we discuss the development and implications of the rise of modern industrialization and the commensurate reshaping of institutional forms. The institutionalization of time in the mechanization and management of many forms of work practice and the normative acceptance of these practices by workers and management in the industrial revolution are presented in some detail in Chapters 3 and 7, in which the work of Taylor and forms of scientific management are shown to be the watershed from which modern conceptions of industrial time proliferated. The importance of Taylor's work in this regard should not be underestimated; for example, Hassard (1989: 20) suggests that Taylor became the 'high priest of rational time-use' by synchronizing work with time; labour was separated from the rhythms inherent within craft work and practices as 'clock rhythms replace fluctuating rhythms; machine-pacing replaces self-pacing; labour serves technology' (1989: 20). Without Taylor's work in explicitly and comprehensively studying the means of maximizing productivity by linking the timing of efficient worker activities to clock time and later embedding time measurement within the machinery itself, it is doubtful if contemporary work and institutions would have taken the shape they now have. It is by the embedding of clock time in the very fabric of contemporary forms of work that time itself becomes an objectified commodity, and it is the commodification of time that forms the basis of later developments in the digital, globalized forms of contemporary work. The implications of the institutionalization of commodified time in these contemporary forms are as Hassard (1989: 19) suggests, that 'industrial sociology has come to view modern conceptions of time as hegemonic structures whose essences are precision, control, and discipline'.

Adam's Five Cs of Industrial Time

To understand conceptualizations of time and their uses in contemporary society, it is necessary to show the interrelationship of a number of conceptions of time and their mutually constituting relationship. We consider that Adam, in her development of the five Cs, including creation, commodification, compression, colonization, and control, provides an excellent framework in which to discuss the multiple, entangled mutually constituting processes, structures, and practices at work in contemporary, institutionalized forms of time.

First, the 'creation of time' refers to time created to human design. As we have shown in this chapter, natural or embedded time, what Adam refers to as 'God's time' (2006), designed into the rhythms and woven into the practices of all matter, is different from the time created through the advent of clock time in the Middle Ages (Adam, 2003). A key difference is that natural time affords variance, whereas 'the hourly cycle of the clock is invariable and precise' (Adam, 2003: 62). Natural time is embedded in living beings, such as plants and animals, whereas clock time is extrinsic to life and inscribed in material objects (Birth, 2012). The growth of industrialization was inseparable from increasing precision of time measurement and time measurement devices, including but not limited to clocks. An excellent example is that of the development of the instruments to measure longitude by John Harrison as documented by Dova Sobel (1995).

Second, perhaps the most influential and dominant change in how time is conceived in the modern and contemporary periods is discussed in

Adam's second C: 'commodification of time'. The notion of labour time being equated with profit and as having an intrinsic business value led to the calculative economy of time. Adam (2006) shows how Marx's work (see Chapter 7 for discussion of this work) provides the theoretical justification for the commodification of time in capitalism. She then goes on to discuss how the development of the modern industrial capitalist notion of time is related to the development of what she terms 'empty time', or time 'as a resource' or the 'creation of non-temporal time' (Adam, 1995: 90). This move, she suggests, is a 'slow shift from working *in* time to working *with* time' (Adam, 1995: 87). 'Such action implies an expectation of predictable and controllable regularity within a universally applicable time, an empty time which measures the same abstract units anywhere and everywhere, a time that is applicable equally to work, leisure and caring activities' (Adam, 1995: 88). This rationally calculable action over time leads to the idea of pre-dictability and is related to punctuality. She goes on to discuss the exchange of commodified time and the implications in terms of speed and flexibility. The link is tightened between time and money as a precondition of modern industrial economics. It is evident in many aspects of modern work such as overtime, absenteeism, and strikes, each of which are only possible in empty time—time separated from context and content. Time is a quantity, and optimization of speed and intensity are constantly sought. 'Any time of work and production that is not easily translatable to money falls outside its framework of evaluation: the time of children and the elderly, the time of mothers and fathers and of those who care for their spouses in the home, the time of prisoners and the unemployed' (Adam, 2003: 66). She also makes the point strongly that the environment is excluded and made invisible in this sort of temporal reckoning (1998, 2003).

Hassard (1989) agrees with this view of the relentless spread of industrial-ization and forms of industrial capitalism, 'Time like the individual became a commodity of the production process. . . . It is homogeneous, it is objective, measureable and infinitely divisible; it is related to change and the sense of motion and development; it is quantitative' (Hassard, 1989: 17). He goes on to suggest the central industrial organizing processes and practices: syn-chronization of labour with machinery, specialization, and segmentation of parts and activities, inter- and intra-organizational coordination were all re-defined by clock times in the industrialization process (Hassard, 1989). In turn, the efficient and effective operation of these scheduled processes supported predictability that increased the accuracy of forecasting.

Third, the 'compression of time' in which it is considered that the inexo-rable quest for improvement in all domains, time is speeded up. In economic terms Adam (2006: 128) suggests:

> Where (clock) time is equated with money, speed becomes an important economic value, since the faster a product can be produced, the less money-time is tied up in the process in forms of machinery, interest

payments and labour costs. The faster the product can be moved
through the system from production to consumption the higher is the
profit potential. An alternative way of expressing speed is time compression, the preferred term of Karl Marx and more recently David Harvey.

Over the past few decades, changes associated with computers and particular Internet technologies and computer networks as watershed technologies
have fundamentally changed society. The knock-on effect has profoundly
influenced work practices including the changing relationship between
space and time in the contemporary era (Hassan, 2007). Ideas, such as timespace compression associated with globalization and the information and
communication technology (ICT) revolution are seen to be supporting a
re-conceptualization of the world, the 'shrinking of the planet' into a global
village, or more accurately a 'market place' in which 'action occurs at a distance through ICT's' (Hassan, 2007: 41).
    The development of the global network has been comprehensively docu-
mented in Castells' landmark work *The Network Society* (Castells, 2000). He
argues that the mark of the move from one period to another—industrialized
to modern or modern to network society—is that time is being emptied
(Adam, 1990, 1995). He cites the story of changes to the conception of time
in Russia under Peter the Great as he sought to link Russia to Europe by
adopting European time (Castells, 2000: 463). These links were to continue
in the Soviet years as Lenin, like Henry Ford, was influenced by Taylorism,
albeit for different ends—Ford for profit and Lenin for "ideological motivation" (Castells, 2000: 463).
    Thus he proposes that 'modernity can be conceived, in material terms, as
the dominance of clock time over space and society' (Castells, 2000: 463).
He thinks there is 'a relativization of time in society. The transformation is
more profound . . . the mixing of tenses . . . creating a forever universe' as
capitalism inevitably seeks to free itself from all constraints (464). He thus
posits 'the patterns in the emergence of a new concept of temporality, which
I call *timeless time*' (465). Hassan (2007: 42) discusses the implications of
network time some years later, for him, the network in which the virtual,
shared space creates new relations of time in the use of a common real time
that is separate and transcends the clock time(s) and embedded times of
individual users. The network is said to be a new ecology—living through
and within the multiple users operating in a 'connected asynchronicity' (51).
    In her discussion of the compression of time, Adam (2006) draws upon
the extensive work of Virillio in discussing the 'speeding up of time' as well
as Castells' views on the importance of networked time. However, while
the assumption of time compression and intensity resonates with everyday
experience, Wajcman (2015) cautions that in contemporary accounts, there
is an overemphasis on the quantitative rather than qualitative characteristics
of time that promotes feelings of hurriedness and detracts from our understanding of multi-temporality in the way that we live and make sense of our

lives. She argues that there are noticeable inequalities in time sovereignty that are ultimately linked to money, status, and power. Employees are expected to give up ever more of their time in the intensification of work and employment, and yet, this is not evenly distributed across society. She argues that there are no uniform experiences of time and that time poverty is unevenly distributed (she uses the example of time scarcity among working single parents). In the office and among professional workers, she notes how connectivity and email are changing the temporal density of work stating, 'Emblematic of this truncation of time spans is the spread of performance management systems, which audit individuals on current performance, without regard to a person's history of effort. Such seismic shifts in the wider culture inform our overall sense that time is telescoping' (Wajcman, 2015: 109).

Wajcman (2015) argues that the conventional timescape of a networked 24/7 world distorts our relationship with time and blinkers a broader understanding of temporality. She contends that people are too ready to conflate the speed of rapid-fire change with inventiveness, progress, productivity, and efficiency. This acceptance of the inevitability and need for accelerated change—which links with people's subjective sense that time has intensified, been squeezed, and compressed—deflects criticism from existing social arrangements and prevents consideration of more humanistic and balanced future work trajectories.

Fourth, the 'colonization of time' is described by Adam (2003: 71) as both 'the global imposition of industrial time and the contemporary incursion into the times of predecessors and successors'. To demonstrate this distinction, she employs the terms 'colonization *with* time' to refer to the former and 'colonization *of* time' for the latter. Colonization with time is said to have occurred as nations have by economic and or political necessity been forced to become part of the global community in which Western industrial time—commodified time—dominates. Global financial markets and technologies use the standardized and digitized world time to coordinate business activities across the globe without exception. In this 'unified' modern world, both Adam (2006) and Wajcman (2015) argue strongly that there are winners and losers, and the distribution of time and therefore money is far from equal. Adam suggests that it divides as much as it unifies. In relation to the colonization *with* time, Adam uses the examples of genetic manipulation of food in which science has achieved 'the technological equivalent of spatial globalization' (2006) in extending time's reach into the past. Whereas forms of industrial neglect that lead to long-term environmental degradation, the future is colonized by current short-sightedness.

Fifth, Adam (2006) considers the 'control of time' to be the overriding determinant of the other Cs. 'The control of time thus includes the slowing down processes, the rearrangement of past, present and future, the reordering of sequence and the transformation of rhythmicity into a rationalized beat' (2003: 69). As already explained, Adam develops the notion of timescapes to show the 'temporal relations with reference to a cluster of temporal features, each implicated in all the others but not necessarily of equal importance' (Adam, 2006: 142). In depicting that industrial timescape controls contemporary life, she usefully charts the juxtapositions, contradictions, and divisions that continue to resonate under the five Cs of industrial time. She (2003) draws on Beck's work in discussing what he calls 'reflexive modernization [and] the discontinuities that occur as a result of modernist attempts at continuity' (1994, cited in Adam, 2003). They argue that whereas global institutional control of time ought to result in a greater sense of harmony as times are smoothed and synchronized, a paradoxical situation has developed whereby modern society's inexorable drive for commodities has created boundaries, such as, those between rich and poor, divisions between the educated and non-educated, and the separation of culture from nature. The institutionalization of clock time as a replacement for natural time has created a new, changing set of temporal norms that have become embedded in everyday practices both within and outside of the workplace and to such an extent that we almost breathe clock time in the unnoticeable way that Glennie and Thrift (2009) allude to.

Globalized Time in Digital Capitalism and the Network Society

As we have seen, over the past five centuries, a number of key factors have combined to support the institutionalization of clock time and its domination of contemporary culture across the globe. These factors include development in the enlightenment of the linear perspective, the commodification of time through the mass expansion of industrial capitalism, and the proliferation of increasingly sophisticated timekeeping and measuring technologies (Adam, 2003). Contemporary forms of work have adapted to these changes in a number of ways. First, workers themselves have been repositioned and their forms of being forced to change in response to increasingly dominant and powerful work structures and practices. New subjectivities are created as workers internalize these powerful relations in different forms of work. As is discussed more fully in Chapter 7, the creation of cultural controls targeting new forms of worker subjectivity has meant time control also includes workers managing their own internalized consciousness of time and temporal awareness in accordance with workplace norms and values. Second, changes have occurred in how work is undertaken. In particular, the use of digital technologies has led to radical changes as to when and where work is performed. Knowledge work is not restricted by location as long as there is Internet access. The creation of 'simultaneous time' by digital technologies means that business and work can be performed 24/7 and creates a workplace that appears to operate without ceasing (Hassan, 2007). Third, change has occurred in relation to the types and forms of work in use in the increasingly technologized world. For example, the casualization of the workforce and the increasing number of part-time positions together with labour hire and outsourcing of work by Western democracies to developing countries where the cost of labour is much cheaper. Conversely, there is the drive for skilled professionals in Western democracies and their migration, including those from developing countries, to fill labour shortages.

Taking a social shaping approach where technological change is seen to emerge in unforeseen ways, shaped by political, economic, and social forces, Wajcman (2015) concludes that people's subjective sense of time has intensified with perceptions of 'time compression' and 'time squeezed'. However, she questions the pervasive myth of an accelerating world and high-speed society pointing to the 'time-pressure paradox', where the recorded amount of work time—both paid and unpaid—has remained largely stable over the last 50 years whilst most people are living longer and, hence, having more time at their disposal for leisure. But Wajcman (2015) also draws attention to an overemphasis on the quantitative rather than qualitative characteristics of time and how discretionary time is unevenly distributed. Gender relations, wealth inequalities, and changing household compositions are all shown to be factors shaping our feelings of hurriedness—viewed as multidimensional phenomena—and our perceptions of time. Wajcman concludes that the shaping process is a lot more complicated than suggested as there is the possibility for living with multiple temporalities in, for example, high-speed ICT also allowing for engagement in slower time frames, as illustrated by the slow food movement. She notes: 'In the end, the relationship between technological change and temporality is always dialectical: the simultaneous production of fast time spaces with those of remarkable slowness. Speed and slow down have always coexisted in modernity, although the meanings and value attached to them have shifted' (2015: 173).

References

Adam, B. (1990). *Time and Social Theory*. Cambridge, UK: Polity Press.

Adam, B. (1995). *Timewatch: The Social Analysis of Time*. Cambridge, UK: Polity Press.

Adam, B. (1998). *Timescapes of Modernity*. London and New York: Routledge.

Adam, B. (2003). Reflexive modernization temporalized. *Theory, Culture and Society*, 20(2), 59–78.

Adam, B. (2006). *Time*. Cambridge: Polity.

Berger, P. L., & Luckmann, T. (1984). *The Social Construction of Reality: A Treatise in the Sociology of Knowledge*. Harmondsworth: Penguin.

Birth, K. (2012). *The Objects of Time: How Things Shape Temporality*. New York: Palgrave, Macmillan.

Castells, M. (2000). *The Rise of the Network Society* (2nd ed., Vol. 1). Oxford: Blackwell.

Clarke, D. (1989). Trade and industry in Barbarian Europe till Roman times. In M. M. Postan & E. Miller (Eds.), *The Cambridge Economic History of Europe* (pp. 1–70). Cambridge: Cambridge University Press.

Foucault, M. (1977). *Discipline and Punish: The Birth of the Prison*. London: Allen Lane.

Gaffney, V., Fitch, S., Ramsey, E., Yorston, R., Ch'ng, E., Baldwin, E., . . . Howard, A. (2013). Time and a place: A luni-solar 'time-reckoner' from 8th millennium BC Scotland. *Internet Archaeology, 34*.

Gell, A. (1996). *The Anthropology of Time: Cultural Constructions of Temporal Maps and Images*. Oxford: Berg.

Glennie, P., & Thrift, N. (2009). *Shaping the Day: A History of Timekeeping in England and Wales 1300–1800*. Oxford: Oxford University Press.

Grosz, E. (2004). *The Nick of Time: Politics, Evolution and the Untimely*. Durham and London: Duke University Press.

Hassan, R. (2007). Network Time. In R. Hassan & R. Purser (Eds.), *24/7 Time and Temporality in the Network Society* (pp. 37–61). Stanford, CA: Stanford Business Books.

Hassan, R., & Purser, R. (2007). Introduction. In R. Hassan & R. Purser (Eds.), *24/7 Time and Temporality in the Network Society* (pp. 1–25). Stanford, CA: Stanford University Press.

Hassard, J. (1989). Time and industrial sociology. In P. Blyton, J. Hassard, S. Hill, & K. Starkey (Eds.), *Time, Work and Organization* (pp. 13–35). London and New York: Routledge.

Heidegger, M. (1962). *Being and Time* (J. M. E. Robinson, Trans.). New York: Harper Collins.

Hernes, T. (2014). *A Process Theory of Organization*. Oxford: Oxford University Press.

Le Goff, J. (1980). *Time, Work, and Culture in the Middle Ages* (A. Goldhammer, Trans.). Chicago and London: The University of Chicago Press.

Parkes, D., & Thrift, N. (1980). *Times, Spaces, and Places*. Chichester: John Wiley & Sons.

Sobel, D. (1995). *Longitude: The True Story of a Lone Genius Who Solved the Greatest Scientific Problem of His Time*. London: Fourth Estate Limited.

Thompson, E. P. (1967). Time, work and industrial capitalism. *Past and Present, 38*, 56–97.

Thrift, N. (1990). The making of a capitalist time consciousness. In J. Hassard (Ed.), *The Sociology of Time* (pp. 105–129). London: Macmillan Press.

Thrift, N. (2004). Thick time. *Organization, 11*(6), 873–880.

Wajcman, J. (2015). *Pressed for Time: The Acceleration of Life in Digital Capitalism*. London: University of Chicago Press.

Whitrow, G. J. (1989). *Time in History: The Evolution of our General Awareness of Time and Temporal Presence*. Oxford: Oxford University Press.

Zerubavel, E. (1981). *Hidden Rhythms: Schedules and Calendars in Social Life*. Berkeley and Los Angeles: University of California Press.

Part II

Organizational Change

Time and Temporality

5 Episodic Change and Linear Time Sequences in Managing Planned Interventions

Introduction

In examining change as sequences of time in managing planned interventions, the chapter opens with the work of Kurt Lewin (1947, 1951), who is closely associated with the early positivist tradition of organization development (OD). In these early theoretical developments, there is a heavy emphasis on objective time in formulating a progressive series of stages needed for the successful management of change. Change is characterized as moving from some present state of quasi-stationary equilibrium (T^1) towards a future state in which change agents prescribe progressive movements forward towards a desired outcome (purposeful change). On securing their change objectives, the organization is re-stabilized to ensure that a new quasi-stationary equilibrium at point (T^2) is maintained. Following on from this exposition, attention turns to another popular model that centres on the need for organizations to adapt and evolve to changing environments over time (taking an evolutionary time perspective). In this model, Tushman and Romanelli (1994, 1985) draw on objective notions of time in which longer intervals that mark periods of relatively stable incremental change (convergence) are contrasted with shorter episodes of dramatic change (reorientation). These two early theories of organizational change usefully characterize episodic change and progressive time sequences in managing planned interventions.

In examining modernist and postmodernist adaptations to early stage models, the chapter examines the reframing by Kotter (2012, 1996) of his eight-stage model of managing successful change as well as new developments in OD (some commentators refer to these as post-Lewinian, dialogic OD). In particular, attention is given to approaches that take on a social constructionist orientation as exemplified in the work of Cooperrider and Srivastva (1987) and Jabri (2012). Whereas there has been a shift from perspectives that hold an objective rational view of reality in formulating strategies for changing behaviours towards those that focus more on changing mindsets in accommodating multiple subjective realities and continuous change, the sequences and cycles of change remain framed within an objective temporality. Subjectivity arises in the meaning making that surrounds organizational change through discourse and conversations rather than through any explicit incorporation of subjective notions of time. The chapter concludes with an assessment of an important theoretical critique by Van de Ven and Poole (1995, 2005) and the work of Demers (2007) that (indirectly) draws attention to the general absence of time in the change theories that they classify and review.

Temporality and Lewin's Theory of Planned Organizational Change

A well-known model founded on a linear progressive conception of time is the planned three-step model of change developed by Kurt Lewin (which has been variously adapted and modified by scholars over the last 60 years) comprising: unfreezing, changing (or moving), and freezing new group behaviours. In building on his research into individual and group behaviour, Lewin developed field theory, the concept of group dynamics, and action research. He proposed that human behaviour is shaped by two sets of forces: restraining forces that seek to maintain the status quo and driving forces that seek to change the current system. Organizations in which these two sets of forces are in balance are in a quasi-stationary equilibrium and can be changed by either increasing the driving forces (to bring about locomotion) or decrease the restraining forces. This process can be planned and, through active engagement with the recipients of change, achieved in a participative manner that minimizes resistance (by reducing the restraining forces and creating a motivation to change) rather than increasing the driving forces. Through action research, shifts in awareness and understanding can be continually appraised not only in the initial planning for change but also following interventions in the evaluation of outcomes and in the need for further actions to support and drive change in the preferred direction. Involving people in change is seen to maximize the opportunity for achieving these planned objectives. As Lewin (1947: 34–45) described,

> A change towards a higher level of group performance is frequently short lived; after a 'shot in the arm,' group life soon returns to the previous level. This indicated that it does not suffice to define the objective of a planned change in group performance as the reaching of a different level. Permanency of the new level, or permanency for a desired period, should be included in the objective. A successful change includes therefore three aspects: unfreezing (if necessary) the present level L^1, moving to the new level L^2, and freezing group life on the new level. Since any level is determined by a force field, permanency implies that the new force field is made relatively secure against change.

Central to managing this change process is creating a felt need for change so that people start to question current practices (loosening behaviours embedded in routines) to then introduce change and re-establish permanency by ensuring that the new ways of doing things become habitualized (Lewin, 2009). The likelihood of group life returning to old ways of doing things is seen as a threat and a real possibility (Lewin, 2009: 76), but for Lewin, this needs to be avoided at all costs as any lapse undermines the planned change and threatens the health and survival of the organization. Consequently, the group is viewed as an essential vehicle for change and especially to long-standing change. Lewin was interested in why groups behave in the way they do in response to the forces they experience and how these forces can be managed and planned to ensure they produce desirable behavioural responses. He strongly believed that the behaviour of the group rather than the individual should be the main focus during change. In a reappraisal of his work, Burnes highlights how the dynamics of the group was central and that 'it is fruitless to concentrate on changing the behaviour of individuals because the individual in isolation is constrained by group pressures to conform' and that group level change should concentrate on, for example: "group norms, roles, interactions and socialization processes"' (2004: 983). In a later review with Cooke (2013: 420), they argue that participative learning through interaction enables groups and individuals to map out their current life space and construct a new, more desirable reality. In bringing the concepts of group dynamics and action theory together with his field theory—the forces in a person's life space that shape behaviour—Lewin advocated that change can be planned to minimize resistance in the transition to new ways of work, resulting in improved organizational effectiveness (see also Dawson & Andriopoulos, 2014: 156–161).

In this stability-change-stability model, time moves forward, but to ensure that the changes introduced endure, new attitudes and behaviours must be integrated into a new set of group norms to sustain new work practices (Schein, 1996). A conventional conception of the arrow of time is evident in which the forces driving change are ever present (that would move the organization forward in time), but these forces are counterbalanced by routine patterns of behaviour that are continually reinforced both through day-to-day interactions and socialization processes, resulting in the embedding of change-resistant group values and norms. There is a past that has been and cannot be changed, the present is characterized as generally being stable due to this balance of driving and restraining forces, and a desired future that can be achieved through a planned sequence of interventions. Like Deleuze's (1994) notion of habitual time, people repeat what they have done before, although it is never exactly the same (the return of difference). Lewin's model is seen to provide an 'effective' planned route to breaking out of the social conditions preventing natural forward movement. The future should be planned, but change does not need to be driven as, by reducing the restraining forces, the natural flow of time will provide the locomotion for change. Underlying this approach, there is a temporal assumption of linear time in moving from a current position (T^1) to a future desired state

(T^2) in which current habits (H^1) are unfrozen and then refrozen into new habitualized behaviours (H^2).

There are interesting similarities between Lewin's approach and the punctuated equilibrium model (discussed in the section that follows) insofar as longer periods of relative stability are followed by shorter episodes of change. However, in this theory, less attention is given to environmental factors (strategic drift), with greater focus on psychological forces (what influences individual and group behaviour) and the importance of group norms and values in shaping individual behaviour. In refreezing, the intention is to set up routines and embed new behaviours to prevent groups returning to past habits and to establish a new period of stability that can counterbalance driving forces. In this, Lewin promotes the importance of establishing a kind of quasi-stationary temporality within the workplace that is intended to maintain the new status quo until such time as another change is deemed necessary, at which point, the pattern of events for change re-enters the prescribed sequence of unfreeze, change, and freeze. In short, there is a linear set of sequences for change that recurs (a cyclical conception of time and change) implicit in this model of planned change.

The Punctuated Equilibrium Model: Cyclical Temporality and Episodic Change

Another widely cited episodic change management model—not associated with the OD camp—is the punctuated equilibrium model of change. This approach was put forward by Tushman and Romanelli (1994, 1985) and draws on concepts from evolutionary biology. Essentially it advocates that organizations gradually adapt to their environments over comparatively long periods of time that are marked by abrupt disruptions or revolutionary episodes in which more radical adjustments are required. Time is cyclical, characterized by long periods of incremental adaptation that are punctuated by short periods of stepped or episodic change when radical interventions are necessary to realign the organization with prevailing competitive conditions (to ensure evolutionary survival). As such, there is a conventional notion of objective linear time that underlies this approach as organizations evolve, continually adapting to their environment in incremental and occasionally radical ways.

Under the longer incremental periods of minor adjustment, managers get settled and take for granted the benefits of particular ways of doing things. A form of inertia arises from the tendency for managers to look for ways to improve accepted ways of operating within the prevailing social, cultural, and political norms of organizational life. During these more stable periods, there is a natural resistance and reluctance to take on board more radical alternatives, and this results in a form of 'strategic drift' (Johnson, 1992). Eventually, the misalignment with the environment becomes critical, requiring strategic reorientation (punctuated discontinuous change) that occurs over a short period of time. Time is marked by a pattern or cycle of events (long periods of small-scale gradual change followed by short periods of large-scale rapid change) in which a paradigm, once established, supports periods of convergence and relative stability that over time, lead to strategic drift and disequilibrium, eventually resulting in the need for more radical, reactive change strategies to bring the organization back in line with the environment. In short, periods of evolutionary change are punctuated by episodes of rapid change.

Under this model, objective linear time is assumed, with the scale and velocity of change increasing significantly within pockets of shorter intervals that repeat themselves over time (cycles of time); these episodes punctuate the evolutionary flow with intense periods of rapid change. But there is no option for regression (survival requires forward evolution) in the linear progressive march of time. Unlike the Lewinian approach, which advocates stability, movement (change), and stability—a stop-and-start approach to organizational change (even if recognising that stability is quasi-stationary)—the punctuated equilibrium model views change as a continuous process that normally occurs in a gradual fashion (evolutionary) but requires rapid adjustment when a major misalignment eventually becomes evident. In this approach there is an inevitable, ever-forward movement (on which rapidity, scale, and intensity vary) as the organization adapts to an ever-changing environment. These cycles of change are ongoing but are marked by noticeable episodes that necessitate organizational responses for company survival as the arrow of time moves companies forward into ever-evolving and changing environments.

The Social Constructivist Orientation in Stage Models of Planned Change

In their review on the history of OD, Burnes and Cooke (2012) claim that whereas OD remains the dominant approach to organizational change, it has moved away from some of the important principles that underpinned Lewin's foundational work. In particular, they note how the centrality of field theory has tended to be misplaced and that this may in part be due to a misstep by Lewin in his attempt to incorporate a more rigorous and mathematical basis to his approach (Burnes & Cooke, 2013: 421). Whatever the reasons, up until the late 1980s, OD developed a wide range of models largely based on a linear sequential time frame of moving through a series of stages from a present state (T^1) to a planned preferred future state (T^2), as illustrated by Hayes in his generic stage model of change (2010: 10) and characterized in the practices associated with Business Process Reengineering (BPR), Total Quality Management (TQM), and Six Sigma (Burnes & Cooke, 2012: 1405).

In their historical review, Burnes and Cooke (2012) describe the decline of conventional OD in the late 1980s and early 1990s, with the rise of more postmodernist and dialogical approaches to change that mark a significant turning point in OD, which has continued to the present day. In an assessment of the diffuse ensemble of OD change models, Marshak and Grant (2008) describe the pluralism of approaches and compare some of their underlining assumptions in evaluating the contribution of organizational discourse to emergent OD theory. They note a shift from a more rational, objective world to one that focusses on multiple realties and the inherent subjectivity of peoples' experiences of change (Marshak & Grant, 2008). In drawing on the earlier work of Argyris (1973), Blake and Mouton (1976), and Chin and Benne (1976), they contrast the positivist (objective) orientation of classical, science-based formulations of change (as punctuated equilibria with episodic transformations) to the more social constructionist (subjective) premises, where change is viewed as continuous and achievable through changing discourses (Doolin, 2003). Marshak and Grant (2008: 17) argue that theories of power (see Mumby, 1988) and discursive processes (see McClellan, 2011) can inform further theoretical developments in the new OD by highlighting how narratives, texts, and conversations can shape the dialogue among participants in creating and sustaining change (see also Grant & Marshak, 2011). Marshak and Grant use the example of Appreciative Inquiry (AI)—in generating dialogue that focusses on positive processes—as a good illustration of this metamorphosis in frameworks for planning group interventions that seek to change mindsets and consciousness (2008: 39). In many ways, AI attempts to build on and re-engage with the humanistic ideals that underpin OD through paying attention to the positive elements at work, rather than on problems and issues, and is also viewed by Burnes and Cooke (2012: 1412) as one of the most prominent new approaches in OD.

The Postmodernist Turn and Appreciative Inquiry

In taking a postmodernist turn, AI is viewed as a new post-Lewinian OD in a shift from a more objectivist to subjectivist ontology. As Marshak (2006) argues, conventional OD assumes that the world is ultimately knowable and that there is an objective reality from which you can obtain data in developing theoretical explanations of the way people behave in the world. The subjectivist position views the world through the way that we experience it rather than as an objective reality. This changes the focus of research questions, methods, and analysis. AI provides a good illustrative example as it starts from the premise that if we focus on what works well (positive-focussed thinking) rather than from an issue or problem-oriented perspective (deficit-focussed thinking), then we are more likely to enlist people in change interventions with extensive participation and stakeholder engagement. In acting as both audience and storytellers, employees are more likely to actively support change, especially where positive stories about the future pervade discussions. These 'feel-good' stories are seen to build cohesion, create new meanings, and promote collective understanding (it is worth noting AI has also been criticized for ignoring issues and problems relating to aspects of employees' subjective lived experiences).

One of the main approaches to AI is the 4D model, based on the four guiding principles of Cooperrider and Srivastva (1987), which promotes a cyclical stage approach to change comprising discovery, dream, design, and delivery. Bushe (2011) argues that AI is one of the first OD approaches to move beyond the Lewinian emphasis on action research and diagnosis towards recognising multiple perspectives through narrative and discourse in the co-construction of meanings through stories. It is founded on the idea of appreciating what is working and co-constructing an ideal future (through discussions and stories) and then translating that desired future state into a statement that is actionable. At the *discovery* stage, all stakeholders are encouraged to fully engage in discussion and debate (inquiry) on the best of 'what is'. *Dream* is the aspirational phase and may result in some graphical representation of a desired future state. *Design* gets down to the actions required in moving forward using techniques such as rapid prototyping and getting people to form into groups in coming up with concrete proposals on how to tackle specific areas. *Delivery* is the final stage in which actions are taken to achieve the design (some prefer the term 'destiny'), encouraging individual actions and energizing self-organizing momentum to ensure some sustainability (Bushe, 2011: 89). Nevertheless, although AI is described as a method of change that does not focus on problems, research suggests that transformational change will not occur from AI unless it also addresses problems of real concern to organizational members (Bushe, 2011: 96). In relation to time, there remains a four-stage cycle that mirrors the classic Deming cycle for implementing new ideas in a controlled way—Plan-Do-Check-Act (PDCA)—and the need to incorporate feedback before committing to implementation. In this, there is a cyclical sequence of stages to be followed from T^1 to T^2 in a linear, forward, progressive movement.

Jabri's Dialogic Social Constructivist Approach

Jabri (2012, 2016) extends Lewin's work through incorporating a more dialogical approach by engaging with complex ideas and concepts whilst attempting to make them understandable and of practical worth. He sets out to develop a new theoretical lens for explaining complex change processes whilst building on Lewin's three stages of change. In adopting a relational perspective and in developing a framework that combines process, dialogue, and social construction, Jabri builds not only on Lewin's work (1951) and his concepts of group dynamics, action research, and field theory but also on Bakhtin's (1981, 1984, 1986) notion of utterance (meaning making through recursive discourses). In using a dialogical lens, he highlights how storying change works well with force-field analysis and action research in managing the change process. Jabri also draws on the more recent debates in information systems through adopting the concept of sociomateriality (Barad, 2007), in which managing change is seen to require consideration of the entanglement between people and matter, especially in the way that change affords 'organizing variation' (2012: 4–5). The possibilities for organizing brings Jabri to consider the dialectical relationship between agency and structure and to compare Foucault's position (see Foss & Morris, 1979), where agency is restricted by the power of discursive language within structures, with Bourdieu (1977), where emphasis is given to the capacity for agency within structures of domination. As Jabri states (2012: 52), 'The adoption of a social constructionist approach to change management emphasizes the need to drive change through an ongoing co-construction of meaning that involves people at all levels of the organization, rather than being restricted to "experts" working through senior management'.

In this development of a more dialogical model, there is a clear link with Lewin in his adoption of force-field analysis in charting the movement from a current state (unfreezing) through changing and organizing to a new desired state (that he refers to as some refreezing in an 'ice-topping' kind of way). This rather peculiar notion of 'ice-topping' is seen to counter the stability criticism levelled against Lewin through incorporating a more process and less linear orientation to change. Nevertheless, there remains a sense of event time and linearity in the ever-forward movement captured by the model, even though recognition is given to the iterative process that connects action (change) with research (understanding) and the way words (utterances) can achieve authentic discussion that can in turn empower people to participate in change. In making sense of utterances through conversations, Jabri draws on Weick's (1995) concept of sensemaking and the importance of using some form of appreciation as a starting point (taking ideas from appreciative inquiry) in co-constructing and projecting a desired future. He claims that 'the challenge for change agents is to work through the utterance of the word and the way in which words are made meaningful through conversations. A change that is led through dialogue is a change that is more likely to take root' (Jabri, 2012: 256).

A Modernist Twist to Kotter's Stage Model of Planned Change

In the popular management literature, Kotter's (1996) original eight-stage model to successful change follows the traditional, sequential OD path (with more recent versions incorporating a more process view). Kotter's well-known model on managing successful change establishes eight key sequential steps that comprise: establishing a sense of urgency; forming a powerful coalition; creating a vision; communicating the vision; empowering others to act on the vision; planning for and creating short-term wins; consolidating improvements and producing still more change; and institutionalizing new approaches. This linear-based temporal frame moves through a set sequence of stages in a prescribed order in changing from a current state to a future desired state. As with conventional OD approaches, there is a series of activities that need to be completed to secure successful and efficient change. However, since 2012, Kotter has started to move away from this linear, sequential stage model of change in embracing some of the more mainstream ideas around process. In building on this earlier work, he identifies seven accelerators centred on the need to create a sense of urgency around a single big opportunity (the first and foundational element of his eight accelerators). These eight accelerators mirror much of his earlier work and consist of the following:

1. Create a sense of urgency around a single big opportunity: Examine market position and competitive situation.
2. Build and maintain a guiding coalition: Bring together a group of people who have enough power to lead the change effort and sustain the transformation even in the face of resistance.
3. Formulate a strategic vision: Develop change initiatives designed to capitalize on the big opportunity.
4. Communicate the vision and the strategy to create buy-in and attract a growing volunteer army: Without an effective and credible communication strategy (and a lot of it), the hearts and minds of employees will never be won over.
5. Accelerate movement towards the vision and the opportunity: Ensure that the network removes barriers.
6. Celebrate visible, significant short-term wins: Major change takes time, and therefore, waiting until the end of the program before rewarding individuals or groups is a mistake.
7. Never let up: Keep learning from experience, and do not declare victory too soon.
8. Institutionalize strategic changes: Embed the new approaches and behaviours into the culture of the organization.

Kotter argues that modern organizations need to sustain two complimentary systems that should work in concert: first, an operating system for maintaining efficient day-to-day operations and, second, a strategy system for identifying opportunities and developing strategies. The operating system focusses on control performance and effectiveness in designing structures and reporting systems that support operational efficiency. The strategy system looks outside daily operations for new opportunities and innovations in utilizing employees' extramural strategic thinking. It is a network staffed by volunteers (around 10 percent of managerial and other employees) who engage in the strategic change game. There needs to be a shared sense of purpose and leadership abilities combined with the authority to develop strategy and the energy and enthusiasm to do so. The network identifies opportunities, creates vision, and inspires action; it is not concerned with reporting relationships, budget reviews, or project management (2012: 49). He contrasts his new framework with his traditional stage model for managing episodic change in the following way (2012: 47):

> There are three main differences between those eight steps and the eight "accelerators" on which the strategy system runs: (1) The steps are often used in rigid, finite, and sequential ways, in effecting or responding to episodic change, whereas the accelerators are concurrent and always at work. (2) The steps are usually driven by a small, powerful core group, whereas the accelerators pull in as many people as possible from throughout the organization to form a 'volunteer army.' (3) The steps are designed to function within a traditional hierarchy, whereas the solution is a second operating system, devoted to the design and implementation of strategy, that uses an agile, network like structure and a very different set of processes. The new operating system continually assesses the business, the industry, and the organization, and reacts with greater agility, speed, and creativity than the existing one. . . . Strategy should be viewed as a dynamic force that constantly seeks opportunities. . . . I think of that force as an ongoing process of 'searching, doing, learning, and modifying;' and of the eight accelerators as the activities that inform strategy and bring it to life. The network and the accelerators can serve as a continuous and holistic strategic change function—one that accelerates momentum and agility because it never stops.

In this new approach, Kotter (2012) has gone beyond his previous focus on episodic change and linear time sequences in managing interventions towards continuous cycles of activities within two separate but interdependent systems. The conventional hierarchical operating system is based around Tayloristic forms of organizing that are regulated and controlled by clock time. Time is viewed as a cost linked directly to measurements of efficiency; work time is tightly constrained and monitored, with a focus on the present. The strategy system however is based on future opportunities and with engaging the minds of employees in their free time (nonwork-monitored time) outside of their daily work activities and routines (see Chapter 7 for a discussion of hegemony, management techniques and political time). The efficiency of production must not be disrupted by other time-consuming activities that detract from maintaining price-competitive outputs of goods and services. Employees are expected to put on hold considerations of the past and future in their total engagement and commitment to the tasks assigned to them at work. Once free from the daily clock time regimes of work, they are expected to engage in creative thoughts generating new ideas for future strategic opportunities. Employees are encouraged to project beyond the present and past to identify potential trajectories and competitive possibilities that, if deemed worthy, can be operationalized and established within the operating system. Taken as a whole, this dual operating system is seen to capture the best of both worlds, namely, tightly regulated Taylorist forms of work organization in the production of goods and services and loosely coupled creative networks and spaces for generating new ideas and strategic thinking. Although Kotter (2012) characterizes this dual operating system for making change happen in an accelerating world as an ongoing process (in contrast to managing episodic change as an eight-stage sequence), his underlying conception of time remains unchanged. The focus is still on objective time in his notion of the need for continuous change in a rapid-fire, competitive world whilst finding 'space' for strategic thinking. Subjective time remains absent; to use Shipp and Cole's (2015) terms, there is a 'temporal blind spot' as these new, conceptual developments fail to move beyond a simple view of time as merely a medium through which change happens. In practice, the expectation that people work like automatons in the hierarchy during the day and then are refreshed and engage in the network at night is a little naïve. Under this scenario, individual time perspectives collapse into a temporality of work time in which time is not only money, but the employee's time becomes work time both in the office and in the home environment.

The General Absence of Subjective Time in Theorizing Change

Whereas all the change models and theories explained in this chapter adhere to a concept of time as a forward-moving phenomenon that is seen as inevitable, irreversible, and progressive, their focus has shifted with the incorporation of new concepts and perspectives from more objective, rational models to more subjective meaning-making frames. Interestingly, there is a general consensus that time is telescoping, intensifying, compressing, and accelerating (see also Adam, 2004; Wajcman, 2015). Whereas these theories do little to try and explain these assumptions—time remains implicit, and the growing rapidity of change is taken as self-evident—they are having a significant influence on these developments. As such, it is worth looking back on a well-cited article by Van de Ven and Poole (1995) that examines the underlying assumptions of change management theories to see if this sheds any light on these developments and the place of time and temporality in theorizing organizational change.

Van de Ven and Poole (1995) propose four foundational theories of change in organizations; these comprise the life cycle, evolutionary, dialectical, and teleological approaches. Life-cycle theory builds on the notion of sequential stages of development in a forward direction; as with the arrow of time, there is no possibility of reversal. From this perspective, organizations go through a number of stages from early start-up through maturity to eventual decline, in which change is linear and occurs in a prescribed order. Evolutionary theory uses a cyclical notion of time (Ancona, Okhuysen, & Perlow, 2001) and builds on the biological metaphor claiming that populations of organizations persist through variation and retention, in which certain forms continue over time and others fall by the wayside (noting that who these are cannot be predicted in advance). Dialectic theory, in drawing on the work of Hegel, Marx, and Freud, recognises that contradictory forces reside within organizations and their environment but that when these are in balance, stability occurs; over time, however, struggles between opposing entities shift the balance of power, and old ways of doing things (thesis) are challenged (antithesis), eventually resulting in a new state of balance where the conflicts are temporally resolved (synthesis). Although this may appear to fit with Deleuze's three temporal modalities and synthesis, it is based on an active synthesis of resolving resolution rather than a passive synthesis and the affirmation of difference that is central in Deleuze's work (see Chapter 11 for the discussion on Deleuze's view of synthesis). It can also be seen as a cyclical (recurring) sequence in the sense that this dialectic will continue to occur over time, even though the timing of the reoccurrence cannot be predicted. The cyclical time implicit in teleological theory centres on the notion of specific goals or objectives used to drive purposeful change. A desired state is clearly envisioned, and yet sequences are not predefined, but rather, modifications and adaptations are made along the way to ensure that the desired end state is achieved. This theory of change is based on the achievement of goals through cooperation and consensus (see Van de Ven & Pool, 2009: 863).

Van de Ven and Poole (1995) claim that there are different generating mechanisms that operate on different units of change (i.e., single entity or two or more entities) and modes of change (whether change is predictable and prescribed or unpredictable and emergent). Predictable patterns are associated with life-cycle and evolutionary theories, whereas a movement towards a new synthesis or desired state is associated with a constructive, unpredictable modality. On units of analysis, teleological and life-cycle theories focus on changes to an entity, whereas evolutionary and dialectical theories deal with multiple entities. They use the example of the punctuated equilibrium model of change (Romanelli & Tushman, 1994) to demonstrate how particular theories of change management are composed of two or more motors. In this example, purposeful action by management (teleological modality) is seen as the main driver for radical change, whereas the longer periods of minor adaptation and general stability are explained by the evolutionary modality.

Whilst useful, time and temporality are under theorized and underplayed in this analysis of theories of organizational change. In their four theoretical formulations, a cyclical notion of time predominates that is differentiated by the degree to which recurring sequences occur in a predictable preset fashion or to the extent to which sequences cannot be predefined and outcomes cannot be predicted. For example, in the life cycle, ideal-type change is temporalized as a linear sequence of prescribed stages, whereas the latter three are based on recurrent sequences centred on: variation, selection, and retention in evolutionary theory; confrontation, conflicts, and synthesis in dialectical approaches; and goal setting and implementation to a desired state under the teleological frame. Time and temporality are represented by the forward flow of time in which episodes reoccur that produce different configurations and outcomes through natural selection, oppositional forces, and purposeful goal attainment, whereas within the prescribed sequences, time is represented as continuing cycles of linear stages. The framework presents a predefined temporality either through prefigured sequences or through more open configurations of episodes that will occur and repeat themselves, even if the exact timing and sequencing of events remain unclear. Unlike Bergson (1913) or Deleuze (1994), there is no attempt to understand differences in the internal passage of time or the way in which memories of the past and anticipated futures may continually shape our temporal experience.

Interestingly, By's (2005) review of the change management literature identifies the speed or rate at which change occurs as a defining characteristic. He argues that scholars who view change as stopping and starting in a series of episodes construct discontinuous theories of change (that generally support stasis and the quasi-stationary view), whereas at the other end of the continuum, writers who view change as a never-ending dynamic (ceaseless change, fluidity) develop continuous theories of change. In drawing on Grundy's work (1993), he adds the notion of momentary acceleration that can result in 'bumpy incremental change' and 'bumpy continuous change' (2005: 372)—this modification attempts to accommodate the situation where most models refer to two or more rates (Burnes, 2009; Senior & Swailes, 2010). This takes us to another main characterization, namely, the scale of change, which is seen to range along a continuum from fine-tuning through to corporate transformation and the extent to which change emerges in a continual state of becoming or is the outcome of the purposeful pursuit of a desired state through planned change initiatives (By, 2005). These different views are seen to reflect the flux or fixity positions where, on the one hand, change is seen as a continuous process capable of bringing about fundamental change, whereas on the other hand, to achieve a desired change, there is a need to unfreeze the status quo and manage the process towards a clearly defined end point. Common to both is a conception of time as progressive movement from point T^1 to point T^2 in which subjective elements of time remain largely absent.

Demers (2007), who uses an historical frame for classifying developments in organizational change theories, also argues that the destinction between continuous and episodic change is a defining characteristic of alternative approaches. In charting developments from the 1950s to the early 2000s (leaving aside OD), she identifies a shift in dominant themes from a concern with whether change is determined by the environment or made through choice (see Child, 1997), to a concern with more radical change initiatives in the 1980s and the issue of whether change is evolutionary or revolution-ary, to a more recent shift to a process view of organizational change. This move towards process has resulted in a greater amalgamation of ideas and combinational approaches that attempt to combine previously separate ele-ments. She claims that the tendency for authors from different traditions to use the same words to mean different things has resulted in fragmentation and confusion that is making it increasingly difficult to position approaches and synthesize change frameworks (Demers, 2007).

From examining attempts to classify and characterize theories of organi-zational change, we can discern the tendency to either temporalize change using linear sequential and recurrent cyclical assumptions or to view change as emergence in which an under explored process temporality is seen to underpin theorization (see Chapters 9, 10 and 11). The most common com-parison arises between models that view change as a sequential series of stages or punctuated episodes and those that take a more process orientation in characterizing change as emergent. The central question here is whether we work from an assumption that there is a linear sequence to the passage of time, making it possible to prescribe a future pathway in the n-step man-agement of change, or whether we recognise that 'with the best laid plans of mice and men things will go awry' and that the unexpected will occur, with many of these unforseen processes emerging around planned interventions. In the latter chapters, we examine process approaches to change and tempo-rility in more depth. Although traces of the process approach have emerged among OD perspectives, the focus remains rooted in conventional notions of time and temporlity with a shift from more positivist to social construc-tionist approaches.

Discussion: Objective and Subjective Time in Managing Change

In developing frameworks and models for managing change, the tendency has been to view time as simply a medium through which change happens rather than being a central explanatory concept of significant theoretical importance. As Shipp and Cole argue, objective time is emphasised heavily in planned approaches to change with little if any notice being paid to sub-jective time. They claim that the main focus is on absolute notions of homog-enous, unidirectional time with an absence of attention to the different ways people experience time (interpretive notion of heterogeneous, multidirec-tional time). They advocate the need for new theory development in the field of organizational change to go beyond time as a background variable; as they state (2015: 251), 'incorporating a completely temporal view with both objective and subjective time can help researchers (in many streams of research) elaborate on organizational phenomenon in greater depth'. Similarly, Bartunek and Woodman (2015: 158), in drawing on the work of Bushe and Marshak (2009), are critical of planned sequenced change models mirroring Lewin's linear stages: 'To put it briefly, we suggest that the unfreeze-change-refreeze sequence represents a partial, linear, monophonic understanding of change'.

These scholars suggest that the need to move away from a singular focus on clock time in developing stage models of change towards frameworks that can accommodate how people think about time, for example, how far people look into the past or think forward to shorter or longer term futures—what Bluedorn and Jaussi (2008) refer to as temporal depth. Shipp and Cole (2015) suggest future research should move beyond objective time as a convenient metric and accommodate other neglected issues, such as time lags, rates, and patterns (linear and non-linear trajectories), duration, and timescales in theorizing change. The need to bring subjective elements more fully into concept development is illustrated through their example of the differential human experience of workdays (e.g., how people typically feel about Mondays compared to Fridays) and in using Tjosvold, Wong, and Chen's (2014) process-based view of conflict, noting,

> The conflict literature has seemingly overlooked the roles of recollected conflict and anticipated conflict. These aspects of subjective time are important for understanding an individual's response to a current conflict. For example, two individuals may experience the same present-day conflict, but their reactions may differ if for one individual this was the first instance of conflict, whereas the other individual recalls a previously experienced conflict. . . . Alternatively, an individual's response to a present-day conflict could differ when additional conflict is anticipated. . . . Thus, examining individual's retrospection and anticipations of conflict may better explain how individuals react to current conflict.
>
> (Shipp & Cole, 2015: 251)

Shipp and Cole (2015: 250) present a four-quadrant figure that summarizes scholarly focus with one axis representing the importance of objective time and the other the importance of subjective time. Those high on objective time take a positivistic clock-time view, whereas those high on subjective time take a more interpretative approach, with studies low on both dimensions being represented with the notion of a temporal blind spot. They argue for the need to build a completely temporal approach (high on both dimensions) to ensure the field of organizational change enters into the next stage of theoretical and empirical sophistication (2015: 254).

Conclusion

From this overview of episodic and linear stage models of change and the replacement of positivist with constructionist OD approaches, a shift has been highlighted from science-based, planned interventions under conventional change models characterized by a prescribed sequence of events towards more social constructionist and dialogic accounts that attempt to accommodate peoples' subjective experiences of change. Under the conventional approach, time is seen as linear and represented by the clock and Gregorian calendar. There is an ever-forward movement represented by a progressive series of stages from the commencement to the ending of change. These cycles of change repeat episodically with future change interventions but are nevertheless positioned along the arrow of time. Cycles of events and stages can be mapped out on a linear timescape of change (with different models and theories putting forward different stages that need to be sequenced in a prescribed order). As Hendry (1996: 624) notes,

> Scratch any account of creating and managing change and the idea that change is a three-stage process that necessarily begins with a process of unfreezing will not be far below the surface. Indeed it has been said that the whole theory of change is reducible to this one idea of Kurt Lewin's (1952). Most accounts of organizational change implicitly follow this pattern, and describe or employ of mix of cognitive and political strategies through successive phases of unfreezing, change, and refreezing.

The influence of contemporary notions of time compression and an accelerating world have shifted attention to the need for continuous change (see Kotter, 2012); developments in AI have highlighted the importance of building on already existing positive elements of organizations in managing cycles of sequenced change (see Cooperrider and Srivastva, 1987), whereas the narrative turn in the social sciences has drawn attention to the importance of sensemaking and dialogue (see Jabri, 2012). The focus in all of these nevertheless remains on processes that support cycles and stages in the progressive movement from a current state to a new, desired state. In these examples, managing change is in response to: big opportunities from a strategy system composed of a volunteer army (Kotter, 2012); an AI-stage cycle of discovery, dream, design, and delivery (Bushe, 2011); or through a sensitive force-field analysis that supports and responds to authentic dialogue in the co-construction of desired objectives (Jabri, 2012).

The growth in the range and type of perspectives that currently coexist within the OD camp has brought about hybridization and fusion, resulting in a certain degree of ontological and epistemological confusion as well as concerns over the incommensurability of these new approaches. The diversification of OD has rendered the perspective problematic for some, with a call to return to basic roots by others, it has led to attempts to reposition OD in a more positive light (AI), and it has resulted in eclectic approaches that draw on a variety of concepts from a range of perspectives. For Marshak (2006) a separation can be made between conventional OD and post-Lewinian OD approaches. The former base theorization on the notion of single, discoverable 'truths' unearthed through rational and systematic analysis of an objective reality. Under this perspective, change is planned, linear, episodic, and actioned by change agents. In contrast, the post-Lewinian view is more concerned with subjective realities in the social construction of meanings through discourse and narrative (see Burke, Lake and Paine, 2009). Change is ongoing and cyclical, and reality reflects power-political relations and is often negotiated and contested (Marshak, 2006: 839). As Dawson and Andriopoulos (2014: 176) note, 'In these later developments there is a movement away from more linear snap-shot models and n-step guides to a recognition of contextual dynamics and the way that change strategies need to be revised and modified during the course of managing an organizational change initiative'.

In the case of the punctuated equilibrium model of change, time remains rooted in onward evolutionary progression in which critical junctures (episodes) require action and radical change to correct organizational drift in line with a changing environment. In all these approaches, objective time is paramount acting as a background context—a medium through which change happens. Change as progression along the arrow of time from a past to a present and a future is the commonly held view even among those with a more social constructionist orientation. Non-linear time and notions of multiple temporalities (as opposed to multiple realities) are largely absent from these discussions and rarely raised or explained in the theories outlined in this chapter. Time remains integral yet hidden to these developments, and in the chapter that follows, we examine organizational change and temporality through the work of scholars who have focussed on technology and the complex relationships between socio-human and technical-material aspects of our experience of transformation and change in organizations.

References

Adam, B. (2004). *Time*. Cambridge: Polity Press.

Ancona, D. G., Okhuysen, G. A., & Perlow, L. A. (2001). Taking time to integrate temporal research. *Academy of Management Review, 26*(4), 512–529.

Argyris, C. (1973). *Intervention Theory and Method: A Behavioral Science View*. Reading, MA: Addison-Wesley.

Bakhtin, M. M. (1981). *The Dialogic Imagination*. Austin: Austin University of Texas Press.

Bakhtin, M. M. (1984). *Problems of Dostoyevsky's Poetics*. Minneapolis: University of Minnesota Press.

Bakhtin, M. M. (1986). *Speech Genres and Other Essays*. Austin: University of Texas Press.

Barad, K. (2007). *Meeting the Universe Halfway: Quantum Physics and the Entanglement of Matter and Meaning*. London: Duke University Press.

Bartunek, J. M., & Woodman, R. W. (2015). Beyond Lewin: Toward a temporal approximation of organization development and change. *Annual Review of Organizational Psychology and Organizational Behavior, 2*, 157–182.

Bergson, H. (1913). *Time and Free Will: An Essay on the Immediate Data of Consciousness*. London: George Allen & Company.

Blake, R. R., & Mouton, J. S. (1976). *Consultation*. Reading, MA: Addison-Wesley.

Bluedorn, A. C., & Jaussi, K. S. (2008). Leaders, followers, and time. *Leadership Quarterly, 19*(6), 654–668.

Bourdieu, P. (1977). *Outline of a Theory of Practice.* Cambridge: Cambridge University Press.

Burke, W. W., Lake, D. G., & Paine, J. W. (Eds.). (2009). *Organization Change: A Comprehensive Reader.* San Francisco: Jossey-Bass.

Burnes, B. (2004). Kurt Lewin and the planned approach to change: A re-appraisal. *Journal of Management Studies, 41*(6), 977–1001.

Burnes, B. (2009). *Managing Change: A Strategic Approach to Organisational Dynamics* (5th ed.). London: Prentice Hall/Financial Times.

Burnes, B., & Cooke, B. (2012). The past, present and future of organization development: Taking the long view. *Human Relations, 65*(11), 1395–1429.

Burnes, B., & Cooke, B. (2013). Kurt Lewin's field theory: A review and re-evaluation. *International Journal of Management Reviews, 15*(4), 408–425.

Bushe, G. R. (2011). Appreciative inquiry: Theory and critique. In D. Boje, B. Burnes, & J. Hassard (Eds.), *The Routledge Companion To Organizational Change* (pp. 87–103). London: Routledge.

Bushe, G. R., & Marshak, R. J. (2009). Revisioning organization development: Diagnostic and dialogic premises and patterns of practice. *Journal of Applied Behavioral Science, 45*, 348–368.

By, R. T. (2005). Organisational change management: A critical review. *Journal of Change Management, 5*(4), 369–380.

Child, J. (1997). Strategic choice in the analysis of action, structure, organizations and environment: Retrospect and prospect. *Organization Studies, 18*(1), 43–76.

Chin, R., & Benne, K. D. (1976). General strategies for effecting change in human systems. In W. G. Bennis, K. D. Benne, R. Chin, & K. E. Corey (Eds.), *The Planning of Change* (3rd ed., pp. 22–45). New York: Holt, Rinehart and Winston.

Cooperrider, D. L., & Srivastva, S. (1987). Appreciative inquiry in organizational life. In R. W. Woodman & W. A. Pasmore (Eds.), *Research in Organizational Change and Development* (Vol. 1, pp. 129–169). Stamford: JAI Press.

Dawson, P., & Andriopoulos, C. (2014). *Managing Change, Creativity and Innovation* (2nd ed.). London: Sage.

Deleuze, G. (1994). *Difference and Repetition.* New York: Columbia University Press.

Demers, C. (2007). *Organizational Change Theories: A Synthesis.* CA: Sage.

Doolin, B. (2003). Narratives of change: Discourse, technology and organization. *Organization, 10*(4), 751–770. Retrieved from http://search.ebscohost.com/login. aspx?direct=true&db=buh&AN=11742373&site=bsi-live

Foss, P., & Morris, M. (Eds.). (1979). *Michael Faucault: Power, Truth, Strategy.* Sydney: Feral Press.

Grant, D., & Marshak, R. J. (2011). Toward a discourse-centred understanding of organizational change. *Journal of Applied Behavioral Science, 47*, 204–235.

Grundy, T. (1993). *Managing Strategic Change.* London: Kogan Page.

Hayes, J. (2010). *The Theory and Practice of Change Management* (3rd ed.). New York: Palgrave Macmillan.

Hendry, C. (1996). Understanding and creating whole organizational change through learning theory. *Human Relations, 49*(5), 621–641.

Jabri, M. (2012). *Managing Organizational Change: Process, Social Construction and Dialogue.* Basingstoke: Palgrave Macmillan.

Jabri, M. (2016). *Rethinking Organizational Change: The Role of Dialogue, Dialectic & Polyphony in the Organization.* London: Routledge.

Johnson, G. (1992). Managing strategic change—strategy, culture and action. *Long Range Planning, 25*(1), 28–36.

Kotter, J. P. (1996). *Leading Change*. Boston, MA: Harvard Business School Press.

Kotter, J. P. (2012). How the most innovative companies capitalize on today's rapid-fire strategic challenges—and still make their numbers. *Harvard Business Review, 90*(11), 43–58.

Lewin, K. (1947). Frontiers in group dynamics: Concepts, method and reality in social science, social equilibria and social change. *Human Relations, 1*(1), 5–41.

Lewin, K. (1951). *Field Theory in Social Science: Selected Theoretical Papers*. New York: Harper & Row.

Lewin, K. (1952). *Field Theory in Social Science. Selected Theoretical Papers*. London: Tavistock Publications.

Marshak, R. J. (2006). Emerging directions: Is there a new OD? In J. V. Gallos (Ed.), *Organizational Development: A Jossey-Bass Reader* (pp. 833–841). San Francisco: John Wiley & Sons.

Marshak, R. J., & Grant, D. (2008). Organizational discourse and new organization development practices. *British Journal of Management, 19*, S7–S19.

McClellan, J. G. (2011). Reconsidering communication and the discursive politics of organizational change. *Journal of Change Management, 11*(4), 465–480.

Mumby, D. K. (1988). *Communication and Power in Organizations: Discourse Ideology and Domination*. Norwood, NJ: Ablex.

Romanelli, E., & Tushman, M. (1994). Organizational transformation as punctuated equilibrium: An empirical test. *Academy of Management Journal, 37*(5), 1141–1166.

Schein, E. H. (1996). Kurt Lewin's change theory in the field and in the classroom: Notes towards of model of management learning. *Systems Practice, 9*(1), 27–47.

Senior, B., & Swailes, S. (2010). *Organizational Change* (4th ed.). Harlow: FT Prentice Hall.

Shipp, A. J., & Cole, M. S. (2015). Time in individual-level organizational studies: What is it, how is it used, and why isn't it exploited more often? *Annual Review of Organizational Psychology and Organizational Behavior, 2*, 237–260.

Tjosvold, D., Wong, A., & Chen, N. (2014). Constructively managing conflict in organizations. *Annual Review of Organizational Psychology and Organizational Behavior, 1*, 545–568.

Tushman, M. L., & Romanelli, E. (1985). Organizational evolution: A metamorphosis model of convergence and reorientation. In B. M. Staw & L. L. Cummings (Eds.), *Research in Organizational Behavior* (Vol. 7, pp. 171–222). Greenwich, CT: JAI Press.

Van de Ven, A. H., & Poole, M. S. (1995). Explaining development and change in organizations. *Academy of Management Review, 20*(3), 510–540.

Van de Ven, A. H., & Poole, M. S. (2005). Alternative approaches for studying organizational change. *Organization Studies, 26*(9), 1377–1404.

Van de Ven, A. H., & Poole, M. S. (2009). Explaining development and change in organizations. In W. W. Burke, D. G. Lake, & J. W. Paine (Eds.), *Organization Change: A Comprehensive Reader* (pp. 859–892). San Francisco: Jossey-Bass.

Wajcman, J. (2015). *Pressed for Time: The Acceleration of Life in Digital Capitalism*. London: University of Chicago Press.

Weick, K. E. (1995). *Sensemaking in Organizations*. Thousand Oaks, CA: Sage Publications.

6 Technical, Social, and Material
Assemblages of Changing Times

Introduction

Studies on the process and impacts of technological change and research into the relationships among people, technology, and the organization of work has generated a number of different perspectives and theories (Preece, McLoughlin, & Dawson, 2000). This long-standing interest in technology, change strategies, and work reorganization covers a very broad area, and in this chapter our attention focusses on the movement from social constructivist to relational perspectives of a selective group of studies concerned with transition and change (with implicit and explicit notions of time and temporality) through the uptake and use of new technologies. Following a brief discussion of early debates, we examine time, technology, and change in relation to constructivist, network, performative, and practice approaches as well as the growing recent interest in quantum mechanics that has produced considerable conceptual debates around notions of relational entanglement and sociomateriality.

The Time Matrix of Industrialization: Some Early Debates

Early studies into technology at work tended to view technology as something distinct and identifiable that had impacts on organizations (Wilkinson, 1983: 11). Technological determinism is a well-touted explanation for this group of work where political process and social choice was seen to be downplayed in a general acceptance of the inevitability and commercial need for the introduction and adoption of new technology (for a discussion, see McKenzie & Wajcman, 1985; McLoughlin & Clark, 1994). In studies charting the technological impacts of the industrial revolution with, for example, the growth of new, mechanized factories in the textile industry, technology was seen to be the determining driving force (Gill, 1985). However social historians such as Hobsbawn (1964) illustrate how transformations in the workplace were not simply determined by technology but by a rich combination of sociopolitical and economic factors. He claims that the early Industrial Revolution was 'technically rather primitive' and that it was the way that the technology was developed and applied under different sociopolitical and contextual conditions that brought about this revolutionary change (Hobsbawn, 1969: 60). During this period, the steam-powered machines of the Industrial Revolution freed production from the biological constraints of physical exhaustion and radically changed people's experience of time. As Frank (2012: 104) notes,

> The factory system formed an entirely new time matrix. . . . Time became compressed and abstracted for both worker and manager alike. For the first time in human history, minutes became a temporal unit of exchange—they counted and they could be counted. They became crucial as factory owners sought efficiency in production and workers resisted the push to turn their bodies into mere extensions of machines.

A central artefact and technical device that became an explicit part of the engagement of labour in factory work was the clock. As explained in Chapter 3, the regulation and control of work was increasingly underpinned by a clock-based discipline where the work of employees was precisely timed. Clocks became a key industrial machine for controlling the pacing of work and payment through synchronizing work with time (see also Chapter 7).

The techniques of Taylorism (Littler, 1982), which even today continue to influence many of the features of work design (Pruijt, 1997), combine the systematic use of clock time with the design and control of work characterized by a detailed division of labour (work broken down to basic component parts) that sets about extracting the conceptual aspects of work through decoupling the work process from the skills of employees (Edwards, 1979). Braverman, who presents a neo-Marxist analysis of technology and change in the workplace, charts the capitalist drive for profitability and productivity in the widespread uptake of Taylorist forms of work organization and the use of stopwatches to control work (1974: 207) that was later refined by Gilbreth in his time and motion studies (Rose, 1988). As Braverman (1974: 119–120) describes,

> Taylor popularized time study as part of his effort to gain control over the job. Time study may be defined as the measurement of elapsed time for each component operation of a work process; its prime instrument is the stopwatch, calibrated in fractions of an hour, minute, or second. . . . Gilbreth . . . added to time study the concept of motion study. . . . Motion study catalogs the various movements of the body as standard data, with the aim of determining time requirements.

By the 20th century the use of Taylorite time and motion studies to break jobs down into highly specialized and repetitive tasks started to take hold, removing knowledge about how work should be done from the workplace. Breitbart (1981) in a film documentary on Taylor and scientific management (titled *Clockwork*) provides some original footage on the way that employee movements were captured using motion-picture cameras—the work of Frank Gilbreth—and then calibrated by clocks into the smallest of motions. This early work paved the way for modern work regimes in establishing clock-based hegemonic structures that continue to regulate behaviours within and outside work settings. These changes marked a transition from the cyclical rhythms of time associated with pre-mechanization prior to the growth of urban cities, when the physical capacity to engage in work in daylight hours was the major regulatory influence. The natural cycles between the seasons, the flow of day into night, and the strong association of night-time with sleeping were forever disrupted with industrialization and the advent of electric artificial lighting. Prior to this, candles and oil lamps were the main mechanisms for providing artificial light to the home, but by the 20th century illuminated cities and 'brightly lit factories ran twenty-four hours a day' (Frank, 2012: 109). As much as the culture of the day was influencing the development and use of technology, so was the technology changing the culture and establishing a long-lasting Western relationship with clock time and commerce.

The links among technology, commerce, and time became highly visible during these early phases of industrialization and were represented in the bodily constructs of new industrial towns, railway engineering projects, the machine application of steam engines, and the use of clocks. Unregulated working hours became a social concern as the welfare of children was jeopardized in the pursuit of profits under time-paced work regimes that sought to ensure that employees were constantly engaged in work activities. Clock time as the bastion of commerce and industry became embedded in a growing industrial culture of time work discipline. Debate, resistance, and negotiation did not arise over the nature of time but rather on change in the value and regulation of time—in for example the campaign to establish a 10-hour working day (Henriques, 1979)—and in the imposition of synchronized time through conventions that could bring continuity to the hodgepodge of local time differences, which were common in this period. Railways were a major driver in reshaping people's experience of time and the import of punctual behaviour as electrically coordinated time engineered a new temporal order that is now largely taken for granted in modern Western cultures. These changes were contested at the time, for as Levine describes, there was considerable resistance to the Gregorian calendar in France, and many Americans consciously resisted standard time (2006: 72):

> By the early twentieth century, particularly in the United States clock time had been firmly established as the regulator of public life. But not everyone greeted the new time with open arms. Many people understood the profundity of temporal standardization and feared its consequences.

They recognized that it established new conceptions of time reckoning and, most critically, that it would mean new priorities for the social order. Some of these criticisms targeted the act of standardization; others focussed on the more general tyranny and rigidity of the clock.

Time as a publicly contested terrain is less in evidence today, but what is interesting is the place of time—which is present in its absence—underlying the shifting debates on the relationship between technology and organization. There has been a noticeable turn in focus from clearly demarcated boundary approaches in which characterizations of technology as objective artefact and time as an objective standard measurement of intervals are common towards perspectives that speak of mutually shaping, interweaving, and entangled relations between, for example, technology and temporal structuring in organizations (Orlikowski & Yates, 2002). McLoughlin charts these developments in asking the rhetorical question of whether technologies shape organizations or organizations shape technology. He claims that many of the debates around technology rest on different conceptualizations that range from well-defined and bounded definitions to more expansive conceptions of technology as a network of relations with no clear boundaries (McLoughlin, 1999: 5–7). Our focus is not with the early technological determinist perspectives (for a discussion, see Wilkinson, 1983) but with the move from social constructivist to more relational approaches (e.g., Barad, 2003; Leonardi & Barley, 2008; Mutch, 2013) that view technology as networks, entangled relations, and sociomaterial assemblages. In this move the binary divisions of time are implicitly replaced by a more relational perspective, yet time still often remains the ghost in the materiality of these reconceptualizations.

The Social Reconstruction of Time, Technology, and Actor Networks

The interconnectivity between time as a concept and time as represented by a technological artefact, such as a sundial, clock, or timepiece, is brought into clearer focus through the lens of the Social Construction of Technology (SCOT) approach. Advocates of this perspective argue that the process of social construction is central in that 'technology does not have any influence which can be gauged independently of human interpretation' (Grint & Woolgar, 1997: 10). The purpose of a clock is not transparent in the character of the machine but only within the social context of the meaning ascribed to clocks by others and through their social use. A SCOT analysis would pose the question: How do we know the capability and place of a timepiece once we remove it from the context in which it has purpose and meaning? From this perspective what a clock can do and how it is used are not integral to the artefact per se but arise from attributes afforded to the machine by humans. Our knowledge of a sundial, clock, or timepiece is essentially social—the outcome of a process of social construction—and does not derive from a set of objective capabilities integral to the machine itself. SCOT emphasises that there is no clear boundary between the technical (non-human) and the social (human) and that any boundaries that are in evidence are essentially socially defined (Grint & Woolgar, 1997). Bijker and Law (1992) argue that technologies are a heterogeneous assortment of societal elements (such as social, cultural, psychological, and economic) that both constrain and make possible trajectories that, for a while, remain open and flexible. The concept of 'interpretative flexibility' is used to capture the potentialities of technologies during early development and use that are seen to diminish over time as alternative design options are gradually eliminated from this process. This permeability and flexibility is made obdurate through the establishment and legitimation of a common set of understandings and interpretations that sets a socially constructed boundary—a form of 'closure'—on what a technology is and is not (Pinch & Bijker, 1984). Alternative interpretations are excluded, and the timepiece and clock become 'stabilized' and taken for granted. Their purpose and place within society become routinized and unquestioned. Natural time is replaced by socially constructed time, which is epitomized by the clock and timepiece.

But one could question whether the technology of time is ever fully closed; for example, the discovery of quantum mechanics, and the invention of the atomic clock and Planck time, has enabled scientists to uncover reversible time and to divide time up into ever smaller intervals, leading to questions about what time actually is. Long-held assumptions about time are called into question, and a more relational, interconnected view of the universe emerges in the re-representation of time in scientific discourse (Hawking, 2011; Penrose, 2011) and public debate (Peake, 2012). As such, social constructivist accounts that counterbalance the technological determinism of earlier perspectives are increasingly called into question as developments in quantum mechanics influence scholars in technology studies and information systems. McLoughlin (1999: 94–104), for example, argues that approaches that view either the technical or the social as ultimately determining are reductionist and fail to appreciate the network of relations that exist. On this count Bruno Latour (1991) announced in what has become a well-cited quotation—that 'technology is society made durable'. He provides a brief account of hotel keys and the use of a large, metal weight to encourage residents to leave their keys at the desk, arguing that through a process of translation, customers no longer need to respond to a request to leave their keys as they now willingly leave a large, unwieldy object (Latour, 1991: 104–110). The essential argument is that social relations and objects (like a mechanism or a machine) are always integrated into longer-term sociotechnical networks within which we can, through deep examination, chart fine differences whilst eliminating traditional binary divides between, for example, the social and technical or human and non-human (Latour, 1991).

In furthering this analysis of a chain of interactions between a network of human and non-human actants—in which technology may achieve some form of transitory primacy—Latour (1991), in conjunction with Callon (1999), is associated with a perspective known as Actor Network Theory (ANT). ANT adopts a relational epistemology that rejects the view that humans and non-humans exist in and of themselves and can be explained either through recourse to nature (realism) or to society (social constructivism). ANT moves beyond this form of dualism in viewing reality as a transitional becoming, in which interacting heterogeneous elements (people, texts, training, rooms, artefacts, and weather) form networks of human actors and non-human participants (actants) (Law & Hassard, 1999). Attention is given to the process of translation (problematization, interessmant, and enrolment) by which disputes in science become 'resolved' and stabilized in the attributes society may ascribe to, for example, the technical artefact of a bicycle (Pinch & Bijker, 1984). In his book *Reassembling the Social*, Latour calls for a reassessment of sociology through feeding off controversies and using ANT to render social connections traceable by following the work done to stabilize the controversies (Latour, 2005). Whereas Law, in reflecting on this approach, argues that the use of 'actor' and 'network' was 'intentionally oxymoronic', the term 'elides the distinction between structure and agency' (1999: 1) in centring on a relational materiality that rejects essentialist divisions (human and non-human) and on performativity, that is, on the way things are performed into relations made durable (Law, 1999: 3–4).

Although these scholars never directly addressed the issue of time and temporality, an examination of clock time—through the perspective of ANT—would investigate the interacting networks of human and non-human elements (e.g., people, organizations, clocks, conventions, standards, and computers) in the translation of controversies and disputes into a more durable collective understanding of time. In Western clock-oriented cultures and with the advent of computers and digital technologies, standard time has become embedded as an unquestionable part of everyday existence. But how stable is this? Is the performance of a conventional watch, in which moving hands indicate time passing (objects moving in space like the rotation of the earth), materially significant when compared with digitalized time that has been dematerialized? Although SCOT speaks to the social construction of time and timepieces, and ANT draws attention to the inseparability of assemblages of human and non-human networks, neither directly addresses issues about time and temporality that remain strangely absent in their presence. From applying this framework, however, digitalized time would be seen as constituted through and supported by networks that would include specific material devices, such as iPads, smartphones, and a range electronic equipment, for example, cars, airplanes, and air control systems, as well as the routines and practices of people and the array of concepts, conventions, and models that support and shape these networks of heterogeneous actants—a view of time and temporality as ever changing through the constitutive flows of actor networks.

Agential Realism, Performativity, and Timelessness

Building on the work of Latour and ANT, a number of scholars have been oriented towards a post-humanist position in which agency is not seen to centre on the intentionality of humans as a subject separate from the world around them (Braidotti, 2013). The human and non-human are actants, and as such, technology is integral to human identity being mutually dependent in a co-evolving world (Law & Hassard, 1999). The representation of boundaries between objects in a separatist world is rejected, and the human is recontextualized into an assemblage, entangled, social-material (post-humanist) world. There is an ongoing mutual constitutive becoming (ontology of becoming) in which the human is not sovereign but a hybrid of the machine and organic body: 'a place of decentred human and non human becoming' (Pickering, 2008: 13). Haraway (2015) develops this human and non-human assemblage to suggest the possibility for a world that moves beyond the conventional conceptions of gender, which are continually reaffirmed through social constructions that represent a male-female divide. Along with a number of other feminist writers, Haraway (2015) objects to the naturalized, essentialist understanding of gender and gender differences (as well as various other dichotomous categories) and, through the figure of the 'cyborg', attempts to destabilize dominant gender categories and stereotypes.

In building on this work (Haraway, 2015) and ANT (Callon, 1999; Latour, 2005), Barad (2007) in her book *Meeting the Universe Halfway* is also critical of the tendency to give primacy to human agency and to represent the human and non-human as distinct elements that cement a nature-culture dichotomy. She comments on and engages with the work of Niels Bohr, whom she claims insightfully rejected representationalism in his early work on atomic theory (2007: 31). She uses the example where Bohr argues against Einstein's view that objectivity is not possible if we are unable to separate the world (the observer and object). Bohr suggests that even if we accept quantum physics' non-separability, objectivity remains possible if we can reproduce an 'unambiguous measurement of one part of the phenomenon (the object) by another part (the agencies of observation)' (Barad, 2007: 339). Barad takes hold of this line of reasoning and argues that humans are not a 'special separate system' but are entangled and emerge along with other physical systems. Within this broader view, intra-actions make phenomena meaningful and allow for agential separability in which measurements are not the outcomes of humans in laboratories but are causal intra-actions. As Barad notes,

> The reproducibility and unambiguous communication of laboratory results are possible because the agential cut enacts determinate boundaries, properties and meanings, as well as a causal structure in the marking of the 'measuring agencies' ('effect') by the 'measured object' ('cause') within the phenomenon. . . . Objectivity is based not on an inherent

ontological separability, a relation of absolute exteriority, as Einstein would have it, but on an intra-actively enacted agential separability, a relation of exteriority within phenomenon.

(2007: 340)

For Barad, there is an ongoing inseparability in conjunction with a dynamic 'intra-action' in which agencies are entangled and mutually constituted; nevertheless, through agential cuts we can enact boundaries and present reproducible explanations. Or to use Barad's words for explaining her 'agential realist' position (2007: 33), '*phenomena* are the *ontological* inseparability of agentially intra-acting components'. To put it another way, the very nature of matter is entanglement, and intra-action matters in the reconfiguring of these entanglements with the boundaries of human and non-human not being determinate but co-constituted—they are constituted along with the world. Barad thereby contends that they are not something in the world; that is, they are not given—why should our bodies end at the skin—or determined, for example, by sight (our daily use of visual representations)—but, rather, are constituted as being of the world (2007: 156–160). This again highlights Barad's rejection of conventional representations in which the world is seen to be broken up into distinct entities that are independent and separate (and in this her relational position aligns with ANT). For example, the social and scientific realms are viewed as co-constituted rather than comprising a set of distinct material practices. Moreover, whereas they are made together, they are not fixed but dynamic and open, ongoing, entangled material practices in which boundaries are ever changing.

Under the rather verbose label of a 'posthumanist performative account of technoscientific and other naturalcultural practices' (2007: 32), Barad maintains that the 'entanglement' of ideas and materials cannot be understood by conventional, reflexive, representational methodologies (that align with a separatist ontology) but, rather, require a diffractive methodology (more in keeping with an ontology of constitutive becoming) that offers a more performative account. She also notes how her use of 'posthumanist' is not linked to 'human' or any idea of the death of the 'human' in a cybernetic world but, rather, rejects separateness of 'things' or natural divisions between culture and nature, in being interested in how boundaries are actively configured and reconfigured. From this position, matter is never fixed nor is it simply the end point of a certain sequence of processes; it is agentive (2007: 137). As Barad states (2007: 392–393),

> In my agential realist account, matter is a dynamic expression/articulation of the world in its intra-active becoming. All bodies, including but not limited to human bodies, come to matter through the world's iterative intra-activity—its performativity. Boundaries, properties, and meanings are differentially enacted through the intra-activity of mattering. . . . The very nature of materiality is an entanglement. Matter itself is always

already open to, or rather entangled with, the "Other". The intra-actively emergent "parts" of phenomena are co-constituted.

On the question of methodology, the concept of diffraction (that is taken from the diffraction of a beam of particles in the double-slit experiment) is drawn from physics, where it is used to describe the wave behaviour displayed by particles following an encounter with an obstruction, in which the waves interact and either combine to reinforce each other and or cancel each other out, resulting in a distinct and characteristic pattern. It is used to replace reflection as a metaphor for thinking—which is deemed to be about mirroring and likeness—to draw attention to patterns of difference and, in particular, to 'the entangled nature of differences', and especially of those differences that matter (Barad, 2007: 36). The performative approach is used to emphasise matter's dynamism and to move away from descriptions that represent reality (i.e., those descriptions that ask the question: How well do these descriptions align with our observations of nature or culture?) to actions, practices, and doings. As Barad explains (2007: 133),

> A performative understanding of discursive practices challenges the representationalist belief in the power of words to represent pre-existing things. Unlike representationalism, which positions us above or outside the world we allegedly merely reflect on, a performative account insists on understanding thinking, observing, and theorizing as practices of engagement with, and as part of, the world in which we have our being.

Barad stresses the interconnectedness of being, emphasising how our intra-actions matter in reconfiguring the world in its becoming. Traditional conceptions of space and time—of this led to this that led to this—that underpin conventional cause-and-effect explanations are questioned. From this viewpoint the future is not the end point of a sequence of actions; 'it is a cascade experiment' (2007: 394) in which 'the world and its possibilities for becoming are remade with each moment' (2007: 396), and as such, Barad suggests: 'We need to meet the universe halfway, to take responsibility for the role that we play in the world's differential becoming' (2007: 396). In her agential realist account, agency is not aligned with human intentionality as the openness of the future is inherent in the nature of intra-activity. In Barad's words 'Agency is "doing" or "being" in its intra-activity. It is the enactment of iterative changes to particular practices. . . . It is an enactment, not something that someone or something has' (2007: 178). She forwards the notion that discursive practices are mutually implicated and articulated with material phenomena and that these do not stand in relationship to each other. Their reconfiguring does not simply result in different descriptions of the world but in different diffraction patterns that comprise different configurations of space, time, and matter. In this sense, 'Becoming is not an unfolding in time but the inexhaustible dynamism of the enfolding of mattering' (2007: 180). Agency changes the possibilities of change.

This ontological shift is seen by many to offer new possibilities for explaining the long-standing problematic associated with social-material dynamics. It acts as a useful counterbalance to the tendency in recent theoretical formulations to privilege the discursive over-material concerns and draws attention (once again) to the need to avoid binary divisions. On a more contentious note, it also highlights the problem of viewing change as a continuous transformation over time rather than as an intra-active dynamic.

> Dynamics are about change. To specify or study the dynamics of a system is to say something about the nature of and possibilities for change. This includes specifying the nature of causation, the nature of the causes that effect change, the possibilities for what can change and how it can change, the nature and range of possible changes, and the conditions that produce change. The study of dynamics, as it is generally conceptualized within the natural sciences, is concerned with how the values of particular variables change over time as a result of the action of external forces, where time is presumed to march along as an external parameter. Agential realism does not simply pose a different dynamics (substituting one set of laws for another); it produces an altogether different understanding of dynamics. It is not merely that the form of the causal relations has been changed, but the very notions of causality, as well as agency, space, time, and matter, are all reworked. Indeed, in this account, the very nature of change and the possibilities for change changes in an ongoing fashion as part of the world's intra-active dynamism.
>
> (Barad, 2007: 179)

The world of quantum mechanics provides a microcosm of how the universe operates in which time does not progress according to the laws of thermodynamics that we often view as inviolable. Time and change are extrapolated from the microworld in which entanglement and uncertainty are seen to capture a wider understanding of reality that has previously been lost by our obsession with a more separatist perspective that seeks to disconnect elements in a world where everything exists in relation to everything else. Drawing on quantum mechanics, time is no longer relative to the observer (Einstein's macro view of space-time) but is part of a performative being in which agencies are intra-actively entangled, inseparable and mutually constituted. Traditional conceptions of space and time are questioned as the moment is in the happening, temporality is displaced, and concepts of time are seen as temporary constructs that people create. It is only through agential cuts (a temporal bracket) that we are able to create delimiters (facilitative boundaries) that enable explanations to be formulated and presented. The focus is on the 'now' of continuous becoming in which there are infinite choice possibilities

(Barbour, 2000), and in this, there is a sense in which temporality is discarded (the world is made of multiple 'nows') in favour of a tenseless notion of time.

Quantum Mechanics Meets Social Practice in the Sociomateriality of Entangled Time

Among scholars in the social sciences, there is growing interest in quantum mechanics and practice-based approaches that are generating productive debates and an intertwining of scholarly ideas across disciplines (Adam, 2004; Carroll, 2010; Frank, 2012), as Adam (1990: 56) explains:

> Whilst Einstein's work has no direct practical application for social science, we need to take note of it at the level of theory since most social scientists understand natural time exclusively through the conceptual framework of Newtonian physics as absolute, objective, spatial, and clock-like. . . . Where Newtonian physicists conceptualised the ultimate reality as hard, material, and permanent, quantum physicists find particles to exist for a while and then to disappear again into a background of energy. They see them as temporally emerging; transient, rather than permanent, displaying simultaneously the characteristics of both particle and wave.

Ideas of a multiverse (multiple space-time worlds) and time reversal (time flowing backwards) have emerged from research into quantum mechanics at the atomic and subatomic levels in which the temporal categories of past and future and the direction of time itself are called into question (Barbour, 2000; Hawking, 2011; Penrose, 2011). For example, Richard Feynman (1999) put forward the idea that antimatter is ordinary matter travelling backwards through time. He explained how the behaviour of things at a small scale (where time is reversible) is so different from the way things behave at a large scale (where time is irreversible), suggesting that we do not have the familiarity or pictures to fully understand and make sense of why the phenomena of the world seems to go in one direction (causality), and yet at the quantum level this directional flow is called into question. Feynman (1999) argues that many of the laws of science, such as the law of gravitation, are reversible in time (in the sense that this would not undermine the fundamental law), even though this is not what we observe in practice (a broken egg does not remake itself through time reversal). Stephen Hawking (2011) also discusses the implications of quantum theory in his discussion of ordinary (real) time that moves along a horizontal line from past to future and imaginary time (that he argues is really the real time) in which all moments in time simultaneously coexist (there are no singularities).

With these developments in quantum mechanics, there is a growing awareness of the inadequacy of clock time for explaining what is occurring at the subatomic level. In quantum mechanics the future is not determined, subatomic particles have an infinite number of choice possibilities, and yet when observed and measured they are 'forced' into making a choice between these multiple options (in the case of an entangled pair, there is the strange finding that the other particle in the pair is instantly 'aware' of the measurement and outcome made on the other). From this perspective, there are no certainties but only probabilities; time-based causality—if you do this, then this will happen—is called into question as there is an innate unpredictability. The conventional meaning of time and space becomes questionable in the way that wave-particles are seen to come into being and where action occurs simultaneously across distances without any apparent cause. The use of distance as a measure of time, therefore, no longer seems to hold sway in this quantum world where relationships and interconnected wholeness takes precedence.

These findings in quantum mechanics draw attention to the contradiction and incompatibility between the indeterminacy of quantum mechanics and Einstein's theory of relativity, which in turn questions the uncritical practice of using standard forms of Newtonian clock time in developing models and theories that seek to explain change and transition in organizations. There is a discrepancy and, as yet, unsolved scientific puzzles arising in the very different space of macro-world and microworld time. These new insights into the workings of quantum worlds and the associated conundrums have also engaged the interests of social scientists and influenced debates on theory and practice (de Vaujany & Mitev, 2013; Leonardi, 2013; Leonardi, Nardi, & Kallinikos, 2012; Orlikowski, 2007; Schatzki, Cetina, & von Savigny, 2001). Boje (2012: 1), for example, suggests that 'quantum physics will mean new approaches to change management and storytelling', whereas Leornardi and Barley (2008) argue for a reassessment of the way the social and material entangle and imbricate in situated practices involving the use and uptake of new technologies.

Drawing on the work of Barad, Orlikowski argues that 'the emergent process perspective inhibits assigning agential power to the distinctive technological capabilities that interact with human interpretations and social action' (2010: 133). In her studies on virtual worlds (Orlikowski, 2010; Schultze & Orlikowski, 2010), she draws on the work of Barad and adopts a performative perspective, claiming that we are what we are through our entanglement with things that we enact in everyday practices and that these sociomaterial realities form and perform organizations as they temporally emerge (Orlikowski, 2010: 137). Whereas there is a focus on performativity and situated relational practices, there remains a notion of temporal emergence, and as with other writers in this area (see Leonardi, 2012, 2013), it is recognised that the empirical study of change and technology in organizations becomes problematic if temporality is too quickly jettisoned and abandoned (see also Kautz & Jensen, 2013).

In this emerging research, various ideas from quantum mechanics and theorist-philosophers such as Barad (2007) and Schatzki (Schatzki et al., 2001) have been developed, modified, and adopted, particularly by scholars who have examined changing technologies (Leonardi, 2011), organizing (Nicolini, Gherardi, & Yanow, 2003) and the way 'socio-material relations and their intermediaries (both human and non-human) not only mediate activities but also propagate practices' (Gherardi, 2006). For example, Schultze and Orlikowski (2010) call for an approach that can accommodate the complex sociomaterial configurations that are an integral part of work activities in organizations. In substantiating this position, Orlikowski (2010) draws on the example of Project Wonderland, which is a virtual, collaborative three-dimensional work environment developed by Sun Microsystems where employees—who manipulate personalized, on-screen representations (avatars) of themselves—engage in real-time interaction using images, text, and audio. Employees in dispersed geographical areas 'co-locate' in this virtual environment, which one could consider as an exemplar of non-materiality in being virtual in composition, and yet, Orlikowski (2010) uses this example to highlight the importance of materiality in everyday organizing and in the performance of contemporary organizations.

These empirical studies of technology, in conjunction with those associated with the broad field of practice-based studies, move beyond divisional, separatist approaches (dualisms) in emphasising the relational and constitutive character of existence, as Schatzki (2001: 12) explains in relation to practice theory:

> Practice theory also joins a variety of 'materialist' approaches in highlighting how bundled activities interweave with ordered constellations of nonhuman entities. . . . Practice approaches promulgate a distinct social ontology: the social is a field of embodied, materially interwoven practices centrally organized around shared practical understandings. This conception contrasts with accounts that privilege individuals, (inter)actions, language, signifying systems, the life world, institutions/roles, structures, or systems in defining the social. These phenomena, say practice theorists, can only be analyzed via the field of practices. Actions, for instance, are embedded in practices, just as individuals are constituted within them. Language, moreover, is a type of activity (discursive) and hence a practice phenomenon, whereas institutions and structures are effects of them.

In a practice-based study of technology, Leonardi (2011) examines the development and implementation of a technology designed to automate computer simulations for crashworthiness of vehicles (using finite element simulation modelling). He argues that most scholars have tended to view human agency as dynamic (in the sense that people make choices and direct activities to achieve particular goals), and material agency as static (in the sense that technology has a fixed technical configuration that does not change across contexts). Under this view, if technology constrains the achievement of certain goals, then people generally revise their way of organizing around the technology or replace the technology with some modified or new version that better serves their needs. Changing their patterns of social action—organizational routines—is a way that human agency may be exercised to ensure desired goals are achieved whilst leaving the technical parameters of the technology unchanged. However from a relational sociomaterial perspective, Leonardi argues that technologies are far more flexible and open to material change than often assumed, noting that 'in many modern organizations it may be as easy for people to change the material makeup of a technology, and hence its material agency, as it is for them to change existing routines' (2011: 149). He claims that in practice there is an interweaving of these human and material agencies (which he refers to as a process of 'imbrication') and that past changes and people's goals (future desires) influence their active construction of perceptual affordances and constraints in the present (Leonardi, 2011: 153–154). The focus is not on the start or end of the process but on explaining how this interweaving (imbrication) occurs and the consequences of change on future actions. In the case of 'crashworthiness', Leonardi tracks developments across the sequence of five imbrications (that alternate from human to material, where technology changes, and then material to human, where routines change), with each constraint being tackled by material agency and each affordance by human agency. He notes how at an empirical level, routines and technologies are relatively easy to observe and distinguish, whereas at an ontological level (when one considers the nature of existence or the essence of the nature of being), these two are seen to blur as indistinguishable phenomena. Though his empirical work he is able to present a very ordered sequence of events that do not align with Barad's ontological view of the world—which may reflect the different focus from empirical observation (micro) to philosophical thinking (macro). In his example, it is still people who choose to change their technologies or routines, spotlighting a limitation to material agency (2011). People can variously interpret the things a technology can or cannot do, but as he states: 'Material agency is limited by its feature set, a toaster simply cannot be used as a cell phone, no matter how much someone wishes it could be' (Leonardi, 2011: 164).

Cecez-Kecmanovic and colleagues (Cecez-Kecmanovic, Galliers, Henfridsson, Newwell, & Vidgen, 2014) highlight the different conceptions and definitions that pervade in the field and the level of controversy, confrontation, and confusion, especially when comparisons are drawn between broader philosophical discussions (macro) and empirical, practice-based studies (micro). Nevertheless, the approach usefully counters the tendency for dualism in much theorizing in the management discipline. The relational character of managerial and organizational practice is emphasised where 'things' exist only when they are in relationship with each other and are not taken to have independent capabilities and characteristics outside of these relationships. It is the ongoing and emergent organizational practices through which 'things' are constituted as material or become materialized and 'entangled' in those

relationships that become the focus for study. Thus, seen through a sociomaterial lens, technology, in the form of a digital timepiece, for example, is not
a separate and independent structure capable of independent impacts and
effects (Orlikowski & Scott, 2008), rather prominence is given to the process
through which innovation in time technologies occur rather than its 'causes'
and 'effects'. As such, a 'clock' can be seen as an 'open' rather than as a 'fixed'
embodiment of structures. Accordingly the meanings associated with such
technologies are open to continual interpretation and reinterpretation by users
and others as a result of ongoing experience and use in practice. This means
that, rather than viewing the technology of clocks as structures that embody
human intentions (e.g., of designers), which are then appropriated (or not)
through their adoption in user domains, they are best viewed as an outcome
(albeit contingent and transitory) of the experience of use in organizational
practice. It is this 'time in practice', rather than structures embodied in technologies of time, that has structurational consequences (Giddens, 1984).

From this perspective, all forms of time (but most noticeably the structural
constraints associated with common perceptions of clock time) should be
viewed as far more open and fluid. The approach provides the basis for a
rather different understanding of the actions and interactions of users. That
is, users enact 'time-in-practice' through individual and collective experience
of use. Such a view invites us to move away from conventional concerns of
thinking about how material technologies of time as discrete artifacts control
and regulate human behaviour to a concern with how actions and relations
are materially constituted in practice. In other words, rather than starting
with the technology of time and the way time artefacts are appropriated by
people as embodied structures, attention should turn to how people enact
emergent structures through their interaction with the technology of time.

This returns us to Gidden's (1984) concept of structuration, in which
actors are central to social processes whilst recognising the duality of structure, that is, the idea that structure is both 'the medium and outcome it recur-
sively organizes' (1984: 374) that enables and constrains actions. In this
approach, people cannot be separated (as an individual) from the context
they produce and reproduce through practices that co-constitute that context. In other words, people create and recreate routinized daily life working
within constraining limitations and enabling possibilities through ongoing
practices. For Schatzki (2001) actions need to be understood within the context of interwoven practices that make up social reality. Both of these practice theorists emphasise mutual constitution and reject dualisms in ensuring
that primacy is not given to agency or structure (social/material, etc.). They
have also generated interest in practice-based approaches by a broad group
of researchers, which Feldman and Orlikowski (2011: 1241) categorize
according to: 'an empirical focus on how people act in organizational contexts; a theoretical focus on understanding relations between the actions
people take and the structures of social life; and a philosophical focus on the
constitutive role of practices in producing social reality'.

In their practice-based perspective on human agency and time in organizations, Orlikowski and Yates (2002) contrast the Newtonian concept of objective quantitative time in which the clock is seen to stand as a 'primary metaphor', with subjective socially constructed 'event' time that is contextual and relative and seen to capture the discontinuity and heterogeneity of this more organic, qualitative form of time. In one of a few studies that directly address the issues of time and temporality, the authors argue that first, there is a need to make an explicit assumption about time and temporality that informs theorizing in organizational research (claiming that these assumption have largely remained implicit) and, second, that the tendency for researchers to either focus on clock-based chronological serial time (*chronos*) or event-based, actor-shaped, kairotic time (*kairos*) is misplaced. They do point to the analytical advantages of these two approaches in providing useful conceptual tools but are highly critical of the tendency to reify taken-for-granted temporal structures that become objectified through routine enactment that can turn socially constituted frameworks into social facts.

Orlikowski and Yates (2002) build on Gidden's concept of structuration (1984) and the practice-based perspective (Schatzki et al., 2001) to forward a view of time as an enacted phenomenon. They use the concept of temporal structuring to capture the way that actors in their everyday activities produce and reproduce temporal structures that shape and are shaped in people's ongoing situated practices. In other words, it is through practice that people create and recreate temporal structures that enable them to engage and coordinate everyday activities. These structures are not separate and independent of human action, nor are they viewed as being wholly determined by human action. As they state,

> Such a view allows us to bridge the gap between objective and subjective understandings of time by recognizing the active role of people in shaping the temporal contours of their lives, while also acknowledging the way in which people's actions are shaped by structural conditions outside their immediate control.
>
> (Orlikowski & Yates, 2002: 684)

They argue that people in organizing activities, for example around academic calendars, reinforce and legitimize temporal structures (although they do note that people may occasionally change their temporal structure to reposition their activities). These structures are seen to provide both the medium through which the timing and form of action takes place and the outcome from ongoing practices. The emphasis in not on how people collectively make sense of their experiences (i.e., socially constructivist accounts of time) but on situated human practices, suggesting that

> by grounding our perspective in the dynamic capacities of human agency we believe we gain unique insights into the creation, use, and influence

of time in organizations. . . . Temporal reflexivity—being aware of the human potential for reinforcing and altering temporal structures—is essential if we wish to act with effect in our world.

(Orlikowski & Yates, 2002: 685, 698)

In a later paper, Kaplan and Orlikowski (2013) demonstrate how in strategy making, projections of the future are always entangled with multiple interpretations of the past and present. They argue that it is the way people make connections (between past, present, and future) and resolve differences in constructing accounts that are plausible, coherent, and acceptable that explains strategic choice and action, claiming that this temporal work in strategy making sheds light on inertia and change in organizations. In these empirical, practice-based pieces, human agency is central to their explanations in which accounts and temporal structures are seen to shape and be shaped by people's ongoing situated practices.

Conclusion

Perspectives on technology draw attention to the relationship between the 'hard' technical and the 'soft' social in their examination of the relationship between organizations and technology. From early studies on the impact of technology on organizations that have been criticized for being technologically determinist, attention has shifted to more socially constructive explanations. However, these studies in turn raise concerns about overly socially determinist accounts in which the only thing that did not seem to matter was matter, that is, approaches in which the technological baby is thrown out with the determinist bathwater (whether of a social or material nature). This has produced wide-ranging debates that have—in various ways—attempted to deal with the long-standing issue of agency (social/human) and structure (material/technological) without getting locked into any account that has or can be tainted by the determinist bogeyman. As we have shown, the SCOT perspective counterbalances the technological determinism associated with earlier impact approaches and provides a useful explanation of the social drivers of change—the way technologies emerge and are used—as, for example, in the development and use of clocks, standardized universal time, and the more widespread use of the Gregorian calendar by highlighting how these social forces shape outcomes under prevailing historical and contextual conditions. SCOT's heavy emphasis on the social in turn led Latour, Callon, Law, and others to develop a relational perspective in which human and non-human actants exist in and of themselves (ANT). The less-flexible and collective understanding of time marks a translation in which controversies are resolved and a stabilized set of attributes may be ascribed to the meaning of time in the Western world. There is inseparability in assemblages of time networks performed into relations made durable by human and non-human actants.

In an approach that parallels many of the issues raised and addressed by ANT, Barad proposes agential realism as a posthumanist performative account of practices in which the social and material are entangled and differentially enacted. Neither material phenomena (matter) nor discursive practices (meanings) take priority; they cannot be separated and used to explain each other but, rather, intra-actively emerge and are mutually constituted. Under this perspective everything is connected with everything else, and it is only through agential cuts that we can present explanations and enact boundaries. There is no linear time as the world and the possibilities of becoming are continuously remade. Barad critiques both social constructivist and traditional realist concepts in which time and temporality are not constructed by people, nor a separable space-time dimension, but the effects of ongoing intra-active materializations in the world's differential becoming.

Two intersecting influences on a growing body of work around the concept of sociomaterial are Barad's (2003) theorizing from her early association with interest in quantum mechanics (she has a doctorate in theoretical physics) and Schatzki's theorizing on social practice, where 'the social is a field of embodied, materially interwoven practices centrally organized around shared practical understandings' (2001: 3). There has been a lot of contestation and definitional/conceptual debate emanating from scholars associated with this relational sociomaterial approach (Kautz & Jensen, 2013), particularly in the field of information systems (Cecez-Kecmanovic et al., 2014). There has been a tendency for more empirically focussed studies to engage with agency in a practice orientation rather than with the agential cuts associated with a more posthumanist, performative perspective. Although there are few studies that directly approach the issue of time and temporality, those that do seek to accommodate the binary divide between notions of linear and cyclical time, objective and subjective time, chronology (*chronos*) and event time (*kairos*), and so forth. Time is part of embodied, materially interwoven practices that, although often appearing fixed, are open to reinterpretation through the constitutive practices of which they are a part. The study of Orlikowski and Yates (2002) was shown to directly address the issue of temporality in putting forward the concept of temporal structuring (mirroring Giddens's structuration view in being seen as medium and outcome) in which people, through everyday actions, produce and reproduce temporal structures that both shape and are shaped through situated practices. An attempt is made to bridge the divide between objective and subjective notions of time through this relational, practice-based approach, but a tension remains, on the one hand agreeing with the analytical usefulness of concepts such as clock time and event time, whereas on the other, arguing for an approach that blurs these concepts through removing boundary definitions. We would support the notion of temporal merging and accommodation, not so much in the entanglement of time but in the fluid, ongoing movement between constellations of separation and merging in the practice and engagement of everyday life.

References

Adam, B. (1990). *Time and Social Theory*. Cambridge: Polity Press.

Adam, B. (2004). *Time*. Cambridge: Polity Press.

Barad, K. (2003). Posthumanist performativity: Toward an understanding of how matter comes to matter. *Signs, 28*(3), 801–831.

Barad, K. (2007). *Meeting the Universe Halfway: Quantum Physics and the Entanglement of Matter and Meaning*. London: Duke University Press.

Barbour, J. (2000). *The End of Time: The Next Revolution in Our Understanding of the Universe*. London: Phoenix, Orion Books.

Bijker, W. E., & Law, J. (1992). *Shaping Technology, Building Society: Studies in Sociotechnical Change*. Cambridge, MA: MIT Press.

Boje, D. M. (2012). Reflections: What does quantum physics of storytelling mean for change management? *Journal of Change Management, 12*(3), 253–271. doi: 10.1080/14697017.2011.609330

Braidotti, R. (2013). *The Posthuman*. Malden, MA: Polity Press.

Braverman, H. (1974). *Labor and Monopoly Capital: The Degradation of Work in the Twentieth Century*. New York: Monthly Review Press.

Breitbart, E. (Writer). (1981). *Clockwork*. Retrieved from http://www.breitbartfilms.com/Clockwork.html, accessed July 2015.

Callon, M. (1999). Actor–network theory: The market test. In J. Law & J. Hassard (Eds.), *Actor Network Theory and After* (pp. 181–195). Oxford: Blackwell.

Carroll, S. (2010). *From Eternity to Here: The Quest for the Ultimate Theory of Time*. Oxford: Oneworld.

Cecez-Kecmanovic, D., Galliers, R. D., Henfridsson, O., Newwell, S., & Vidgen, R. (2014). The sociomateriality of information systems: Current status, future directions. *MIS Quarterly, 38*(3), 809–830.

de Vaujany, F., & Mitev, N. (Eds.). (2013). *Materiality and Space: Organizations, Artefacts and Practices*. Hampshire: Palgrave Macmillan.

Edwards, R. (1979). *Contested Terrain: The Transformation of the Workplace in the Twentieth Century*. London: Heinemann.

Feldman, M., & Orlikowski, W. J. (2011). Theorizing practice and practicing theory. *Organization Science, 22*(5), 1240–1253.

Feynman, R. (1999). *The Pleasure of Finding Things Out: The Best Short Works of Richard P. Feynman* (J. Robbins, Ed.). Cambridge, MA: Perseus Books.

Frank, A. (2012). *About Time*. Oxford: Oneworld Publications.

Gherardi, S. (2006). *Organizational Knowledge: The Texture of Workplace Learning*. Malden, MA: Blackwell Publishing.

Giddens, A. (1984). *The Constitution of Society—Outline of the Theory of Structuration*. Cambridge: Polity Press.

Gill, C. (1985). *Work, Unemployment and the New Technology*. Cambridge: Polity Press.

Grint, K., & Woolgar, S. (1997). *The Machine at Work*. Oxford: Polity Press.

Haraway, D. (2015). *Simians, Cyborgs, and Women: The Reinvention of Nature* (Reprint ed.). New York: Routledge.

Hawking, S. (2011). *A Brief History of Time: From the Big Bang to Black Holes*. London: Bantam Books.

Henriques, U. R. (1979). *Before the Welfare State: Social Administration in Early Industrial Britain*. London: Longman.

Hobsbawn, E. J. (1964). *Labouring Men*. London: Weidenfled & Nicolson.

Hobsbawn, E. J. (1969). *Industry and Empire*. Harmondsworth: Penguin.

Kaplan, S., & Orlikowski, W. J. (2013). Temporal work in strategy making. *Organization Science, 24*(4), 965–995.

Kautz, K., & Jensen, T. B. (2013). Sociomateriality at the royal court of IS: A jester's monologue. *Information and Organization, 23*, 15–27.

Latour, B. (1991). Technology is society made durable. In J. Law (Ed.), *A Sociology of Monsters: Essays on Power, Technology and Domination* (pp. 101–131). London: Routledge.

Latour, B. (2005). *Reassembling the Social: An Introduction to Actor-Network-Theory*. Oxford: Oxford University Press.

Law, J. (1999). After ANT: Complexity, naming and topology. In J. Law & J. Hassard (Eds.), *Actor Network Theory and After* (pp. 1–14). Oxford: Blackwell Publishing.

Law, J., & Hassard, J. (1999). *Actor Network Theory and After*. Oxford: Blackwell.

Leonardi, P. M. (2011). When flexible routines meet flexible technologies: Affordance, constraint, and the imbrication of human and material agencies. *MIS Quarterly, 35*(1), 147–167.

Leonardi, P. M. (2012). Materiality, sociomateriality, and socio-technical systems: What do these terms mean? How are they related? Do we need them? In P. M. Leonardi, B. A. Nardi, & J. Kallinikos (Eds.), *Materiality and Organizing: Social Interaction in a Technological World* (pp. 25–48). Oxford: Oxford University Press.

Leonardi, P. M. (2013). Theoretical foundations for the study of sociomateriality. *Information and Organization, 23*(1), 59–76.

Leonardi, P. M., & Barley, S. R. (2008). Materiality and change: Challenges to building better theory about technology and organizing. *Information and Organization, 18*(3), 159–176.

Leonardi, P. M., Nardi, B. A., & Kallinikos, J. (Eds.). (2012). *Materiality and Organizing: Social Interaction in a Technological World*. Oxford: Oxford University Press.

Levine, R. V. (2006). *A Geography of Time: The Temporal Misadventures of a Social Psychologist or How Every Culture Keeps Time Just a Little Bit Differently*. Oxford: Oneworld Publications.

Littler, C. (1982). *The Development of the Labour Process in Capitalist Societies*. London: Heinemann.

McKenzie, D., & Wajcman, J. (Eds.). (1985). *The Social Shaping of Technology*. Buckingham: Open University Press.

McLoughlin, I. (1999). *Creative Technological Change: The Shaping of Technology and Organizations*. London: Routledge.

McLoughlin, I., & Clark, J. (1994). *Technological Change at Work* (2nd ed.). Buckingham: Open University Press.

Mutch, A. (2013). Sociomateriality—taking the wrong turning? *Information and Organization, 23*(1), 28–40.

Nicolini, D., Gherardi, S., & Yanow, D. (2003). *Knowing in Organizations: A Practice-Based Approach*. Armonk, NY: M. E. Sharpe.

Orlikowski, W. J. (2007). Sociomaterial practices: Exploring technology at work. *Organization Studies, 28*(9), 1435–1448.

Orlikowski, W. J. (2010). The sociomateriality of organisational life: Considering technology in management research. *Cambridge Journal of Economics, 34*(1), 125–141.

Orlikowski, W.J. and Scott, S.V. (2008). Sociomateriality: Challenging the Separation of Technology, Work and Organization. *Annals of the Academy of Management, 2*(1), 433–474.

Orlikowski, W. J., & Yates, J. (2002). It's about time: Temporal structuring in organizations. *Organization Science, 13*(6), 684–700.

Peake, A. (2012). *The Labyrinth of Time: The Illusion of Past, Present and Future*. London: Arcturus Publishing.

Penrose, R. (2011). *What Came Before the Big Bang? Cycles of Time*. London: Vintage Books.

Pickering, A. (Ed.). (2008). *The Mangle in Practice: Science, Society, and Becoming.* Durham, NC: Duke University Press.

Pinch, T. J., & Bijker, W. E. (1984). The social construction of facts and artefacts: Or how the sociology of science and the sociology of technology might benefit each other. *Social Studies of Science, 14*, 399–441.

Preece, D., McLoughlin, I., & Dawson, P. (2000). *Technology, Organizations and Innovation: Critical Perspectives on Business and Management.* London: Routledge.

Pruijt, H. D. (1997). *Job Design and Technology: Taylorism vs Anti-Taylorism.* Abingdon, Oxon: Routledge.

Rose, M. (1988). *Industrial Behaviour: Research and Control* (2nd ed.). Harmondsworth: Penguin.

Schatzki, T. (2001). Introduction: Practice theory. In T. Schatzki, K. Cetina, & E. von Savigny (Eds.), *The Practice Turn in Contemporary Theory* (pp. 10–23). London: Routledge.

Schatzki, T., Cetina, K., & von Savigny, E. (Eds.). (2001). *The Practice Turn in Contemporary Theory.* London: Routledge.

Schultze, U., & Orlikowski, W. J. (2010). Virtual worlds: A performative perspective on globally distributed, immersive work. *Information Systems Research, 21*(4), 810–821.

Wilkinson, B. (1983). *The Shopfloor Politics of New Technology.* London: Heinemann.

7 Political Time as an Instrument of Dominance and Power

Introduction

Early processual studies of change in organizations such as those of Pettigrew and Dawson were grounded on the dual characteristics of process ontology and analysis of the operations of power and politics (see Chapter 9 for a discussion of their work). In recent developments of process organizational studies, however, discussions of power are largely absent or left in the background as refinements of process organizational work have tended to focus on the ontological and temporal views of process philosophers in whose work power was not a feature. It is therefore timely to remember Clegg, Courpasson, and Phillips's warning that 'organization requires power and, while not all power requires organization most does. Power is to organization as oxygen is to breathing' (2006: 3). They go on to suggest that although ubiquitous, 'power is a difficult idea to pin down and has been very widely, ignored, marginalized and trivialized in many discussions of organization' (2006: 6). In the light of this reminder and the strong emphasis on power in early processual studies, this chapter seeks to explore the relationship between time and temporality and the operations of power. We introduce and discuss the dominant theories of power used in organizational studies and then turn to examine their use in analyses of work by attending specifically to how time is used as an instrument of power to control workers through a variety of approaches in the subjugation of their bodies and minds. The chapter is structured as follows: first, we supply a brief introduction to common conceptualizations of power and their relationship to time; second, we turn to the use of time and temporality as powerful instruments for controlling bodies; and third we examine time and temporality as disciplining processes and forms of biopower that shape the soul.

Theories of Power and Their Relationship to Time

As Clegg et al. (2006) say in the earlier quote, power is a difficult concept to understand, although as with the term 'time', it is used as if there is a uniform meaning shared by all. A common-sense notion of power is generally conceived in two ways, either as the 'capacity or ability to act' or as a 'determining force' (Knights, 2009). Whereas these common-sense conceptions can seem relatively straightforward, a number of complex and contrasting philosophical approaches to power have dominated discussions in organizational and sociological studies over the past 60 years, and a brief introduction to this theoretical work is necessary to ground later discussions of their outworking and application.

In the ancient world, rulers and philosophers alike recognised that political authority and governance was strongly linked to the structuring and measurement of time (as was discussed in Chapters 2 and 3). In China, for example,

> The calendar was a prerequisite of sovereignty, like the right to mint coins. Knowledge of the right time and season was power, for it was this knowledge that governed both the acts of everyday life and decisions of state. Each Emperor inaugurated his reign with the promulgation of this calendar, often different from the one that preceded it. His court astronomers were the only persons who were permitted in principle to use time keeping astronomical instruments or to engage in astronomical study. His time was China's time.
>
> (Landes, 1983: 33, cited in Adam, 2006: 111)

Similarly, links among power, as the divine right to rule, the state, and time control are evident in the West; for example in ancient Greece, the rule of kings was linked to the divine authority of the gods. In his *Politics*, Plato emphasises the role of the emperor in creating and maintaining political stability in that the majority of the populace were deemed non-logical and inferior and therefore needed to be ruled by powerful, rational, philosopher kings (Knights, 2009: 146). This control was inseparable from cultic traditions and the seasonal rhythms manifest in calendars that effectively linked everyday social life to the control of rulers and even divine authority. These early sociopolitical systems are the precursors to what Hobbes was to later theorize as the 'sovereign' view of power, premised on a universal time measurement system. Although the sovereign view has been and still is dominant in contemporary organizations, alternative forms of power and control built on very different theoretical approaches commonly operate. Machiavelli, Marx, and Foucault developed explanations of power that were linked to different, sociopolitical formulations premised not only on very different understandings of knowledge and truth but generating radically different reckonings and uses of time.

Philosophical Views of Power and Its Relation to Time

Hobbes' (1651/1968) sovereign view of power is the most common conceptualization of power used in the Western world. His work *Leviathan* provides a comprehensive and systematic analysis of power, particularly as it relates to social order. A major aim of the work was to provide a theoretical structure for peaceful relations at the time of the English civil war. Hobbes emphasises power in relation to sovereignty both in terms of the power of the ruler and the proxy of this power in the state. He termed the structure of the state 'the Leviathan or Common-wealth' and saw the human body governed by the head as its most appropriate metaphor. His conception of human nature positions individuals as reprobate, dominated by their natural instincts, and who, when left to their own devices, become rational egoists pursuing their own 'natural' interests based on their bodily appetites and that this necessarily places them in conflict with one another. The role of the sovereign is to develop and manage the sum of the individuals to curtail the natural conflict in the 'Commonwealth'; the sovereign decrees truth at all levels based on monarchical right, coercion, ecclesiastical law, and ultimately the law and rule of God. The power of the sovereign is centrally controlled and systemically managed and operates through armies and the visible show of force, a view that fitted well with the dominant European monarchies in power from the time of Hobbes to the peak of modernism and its capitalist expressions in the early 20th century (Foucault, 1977). As in early China and Greece, time was controlled by the power of the sovereign and the church.

In contrast, a second major philosophical influence in Western political theory, developed in the turbulent years of the 15th-century Florentine republic, is that of Machiavelli. Like Hobbes, he was concerned with the development and maintenance of order in society, but in contrast Machiavelli (1961), influenced by his role as a diplomat par excellence, details the political practices necessary to achieve it. *The Prince*, his main work dealing with politics, was said by his religious critics, soon after its publication, to be inspired by the devil (Machiavelli, 1961) for its strident criticisms of religious and political orthodoxy and its detailed exposition of the political machinations necessary for effective leadership and control of the state. Whereas such a reaction is not surprising, given the historical context and the radical ideas expressed, it fails to acknowledge his penetrating analysis of state politics. Ironically, his ultimate goal in writing the work was the development of a pragmatic methodology for political stability and rule within the Florentine state.

In contrast to Hobbes's sovereign approach that is clearly evident within the dominant political systems within modernity, Machiavelli's approach is more consistent with that of postmodern approaches in that he considered truth not as universal but partial and determined by history, necessity, and expediency. His view of human nature, though, is similar to that of Hobbes in emphasising the propensity of humans to selfishly pursue their own success even at the expense of others. His understanding of the need for those in power to gain 'willing' consent also anticipates the concept of hegemony developed four centuries later by Gramsci. Machiavelli and his work have been caricatured and misunderstood by many. As Buchanan and Badham (2008) point out, the caricatured version or 'Machiavellian thug' approach can be contrasted with an interpretation of his work that emphasises pragmatic expediency that is not only more fitting to the sorts of games in play within organizations but is commensurate with the way the politics of the everyday world works (Buchanan & Badham, 2008).

The two contrasting philosophical positions of Hobbes and Machiavelli draw upon very different conceptions of time and temporality. Hobbes's sovereign conception of power embedded in tight social structures is supported by the use of a common time (and is evident in Hobbes's favoured metaphor of clockwork), in which individual, organizational, and societal practices take place and by which they are controlled. Time measurement is central to ensure punctuality, synchronization, and scheduling that form the basis not only of the organization of work but of social order. As we will discuss, sovereign power operating through the imposition of clock time, as the one dominant form of time measurement (*chronos*), was an instrumental emphasis in the rise of scientific management in which the behaviours of individuals were subjugated to clocks and time controls embedded in machinery. In contrast, those that draw either implicitly or explicitly on Machiavellian conceptions of power rely more upon *timing* and conceptions of time that link to strategy and temporal distinctions that relate to individual or collective expediency and utility (*kairos*). Here the timing of opportunity is primary and synchronization follows as important for strategy and its implementation. Clock time is only one of a number of times needed for political mastery and manoeuvring, for the timing of rhythm or its negation; the temporality of history, memory, social context, and opportunity; as well as anticipation, planning, and propensity all come into play. This use of what are regarded as subjective approaches to time in which individuals calculate their own timing in relation to action is now highly influential in contemporary approaches to organizational control and forms the basis of the hegemonic and disciplining forms of power developed by Gramsci and Foucault, respectively.

A third dominant philosophical approach to power is that developed by Marx. His work situated as strongly modernist, continues the sovereign, institutional approach to power but critiques accepted links between elites and capitalist interests and their control of workers by truth production expressed as ideology. Knights suggests that for Marx, power is linked to the 'oppressive capitalist state and to ideology and distortions of truth' (Knights, 2009: 146), describing the general views of power for Marx and his later acolytes as follows:

> In the hands of pro- and neo-Marxian theorists, power remains as an oppressive and coercive force that deprives people of freedom and the ability to realize their human potential. For Marx, power was an attribute of owning private property (capital) that determines the wage relation and the exploitation of labor through appropriation of surplus value or profit. Described by Marx as alienation, workers were separated from the products of their labor both materially and symbolically;

they were dependent on the capitalists for their livelihood and only through collective resistance and political revolution would they be able to free themselves from the slavish chains of their wage labor. Knowledge for Marx was systematically distorted by bourgeois (capitalist) ideology in that it concealed the truth about power from proletarian labor—repressing its capacity to advance a revolutionary struggle for emancipation.

Whereas the common tenets of Marx's approach and its influences in labour process are well known, their relation to time is less understood. The work of Adam (2004) is useful here in providing insights into the importance of time in the development of Marxist social and economic theory. She suggests that Marx's conception of time provides an often overlooked philosophical contribution based on his reinterpretation and relocation of Hegel's dialectic from the metaphysical to the historical and material. Whereas Plato and Hegel separated mind, as the locus of engagement with the eternal categories (including time), and body, as the locus of temporal change, Marx saw the categories as products of historical material processes. He didn't write explicitly about the relationship between time and power, but he did write extensively about the historical processes of labour and work *times* and their exchange value. Time is no longer viewed as an external metaphysical category as in Kant and Hegel but is central to his understanding of the material world and therefore crucial in grounding his economic theories. Commodities could be exchanged and value calculated through this exchange on the basis of a third, independent value: money. Time is introduced as an independent value exchangeable for money—time is itself commodified based on its value in exchange for money. This relationship is discussed by Adam (2004: 38):

> Time is the decontextualized, asituational abstract exchange value that allows work to be translated into money. Since, however, money is a quantitative medium, the time that features in this exchange has to be of a quantitative kind as well: not the variable time of seasons, ageing, growth and decay, joy and pain, but the invariable, abstract time of the clock where one hour is the same irrespective of context and emotion. Only the quantitative, divisible time of the clock is translatable into money. Only this decontextualized time can serve as an abstract exchange value and thus be traded as a commodity on the labour market.

Adam (2004) goes on to discuss the implications of Marx's view of time as a central capitalist medium. She argues that he realised that as time was exchangeable with money and that capitalist interests were constantly striving to improve profitability, increases of speed were essential. For if the same commodities could be produced more quickly by mechanization or technology, they could then be produced more cheaply and increase potential returns. Similarly, if labour could be intensified and speeded up and if the same production targets could be achieved in less time, then profitability would likewise be increased and competitiveness maintained. Adam summarizes: 'Commodification compression and intensification were therefore to be sought in the quantification, de-contextualization, rationalization and commodification of time, in the calculation of time in relation to money, efficiency, competition and profit' (Adam, 2004: 40). She shows that for Marx, whereas time is within the historically constituted economic processes, it is the abstract and decontextualized time that is used in exchange. She thus concludes that both 'decontextualized and historical times are entwined in a dialectical dynamic' (2006: 40).

Foucault's (1977, 1980) view of power provides a fourth dominant philosophical approach to power that is strongly contrasted to the sovereign view in that its aim is to shape thinking processes from inside the person, and therefore time and temporal practices are construed as internally driven. His philosophical approach is notoriously inconsistent and changes throughout the corpus of his work (Dreyfus & Rabinow, 1982). Here we are particularly interested in his later genealogical work that examines power as a disciplining process and its relationship to knowledge. His approach is contrasted explicitly to sovereign views of power found in Hobbes:

> It is a mechanism of power which permits time and labour, rather than wealth and commodities, to be extracted from our bodies. It is a type of power which is constantly exercised by means of surveillance rather than in a discontinuous manner by means of a system of levies or obligations distributed over time. It presupposes a tightly knit grid of material coercions rather than the physical existence of a sovereign. It is ultimately dependent on the principle, which introduces a genuinely new economy of power, that one must be able simultaneously both to increase the subjected forces and to improve the force of efficacy of that which subjects them. . . . This type of power is in every respect the antithesis of that mechanism of power which the theory of sovereignty described or sought to transcribe.
>
> (Foucault, 1980: 104)

Influenced by Saussure's structural and linguistic work, he considered power relations inseparable from meaning making and thus a social product embedded in language and not a thing or property that could be possessed by individuals. For Foucault, power was always aligned to knowledge, and this is evident in his neologism 'power/knowledge', which he used not in the sense that knowledge creates power for individuals, or that knowledge is power, but as Knights says, 'They are in a relationship such that when power is exercised it invariably draws on knowledge but is also productive of further knowledge and when knowledge is created it generally stimulates some exercise in power' (2009: 155). He was not interested in the idea of 'the truth'; instead he focussed attention on the discursive practices by which truth comes to be accepted as truth—the conditions of its possibility and production. He conceived of power as a 'cluster of relations': 'But in thinking of power, I am thinking rather of its capillary form of existence, the point where power reaches into the very grain of individuals, touches their bodies and inserts itself into their actions and attitudes, their discourses, learning processes and everyday lives' (Foucault, 1980: 39).

In his genealogical work, he attends to the disciplining processes of power aiming to go beyond what he terms the exercise of 'juridical' power—power possessed and exercised by individuals and social classes and by institutions such as the state, political parties, and the institutional church. He contrasts this genealogical method with scientism and empiricism; the latter are linked to truth and discourse production that unify knowledge in overarching scientific and historic discourses based on homogeneous time, and genealogy aims to disrupt such unities. It attends to the conflicts and ruptures that are smoothed out in discourse production by separating the many subjugated knowledges that have become homogenized in unifying historic discourses. Time and history are thus necessarily fragmented. He deals with the move from sovereign power to power as 'a technique that achieves its strategic affects through its disciplinary character' (Clegg, 1989: 153). Techniques target not only bodies but subjectivities constituted by a 'plurality of disciplinary mechanisms' (Knights, 1990). He thus moves the locus of power from the individual to social practices that produce subject positions or self-disciplining subjectivities. Such power is exercised discontinuously on specific occasions and directed toward specific individuals. As Dreyfus and Rabinow note,

> Foucault's aim is to isolate, identify, and analyse the web of unequal relationships set up by political technologies which underlies and undercuts the theoretical equality posited by the law and political philosophers. . . . To understand power in its materiality, its day to day operation, we must go to the level of the micropractices, the political technologies in which our practices are formed.
>
> (1982: 185)

Time in a Foucauldian approach to power is not the overarching time of juridical or sovereign power found in Hobbes and Marx but arises from within the micro-practices and webs of relations of power: 'Power will be a more or less stable or shifting network of alliances extended over a shifting terrain of practice and discursively constituted interests' (Clegg, 1989: 154). From this perspective, there is no overarching time such as 'empty time' generated by time's commodification. Foucault's work inverts and fragments the sovereign view by examining the local micro-level 'capillary' actions that produce and are produced by power-knowledge (see Chapter 8 for a discussion of time, narratives, and storytelling). This move opens the possibility of multiple and conflicting times and the relationship between subjective and objective notions of time and temporal awareness. The past is not one homogenized and smooth discourse but is constantly ruptured and therefore becomes discontinuous. It consists of multiple, intersecting, and fragmented discourses collected and connected for various purposes of 'truth' production. Therefore the past is multiple and creates the possibility of different versions of the present and future.

Each of the four dominant theories of power and their relationship to time and temporal practices are important in their own right, but also collectively, as they often overlap and coalesce in their use in contemporary forms of organizing.

Key Issues Relating to Power in Organizational Studies and Their Relationship to Time and Temporality

In having introduced the major philosophical frames, this section examines some of the well-known approaches to power in organizational studies, drawing attention to their implicit uses of time, including functionalist, bureaucratic, strategic contingency, and resource-dependent views as well as Lukes's conflict theory. The approaches discussed may be said to hold either negative connotations or 'power over' or positive connotations, as in 'power to'. Göhler suggests that power over

> means power over other people, enforcement of one's own intentions over those of others, and is thus only conceivable as a social relation. *Power to* on the other hand, is not related to other people. It is an ability to do or achieve something independent of others. It is not a social relation.
>
> (2009: 28)

This distinction is useful as we examine theories and applications of power in organizing.

From Functionalism to Strategic Contingency and Resource Dependent Approaches

Early conceptions of power in organizations were influenced by two dominant strands of thought. First, in the U.S. where organizational and management studies began, the field was dominated by functionalist views of power based on the work of Talcott Parsons. In this view power is a circulatory media like money. It is recognised as a legitimate and symbolic medium that is the 'medium of social order for systems' (Clegg et al., 2006). Power operating through the organizational hierarchy is termed authority and is considered to have positive aspects in that it is conceived as part of the normative social order.

A second influence on organizational views of power is that of Weber. He developed an approach to power that aimed to eliminate uncertainty by the enactment of tight organizational structures. His bureaucratic approach embedded power in the organizational structure by combining clear and comprehensive accountability of all roles to those in higher positions and the structured orchestration of work activities to one central and dominant time. Time is homogeneous and abstract in the functionalist and bureaucratic views that draw philosophically upon Hobbes's sovereign approach to power, rearticulated to social and economic theory by Marx and Weber. One unified time, that of management and the bureaucracy, dominates, and workers and their times must comply obediently to these demands during the hours of work. Negotiations in relation to wages, conditions, and other industrial relations are centred on work times such as hourly or daily rates of pay; length of the hours worked in a day or shift; overtime; times and periods of sick, annual, and long-service leave, etc. Work time is regulated by industrial laws that are negotiated by unions or more recently, with the increasing casualization of the workforce, through individual or collective bargaining agreements. Individuals and organizations are thus constrained to comply with these agreed times within which temporal practices must also be aligned.

A second group of approaches cluster around the notion of uncertainty as a source of power. Weber had targeted a reduction in the effects of organizational uncertainty in the development of his ideas on bureaucracy. Two important studies, one by Thompson in 1956 and another by Crozier in 1964 (Clegg, Kornberger, & Pitsis, 2011) extend understanding of uncertainty and its effects in bureaucratic organizations. Interestingly, time-related issues are often overlooked as central components of the uncertainty that support the re-creation of power differentials. In Thompson's study in the tightly prescribed military bureaucracy of the U.S. Air Force, the relationship between the flight and ground crews in a bomber command is examined (Thompson, 1956, cited in Clegg et al., 2011: 256). Whereas the flight crew had greater legitimate authority than the ground crew, their need for aircraft to be safe to fly at specific times made them vulnerable to the ground crew. When the ground crew used this uncertainty to secure their interests, their 'illegitimate' actions put them in a powerful position. So the crew that controlled the source of uncertainty, in this case, safe and flyable planes ready as needed, became powerful (Clegg et al., 2011: 256). The uncertainty had the potential to disrupt flight schedules, causing angst about military capability in which response times were crucial. Crozier's study further linked the study of power to uncertainty (Crozier, 1964, cited in Clegg et al., 2011). Crozier studied a state-owned French tobacco manufacturer in which female machine operators, central to the bureaucracy's routine operations, were paid on a piece rate system. Their productivity and therefore livelihood were tightly linked to operational machines. Breakdowns that required male maintenance staff to rectify created uncertainty that was ruthlessly exploited. Their technical expertise created the opportunity for the maintenance workers to control the source of uncertainty, and thus they became powerful. Again, breakdown affected schedules; in this case production schedules were made uncertain. This uncertainty was related to lack of control of organizational schedules, which poses a major risk to organizations in which delivery contracts contain production and delivery schedules for customers. When the sovereign view of time is disrupted by the political actions of workers, uncertainty ensues and time becomes a contested terrain. Powerful use of the creation and manipulation of uncertainty can thus be seen as inseparable from the control of time.

Following this study Hickson, Hinings, Lee, Schneck, and Pennings (1971) developed the strategic contingency theory of organizational power that created the means to measure the power of uncertainty. The organization is considered to comprise subunits: production, marketing, maintenance, and finance, that although interdependent, competed for power. The subunits most dependent on the others have the greatest uncertainty and therefore the least power. A similar theory is the resource dependency theory, where organizations compete for control of scarce resources. Pfeffer and Salancik (1978) examined the influence that organizational subunits had on decision making in relation to resource allocation. Organizations were also shown to attempt to influence other organizations on which they were dependent for resources. In these cases power is reified and considered to operate in a positive-sum transaction, where those that possess the scarce resource possess power over uncertainty and are in a position to produce more (Clegg et al., 2011).

Time and Lukes's Conflict Theory of Power

Many discussions of power in organization studies (Clegg, 1989; Clegg et al., 2006; Hardy & Clegg, 1996; Haugaard, 1997) emphasise the three dimensions of the conflict approach of Steven Lukes (1974) in his work *Power a Radical View*. In the first dimension, Lukes (1974) uses the work of Dahl to illustrate a conflictual model of power in which power is the capacity of A to get B to do something that they may not wish to. Dahl contested the view espoused by C. Wright Mills and others, who argued that elites are powerful by virtue of their privilege and status in society (Haugaard, 1997). He argued that power resources such as wealth and status are different from power in that power becomes what it is only when it is exercised. Dahl's empirical study in 1961(Dahl, 1961, cited in Haugaard, 1997) demonstrates that the power of elites in the U.S. is countered by pluralism in which diverse groups and individuals compete for power and that the enactment of this pluralism mitigates the concentration of power (and linked to their control of resources) of elites in democratic societies. This debate is reminiscent of the differences between Hobbes's sovereign view of power and the Machiavellian view that sees time as contested by competing powerful narratives. Haugaard (1997) illustrates this point using the example of the car park attendant and the professor at Yale to show that both can exert power but that because they operate in different domains and at different times, power is difficult to align to control students' activities. Time and space are seen to militate against the concentration of power of the elites. Again, time is linked to space and context where the disruption of sovereign time disperses concentrations of power.

In the second dimension, Lukes (1974) draws on the work of Bachrach and Baratz, who refuted Dahl's argument by suggesting that the exercise of power can happen not only by organizing things *in* but by organizing things *out*. They suggest that in agenda setting, power is exerted by the omission of issues from explicit discussion. Who sets the agenda for discussion and on what basis become areas of power that operate implicitly. Elites may therefore exert power by controlling what issues are debated and therefore whose interests prevail. Non-decision making is therefore powerful and is the consequence of specific actions or choices not to act. Here again, it is the operation of temporal practices of agenda setting by anticipating future decision making as to who is invited to attend meetings and what items are listed on the agenda. If future decisions can be orchestrated by the inclusion or exclusion of certain decision makers or agenda items, then control is exerted. This political use of time is again reminiscent of the tactical manoeuvring associated with Machiavelli in the political use of temporal practices for anticipating future outcomes by powerful players.

Lukes (1974) added a third, what he called the 'radical', dimension that draws on Marx's famous statement:

> Men make their own history, but they do not make it as they please; they do not make it under self-selected circumstances, but under circumstances existing already, given and transmitted from the past. The tradition of all dead generations weighs like a nightmare on the brains of the living. And just as they seem to be occupied with revolutionizing themselves and things, creating something that did not exist before, precisely in such epochs of revolutionary crisis they anxiously conjure up the spirits of the past to their service, borrowing from them names, battle slogans, and costumes in order to present this new scene in world history in time-honored disguise and borrowed language.
>
> (1852: 5)

Lukes argues that power can be exerted by manipulating forms of false consciousness and consent by drawing on the notion of hegemony, first developed by the Italian Marxist Antonio Gramsci, who was concerned with the relationship between consent and power: 'Hegemony occurs when the ruled consent to their rule and imagining the reality of their everyday existence in terms that cannot do other than reproduce their consent and subordination' (Clegg et al., 2006: 212). In discussing contemporary uses of hegemony, Haugaard suggests:

> In recent times there has been a move away from conceptions of power relying on coercion to those that rely on consent this was clear in Gramsci's own epistemic move away from a view of bourgeois domination . . . to a more nuanced view of domination as rooted in hegemony which constitutes a system of dominant ideas that receive consent from the relatively powerless or subaltern groups.
>
> (2009: 239)

He suggests that the introduction of interests raises the issue of knowledge and what counts for knowledge and why, for power may distort (true) knowledge. He uses the argument that in science, common sense would say that the sun travels around the earth—by watching the rising and setting of the sun. However, science shows that this view is false and that reality is in fact counter-intuitive. He then argues that similarly, in capitalist economics, value appears to be created by the market, whereas in reality, as Marx shows, it is created by workers not being payed the full value of their labour (Haugaard, 1997: 17).

Here as in Foucault's work, knowledge is linked to power, and a type of false consciousness is produced that perpetuates deception. The relationship between time and hegemony is complex but is based on the acceptance or consent to the time or temporal practices embedded in the knowledge that is accepted. Time is no longer the objective, external form but operates subjectively. Temporal practices are adopted by consent, and the willing subject determines the timing of their actions in line with their beliefs and values (Herman & Chomsky, 1988). Manufactured consent (Burawoy, 1979) is the corollary in which Haugaard (1997) suggests that useful examples are tobacco companies in the 1950s and 1960s that promoted smoking while discouraging medical research into the effects of smoking on human bodies, or manufacturers of baby milk who marketed their product in developing countries while suppressing the 'truth' that breastfeeding is a much healthier option (1997: 20).

Time, Temporality, and the Control of Behaviours in the Workplace

The control of workers in the workplace by use of a unilateral, sovereign approach to power developed at the time of modern industrialization. The outworking of the sovereign approach to power and time was discussed in earlier chapters in the use of bells to control prayer and work time in monasteries, where the choices associated with the timing of the most basic bodily functions are controlled by others. Work, eating, sleep, and sexual relations are controlled by externally imposed times and routines associated with domination. The most extreme form of controlling behaviours is in what Goffman termed 'total institutions' (Goffman, 1961) in which the freedom to behave and bodily enact is brutally curtailed by coercion and time control. In the management of slavery, the British system of 'pressing' young men into servility in the navy and military procedures of discipline such as drilling soldiers, time was used as a powerful tool to subjugate and discipline aberrant behaviours. Clegg et al. (2006) suggest that the key driver of the rise of institutionalized methods of domination and control of workers originated in the disciplinary routines used to control aberrant populations such as in the rise of utilitarianism as a response to vagrancy in England after the civil war. The growing numbers of the poor who sought refuge from rural poverty and unemployment in cities and associated rising levels of crime led to the development of The Poor Laws and the poorhouses in which the poor could earn enough to feed themselves and obtain shelter. These developments were in turn, linked to work by liberal reformers such as John Stuart Mill and Jeremy Bentham and the development of utilitarianism. Clegg et al. (2006: 43) describe Bentham's project:

> What Bentham proposed was a program for distilling a certain mode of rationality a system that would produce administrative certainty and perfection for society as a whole by categorizing and reforming the classes of vagrancy and vagabondage.

Here as in earlier chapters, Taylor's scientific management comes to the fore, on this occasion as the exemplar utilitarian project with its embedded sovereign approach to power expressed in ideas of the betterment of society. The goal of developing optimum organizational effectiveness and productivity would translate to organizational profit considered to benefit all. Taylor's conception of scientific management aimed at disciplining the behaviours of individual workers or a 'political economy of the body' and was premised on linking the notions of power and efficiency. Time measurement and principles of surveillance provide the necessary link (Clegg et al., 2006). Taylor emanated from an engineering background and worked on the shop floor in his early career where he learned the craft, politics, and approaches to time that were part and parcel of everyday working life. He observed that workers took shortcuts and collaborated to make their work easier, and he saw the impact of this in the form of reduced productivity that in turn created challenges for organizational competitiveness. These insights led him to become preoccupied with how to improve the design of work to increase efficiency, in which time was a central consideration (Clegg et al, 2011: 315). The actions of workers were timed using stopwatches and then adjusted iteratively to improve performance. Similarly, the use of specific tools was examined both in terms of the speed and effectiveness of achieving particular tasks and the optimum design of the tool for efficiency and endurance. The role of management was to ensure workers performed to their maximum capability and to gather information to calculate the best way to undertake increasingly productive and efficient work practices. Time measured by the clock was an enduring, calculable, and incremental measure that ensured uniformity both of individual bodily performance and potential performance of the workforce. Nonetheless, the pursuit of the ideal floundered in a number of areas, for workers as a whole were never able to fully achieve the ever-increasing, finely-tuned, incremental demands for improvement; the ideal or optimum was illusive, belonging always in the future.

The story of the Ford assembly line shows the move from clocks as measures of time to forms of time control embedded in automated machinery. Ford, drawing on scientific management principles, adapted the moving assembly line used in abattoirs for meat processing to an automobile manufacturing assembly line. Such mechanization, according to Clegg and colleagues, provided another timing mechanism as the timing embedded in the various components of machinery in the assembly line determined workers bodily movements.

> It vastly simplified production through running at a constant speed by which the workman must measure his pace, so that products are delivered at a constant production rate. Each job on the line had to be completed in an amount of time commensurate with this production rate.
>
> (Clegg et al., 2006: 56)

However, in a second time-related innovation, the Ford assembly line provided a watershed in workplace and industrial relations by paying workers daily rates of pay instead of using the piece rate system. Ford was beset by problems of workforce turnover, with annual rates in 1913 running at 400 percent and daily absenteeism running at 10 to 20 percent (Clegg et al., 2006: 57). Here 'good' workers could not be rewarded by incentives as their activities were tied to the production rate calibrated in the timing of the functions of machinery in the assembly line. To stabilize the workforce and increase retention rates and reduce absenteeism, 'good' workers were rewarded by being paid per day. This innovation of linking work to the period of the day, not the hour, would become part of American life and spread across the world. However, the move was risky for Ford in that day rates were used only for workers deemed as worthy or 'deserving'. 'The rules governing eligibility were demonstrating that, if one were a man, one lived a clean, sober, industrious, thrifty life, while for women to be "deserving" they needed to demonstrate that they had relatives who were solely dependent upon them' for income (2006: 57). Ford enforced and policed those deemed to be the deserving workforce utilizing the 'Sociological Department', which was created to provide surveillance of the worker and his/her family outside of work hours and not just the worker in the workplace in the hours of work. In this move, a transition is evident from the use of empty time—the embedding and commodification of clock time in industrial production schedules—to a new form of surveillance of workers that extended to the disciplining of social practices that occurred outside the workplace and work hours. Surveillance was moved from observing workers' use of time at work to their self-disciplining and temporal awareness and practices more generally—a move towards control of individual and collective subjectivities that is usefully theorized in approaches by Foucault (1980).

In summary, the advent of modern industrialization linked to Taylor's scientific management drew on a sovereign view of power reliant on homogenous conceptions of time. One unified time dominated the workplace—production time. The behaviours of workers are collectively and efficiently organized by synchronized and integrated operations that rely on relentless recalibration of work to clock time. The time of the organization dominates workers and subjugates their daily lives (and that of their families) and constrains bodily rhythms to that of the production machinery. Aberrant behaviours are disciplined by the development and repetition of embodied routines that are suggestive of robots that in highly automated manufacturing plants, took over their jobs in contemporary forms of industrial production. The effects of Taylorization on society were enormous and make it synonymous with forms of progress and modernist industrialization that rely on empty time. The extent of its uptake, its links to time's use as an instrument of capitalist interests, and its effects on society in early modern industrialization are clear in Kafka's bleak assessment:

> Time, the noblest and most essential element in all creative work, is conscripted into the net of corrupt business interests. Thereby, not only creative work, but man himself, who is its essential part, is polluted and humiliated. A Taylorized life is a terrible curse which will give rise to hunger and misery instead of the intended wealth and profit.
> (Janouch, 1971: 115, cited in Clegg et al., 2006)

Nevertheless, the influence and spread of forms of Taylorism has continued unabated and continues to be a dominant influence in contemporary controls of work. Recent adaptations such as McDonaldization (Ritzer, 1993), with its four elements of efficiency, calculability, predictability, and control that move the production line into new domains, have been welcomed by organizations and customers alike. For example, Adam's (2003) discussion of the contemporary changes to time reckoning that are marks of contemporary modernization provide important evidence of how such forms of control operate. The five Cs of creation, commodification, compression, control, and colonization, are inseparable from these new forms of organizational control. However, the control of behaviours in early industrial manufacturing focussed on the control of workers' bodies using external forms of time (clocks and machinery), but we must now turn to examine more recent forms of power and control of workers based on subjective notions of time in which workers internalize time controls.

Time, Temporality, and Worker Subjugation

A second mechanism of power used in controlling employees targets the self or subjectivity of workers. Here the control of time relies less on external technologies of time in the form of clocks and mechanized machinery or nego-tiated hours of work. Instead, internalized or subjective conceptions of time and temporality are targeted. The use of these forms of power have grown rapidly over the last 50 years in the shift from industrial to post-industrial society (Bell, 1999). Arising as a result of globalization, these new forms of power are made possible through multiple, overlapping elements such as the development of the global marketplace; 'time-space compression' (Harvey, 1989) and the 'network society' (Castells, 2000) in a world that operates 24/7 (Hassan & Purser, 2007), utilizing global flows of finance, information, labour, and resources (Thrift, 2005).

Forms of post-bureaucratic organizing that have developed in the net-work society require new forms of control of work that are less reliant on tight organizational structures of control based on forms of hierarchical authority. For example, Friedman (1977), from his study of the automotive industry in Coventry concluded that there are two ends of a continuum of strategies open to companies in the pursuit of profit, namely, direct con-trol as found under Taylorist forms of work organization and responsible autonomy, where an individual or group of workers is given discretion over the direction of work with a minimum of supervision for the purpose of maintaining managerial authority. The claim that there has been a grad-ual shift towards strategies of responsible autonomy in modern industrial economies can however be criticized for oversimplifying the levels and types of other forms of bureaucratic (performance management systems), super-visory (visibility), and technical controls found under new organizational arrangements (Dawson, 1994).

The main managerial method of controlling employee behaviour has been usefully summarized by Edwards (1979), who identifies three elements essential to the control of labour, namely: directing the activities of labour; monitoring the activities of labour; and disciplining the non-compliance of labour (Edwards, 1979: 18). According to his historical analysis, the systems of control used by management to coordinate these three elements have undergone fundamental change. He suggests that it is possible to discern a typology of systems of control that have evolved as a result of conflict and contradiction in the management of organizations, that is, from simple forms of personal control systems (entrepreneurial control and hierarchical control) to structural systems of control (technical control and bureaucratic control). Entrepreneurial and hierarchical control involves direct personal control, either by the employer in the former case or by supervisory management in the latter (Edwards, 1979: 25–36). Bureaucratic control is achieved through bureaucratic means in building formalized rules and procedures into the social structure of work (e.g., personnel policies, disciplinary procedures, and formal job descriptions), whereas technical control refers to the achievement of control through technical means that are built into the physical structure of the work process (e.g., the automotive assembly line). In building on this framework, Dawson (1994) provides a series of case studies illustrating how in the transition towards new forms of organization (under e.g., teamwork strategies), there has been an attempt to create new value and belief systems that support collaborative workplace arrangements that obscure traditional areas of concern, conflict and resistance in the development of more subtle methods of control that he refers to as forms of cultural control. In this regard, control and responsibility for aspects of work such as flexitime, working from home, divestment of quality and efficiency issues to workers, new forms of electronic surveillance such as wearable technologies, use of cross-functional and self-managed teams, and so on, all rely on self-supervision and subjectivity in forms or internalized cultural controls (Clegg et al., 2006; Dawson, 1994).

There are two interrelated approaches that clearly illustrate the replacement of earlier forms of control that rely on temporal awareness more than external forms of time. In the first, the consent of the worker is acquired, sometimes by the utilization of forms of hegemony, and in the second, what Rose has termed (following Foucault) 'technologies of the self' (Rose, 1989, 1998, 1999) are employed that rely on disciplinary practice resulting in subjugation in which 'power seeps into the very grain of individuals, reaches right into their bodies, permeates their gestures, their posture, what they say, how they learn, to live and work with other people' (Foucault, 1977: 28, cited in Clegg et al, 2011: 316). As Clegg and colleagues (2006) suggest, the political economy of the body becomes a moral economy as the locus of control moves from bodies to 'souls'.

The idea of the panopticon, an architectural design presented first by Jeremy Bentham and then taken up by Foucault in his work on discipline, shows the move from the use of sovereign power to control of bodies to the subjugation of the 'soul' through control of subjectivities by use of an all-seeing technology. Clegg and colleagues (2006: 44) nicely describe the panopticon and its applications for workers:

> The Panopticon was designed as an efficient cause. . . . It consisted of a central observation tower from which any supervisor, without themselves being seen, could see the bodies arranged in the various cells of the building. In each cell, the occupants were backlit by natural light, isolated from one another by walls and subject to scrutiny by the observer in the tower. Control was to be maintained by the constant sense that unseen

eyes might be watching those under surveillance. You had nowhere to hide, nowhere to be private, and no way of knowing if you were being watched at any particular time.

The principles embodied in the Panopticon had widespread influence. The key principle was inspection by an all-seeing but unseen being—rather like a secular version of God. And it did not matter if the inmates were actually being watched at any specific time: they would never know, but they did know that they were always at risk of being watched. The principle of inspection or surveillance instilled itself in the moral conscience of those who were being overseen. The aim of the Panopticon was to produce a self-disciplining person subject to an asymmetrical experience of knowing you were possibly being watched, but not when and if you were. It was designed to produce employees socialized into submitting their will to the task at hand; the alternative to imposed self-adjustment was the fear of being corrected or disciplined.

The most effective means of power and control is said to occur when it goes unobserved and is aligned with willing subjects. It is also a form of total control in that the subject soon internalizes not only what should be done but when. And so power is linked to time in that timing and temporal controls exceed the boundary of work hours as they are controlled by the discipline of the individual subjectivity or in forms of hegemony. The panopticon encapsulates this move in the operation of power relations expressed in a range of forms in contemporary organizations. Post-bureaucratic forms of organizing that adopt techniques such as TQM, Human Resource Management (HRM), BPR, and concertive control have been well analysed by organizational scholars, and these are discussed in the following section.

In the transition that occurred to new forms of industrial organization that was sometimes referred to as Japanization, emphasis was placed on workers' control of quality, not just quantity. Organizations required greater flexibility (Dawson, 1994) and aimed to achieve this through collaborative relations including those between trade unions and management and the restructuring of workers into work teams (Dawson, 1994). Under this movement towards teams, 'The primary mechanism for control stems from the creation of a new set of values and beliefs (cultural control) which serve to reinforce cooperative teamwork and group regulation' (1994: 30). A number of post-bureaucratic organizational processes were developed over the past three decades in which workers' temporal practices are controlled subjectively.

First, in an early study of change using TQM, Dawson charts the transition in methods used by management to control employees at work. He suggests that earlier forms of organization relied on personal control systems such as entrepreneurial and hierarchical controls or structural systems such as technical and bureaucratic controls and that these were later refined to include further controls that operate on the basis of the control of culture.

These forms of control operate at both the individual and group levels of organization. TQM and JIT management both relied on the 'devolution of control responsibility to the shopfloor' (1994: 34). In this mode, time is both the abstract, empty time commodified in coordination schedules and in the synchronization of team activities, as well as hegemonic time in consent to shared and individual temporal practices, such as repeating or changing past practices in present operations to ensure not only profitability and/or production bonuses but in internalized forms of personal gratification.

Second, in her Foucauldian analysis of HRM, Barbara Townley (1998) suggests, 'The practice of HR activity—job analysis, job evaluation, selection procedures and performance appraisal—so easily dismissed as merely technical procedures are implicated in strategies of power and knowledge' (Townley, 1998: 194). She goes on to argue that the three principle areas of knowledge targeted in management of personnel are knowledge of the workforce, the work activity and knowledge of the person or individual:

> The construction of knowledge through rules of classification, ordering and distribution, definitions of activities, fixing scales, rules of procedure leads to the emergence of a distinct personnel discourse. . . . It 'disciplines' the interior of the organization, organizing time, space and movement within it. In so doing, personnel helps to bridge the gap between promise and performance, between labour power and labour and organizes labour into a productive workforce.
>
> (Townley, 1998: 195)

Here again, the discipline used to control workers relates to time and temporal practices operating through classification—the object of many of Foucault's most penetrating analyses and the disciplining of the subjectivity in line with corporate strategies (Townley, Cooper, & Oakes, 2003).

Third, in his extended ethnographic study of the human impacts of BPR in a large bank in the UK, Darren McCabe (2007) shows that the power of a newly introduced 'strategy discourse' was a driver in setting up the conditions of possibility for large-scale redundancy of workers. He describes the strategy and its use of abstract language that dehumanizes workers, making them commodities or 'androids', disembodied without gender or feelings, and 'consequently, it is easier to disregard such workers and make them redundant' (McCabe, 2007: 16). McCabe shows how the strategy discourse provides the basis for the introduction of BPR and the introduction of a second, companion discourse that provides a technology to transform worker subjectivities (McCabe, 2007: 42). The new discourse emphasises a move to centralization, using techniques of self-managing teams and multi-skilling so that staff will have more time to 'support customers in quality of service' (McCabe, 2007: 48). The two seemingly incongruent discourses are paired; on the one hand the strategy discourse dehumanizes staff so that management can make decisions about mass redundancy with relative impunity.

Whereas on the other hand the discourse of 'excellence', originating in the work of Peters and Waterman (1982), the customer service discourse prioritizes customers and extols the virtues of teamwork and collaboration (McCabe, 2007).

Finally, Barker argues that concertive control operating in and through teams is a more powerful form of organizational control than bureaucratic control (Barker, 1993). Here the locus of control moves from the individual to the team:

> Workers achieve concertive control by reaching a negotiated consensus on how to shape their behavior according to a core set of values, such as the values found in a corporate vision statement. . . . Concertive control reflects the adoption of a new substantive rationality, a new set of consensual values by the organization and its members.
>
> (1993: 411)

Once the agreed collaborative values are in place, then workers reshape their discourse to reflect the normative dominance of the new values. Workers not only accept the new values and norms individually, but they also collectively articulate and enact the normativity in ways that produce and constrain behaviours. For example, workers may agree that it is a good thing to work hard for company success that maintains their income as workers and collectively implement the norm that they should all therefore arrive for work on time and not be tardy with their timekeeping. If workers arrive at work late they are judged by this standard that has been agreed and reinforced by their peers, not by the supervisor's clock. Once this system becomes entrenched rules and punishments are meted out by the team for worker breaches of the norms, such as tardiness in timekeeping. Barker (1993) undertook an empirical study at a manufacturing plant during the introduction of a team structure to replace a production line. He followed workers in the transition from a bureaucratic form of organization to one structured by self-managing teams, finding that workers believed that concertive control was a more complete form of domination than the iron cage of bureaucracy. Ultimately, notions of soft domination provided a strong foundation when linked to technologies for workers to monitor and control their own performance in accordance with management requirements.

Conclusions

In this chapter we have examined the relationship between power and politics and the use of time in organizations. Tracing the development of key philosophical approaches to power and their relationship to time enables us to show how theories of power and time are implicitly woven together in contemporary forms of organizing. It also helps us to recognise how commonly accepted views of power in organizational studies are imbued with time and temporal relations. We discussed how the clock perhaps more than the steam engine was the real engine for new factory work disciplines. But clocks are very stark figures of control as is the automated assembly line and high division of labour evident in contemporary forms of Taylorism, such as McDonaldization, that characterizes many high-profile organizations. Once dominant clock time becomes embedded in our world of being and consciousness, the power to control extends, even more so with technologies that collapse old boundaries—simultaneity, instantaneous, compressed time, and stress from belief in the scarcity of time in the 21st century. There is no (perceived or real) time to resist by those (professionals and employees) who have any semblance of power, rather they participate in reinforcing what appears to them as inviolable—a solid belief in a compressed time reality of this is the way it has to be.

It is with the wide uptake of cultural controls in which new time-regulated behaviours become internalized that individuals become less resistant and more accepting of self-regulatory practices that are continually reinforced through structures, such as semi-autonomous work groups, HRM professionals, TQM, and concertive control systems. Ironically, these new techniques of managerial control that really came to the fore in the 1980s and 1990s associated with three-letter acronyms such as, JIT, TQM, BPR, TPM, and TPS link to a so-called culture of excellence overlaid with a rhetoric of empowerment that in practice is more about disempowerment and time intensification. In this, there has not only been a wider internalized acceptance of time commitments in extended work activities beyond the prescribed working day but also a sense that such time-intensive busyness signals belongingness and a sense of purpose. This relinquishing of time boundaries between work and other life spheres disempowers the individual in the control of time with a range of consequences for those unable to cope, such as stress, related health issues, burnout, and time inequalities— the latter is most notable between those with power and wealth and those seeking to fulfil the expectations of professional careers in paid employment. In the case of professionals, the self-discipline and self-regulation of the working day is no longer limited to nine-to-five, but rather, there is greater self-determinacy in temporal patterns in which temporal freedom is severely curtailed. The question of whether employees really just participate in their own oppression remains open for discussion and debate and on this count; Wajcman (2015) reminds us of the power dimensions evident in the inequality of time when examining historical developments in the distribution of work-life activities and the domestic division of labour and wealth inequalities (see Dawson, 2015; Piketty, 2014). This thinning of time mirrors the thinning of human endeavour in a world where the currency of life— time—is commoditized, pressurized, digitalized, and exteriorized—moving us away from a time worth living.

References

Adam, B. (2004). *Time*. Cambridge: Polity.

Adam, B. (2006). *Time*. Cambridge: Polity.

Barker, J. (1993). Tightening the iron cage: Concertive control in self-managing teams. *Administrative Science Quarterly, 38,* 408–437.

Bell, D. (1999). The axial age of technology. *The Coming of Post-Industrial Society* (pp. Foreword ix–lxxxv). New York: Basic Books. (Reprinted from: Special Anniversary Edition).

Buchanan, D., & Badham, R. (2008). *Power, Politics and Organisational Change: Winning the Turf game*. London: Sage.

Burawoy, M. (1979). *Manufacturing Consent: Changes in the Labour Process under Monopoly Capitalism*. Chicago: Chicago University Press.

Burawoy, M. (2003). Revisits: An outline of a theory of reflexive ethnography. *American Sociological Review, 68*(5), 645–679.

Castells, M. (2000). *The Rise of the Network Society* (2nd ed., Vol. 1). Oxford: Blackwell.

Clegg, S. (1989). *Frameworks of Power*. London: Sage.

Clegg, S., Courpasson, D., & Phillips, N. (2006). *Power and Organizations*. London: Sage Publications.

Clegg, S., Kornberger, M., & Pitsis, T. (2011). *Managing and Organizations: An Introduction to Theory and Practice*. Los Angeles: Sage.

Crozier, M. (1964). *The Bureaucratic Phenomenon*. London: Tavistock.

Dahl, R. A. (1969). *The Concept of Power Political Power: A Reader in Theory and Research*. New York: Free Press.

Dawson, P. (1994). *Organizational Change: A Processual Approach*. London: Paul Chapman Publishing.

Dawson, P. (2015). In search of freedom: legacies of management innovations for the experience of work and employment. *Employment Relations Record, 15*(1), 4–26.

Dreyfus, L. H., & Rabinow, P. (1982). *Michel Foucault: Beyond Structuralism and Hermeneutics*. New York: Harvester Press Ltd.

Edwards, R. (1979). *Contested Terrain: The Transformation of the Workplace in the Twentieth Century*. London: Heinemann.

Foucault, M. (1977). *Discipline and Punish: The Birth of the Prison*. London: Allen Lane.

Foucault, M. (Ed.). (1980). *Power/Knowledge: Selected Interviews and Other Writings 1972–1977*. New York: Pantheon Books.

Friedman, A. (1977). *Industry and Labour: Class Struggle at Work and Monopoly Capitalism*. London: MacMillan.

Goffman, E. (1961). *Asylums: Essays on the Social Situation of Mental Patients and Other Inmates*. Garden City, NY: Anchor Books.

Göhler, G. (2009). Power to and power over. In S. Clegg & M. Haugaard (Eds.), *The SAGE Handbook of Power* (pp. 27–39). London: Sage.

Hardy, C., & Clegg, S. (1996). Some dare call it power. In S. Clegg, C. Hardy, & W. Nord (Eds.), *Handbook of Organization Studies* (pp. 622–641). London: Sage.

Harvey, D. (1989). *The Condition of Postmodernity*. Oxford: Blackwell.

Hassan, R., & Purser, R. E. (Eds.). (2007). *24/7 Time and Temporality in the Networked Society*. Stanford, CA: Stanford University Press.

Haugaard, M. (1997). *The Constitution of Power: A Theoretical Analysis of Power, Knowledge and Structure*. Manchester and New York: Manchester University Press.

Haugaard, M. (2009). Power and hegemony. In S. Clegg & M. Haugaard (Eds.), *The SAGE Handbook of Power*. London: Sage.

Herman, E., & Chomsky, N. (1988). *Manufacturing Consent*. New York: Pantheon.
Hickson, D., Hinings, C., Lee, C., Schneck, R., & Pennings, J. (1971). A strategic contingencies theory of organizational change. *Administrative Science Quarterly, 16*, 216–229.
Hobbes, T. (1651/1968). *Leviathan*. London: Penguin.
Janouch, G. (1971). *Conversations With Kafka*. London: Andre Deutsch.
Knights, D. (1990). Subjectivity, Power and the Labour Process. In D. Knights and H. Willmott (Eds.), *Labour Process Theory* (pp. 297–335). London: Macmillan.
Knights, D. (2009). Power at work in organizations. In M. Alvesson, T. Bridgman, & H. Willmott (Eds.), *The Oxford Handbook of Critical Management Studies* (pp. 144–165). Oxford: Oxford University Press.
Landes, D. S. (1983). *Revolution in Time*. Cambridge: Harvard University Press.
Lukes, S. (1974). *Power: A Radical View*. London: Macmillan.
Machiavelli, N. (1961). *The Prince*. London: Penguin.
Marx, K. (1852). *The Eighteenth Brumaire of Louis Bonaparte*. Retrieved from https://www.marxists.org/archive/marx/works/download/pdf/18th-Brumaire.pdf
McCabe, D. (2007). *Power at Work: How Employees Reproduce the Corporate Machine*. London and New York: Routledge.
Peters, T., & Waterman, R. (1982). *In Search of Excellence: Lessons from America's Best Run Companies*. Sydney: Harper and Rowe.
Pfeffer, P., & Salancik, G. R. (1978). *The External Control of Organizations: A Resource Dependence Perspective*. New York: Harper and Rowe.
Piketty, T. (2014). *Capital in the Twenty-First Century* (A. Goldhammer, Trans.). Cambridge, MA: Belknap Press.
Ritzer, G. (1993). *The McDonaldization of Society*. Newbury Park: Pine Forge.
Rose, N. (1989). *Governing the Soul: The Shaping of the Private Self*. London: Routledge.
Rose, N. (1998). *Inventing Ourselves: Psychology, Power and Personhood*. Cambridge: Cambridge University Press.
Rose, N. (1999). *Powers of Freedom*. Cambridge: Cambridge University Press.
Thompson, J. D. (1956). Authority and power in identical organizations. *American Journal of Sociology, 62*, 290–301.
Thrift, N. (2005). *Knowing Capitalism*. Los Angeles, London and New York: Sage.
Townley, B. (1998). Beyond good and evil: Depth and division in the management of human resources. In A. McKinlay & K. Starkey (Eds.), *Foucault, Management and Organization Theory: From Panopticon to Technologies of the Self* (pp. 191–210). London: Sage.
Townley, B., Cooper, D., & Oakes, L. (2003). Performance measures and the rationalization of organizations. *Organization Studies, 24*(7), 10–45.
Wajcman, J. (2015). *Pressed for Time: The Acceleration of Life in Digital Capitalism*. London: University of Chicago Press.

8 Narrative Time and Stories in Making Sense of Change

Introduction

Time has often been ignored in the narrative turn in social science, and in the related sensemaking literature, temporality has largely remained cast as a linear movement from past to present. Surprisingly, time does not appear at all in the review by Rhodes and Brown (2005) of the literature on narratives and storytelling, whereas in Weick's (1995) sensemaking theory it is time past, through the backward glance in the association of events, that connect through space-time, that takes centre stage. In this latter work, retrospection stands as the distinguishing characteristic; that is, sensemaking is triggered retrospectively by unforeseen and unusual events—that may threaten identities—in which people seek to make plausible sense of what has occurred.

In the narratives and stories used in making sense of change, conventional, taken-for-granted time in the ticking of the clock (clock time) and the organization of business (in the use of the calendar in planning and scheduling operations, meetings, and work practices) have been the mainstay underlying concept development and theorization. Time has remained forever present in its absence in which these concepts of chronological, linear, and business times limit our understanding of narrative time in stories and sensemaking through their tendency to time sequence events, to impose chronological structure on lived experience, and ultimately, to reduce the variety of times and temporalities. On this count, Pederson calls for a need to move beyond linear time in the sensemaking literature and to view narrative time as open time:

> In relation to sense-making, chronological time is not very helpful, because it divides time into small sequential units. Thereby meaning can only be created in short sequences of times. Narrative time is open time, which means that time must be defined; it is left to the storyteller or the listener to define time as, for example, chronological time. Time can be defined in many different ways as historical time or as personal inner time. An example of the latter is that in chronological time, I may be sixty, but in inner time I feel as if I were forty-years-old.
>
> (2009: 392)

This quotation by Pedersen usefully captures the tendency within organization studies to use chronological time as a focal lens for explaining phenomena in which other kinds of experiential time such as adventure time or holiday time remain understated (Bakhtin, 1981; Boje, Hayley, & Saylors, 2015; Gabriel, 2004; Hayley & Boje, 2014). In this chapter we set out to show how time can be defined in many different ways, and these different sorts of time come into play in organizations, especially in relation to storytelling and sensemaking processes. A central aim therefore is to explore the implications of these various sorts of time for understanding narrative time and stories in making sense of change.

   In the backward reflection on successful change interventions, change narratives with plots (including sequential time), characters (often including change champions), and lessons are often constructed around a linear time frame with an implied chronological causality (this led to this, which caused this to happen) with a clear beginning, middle, and end (BME). Objective time is central, enabling divisibility of change interventions into units that can be sequenced, measured, and evaluated not only to inform and direct change but also to create formal plans and retrospective accounts of change. In discussing narrative, Czarniawska and Sevón (1996: 21) explain how 'sequentiality implies causality—in terms of both objective causes and human intentions—and is the basic glue which holds together our narratives'. Practical 'how-to' knowledge distilled from these sequential, retrospective accounts generally spotlight critical turning points (e.g., heroic activities), identify causal chains on how to best manage change (see, e.g., the prescriptive literature on successful change management), and present, well-structured stories with a clear BME (often with a moral twist and identifiable lessons). In these completed stories, where Aristotelean time sequences are used to structure accounts, notions of relative or subjective time remain largely absent (Czarniawska & Sevón, 1996: 21). They contrast with the unfinalized storying (Boje, 2006) that is common among people experiencing change. In these stories, during times of change, there is a far more open and emergent narrative; causality is up for discussion as interpretations mix with explanations among the stories of people trying to make sense of change (Czarniawska & Sevón, 1996: 47). Time is also more loosely conceived as the linear and non-linear intermix in the narrating of stories in the making about individual and group experiences. The polyphony of change as a multi-story process (Buchanan & Dawson, 2007) is evident both in the range of accounts that emerge and in the ongoing storying process that draws not only on the past and the present but also on prospective futures and longer-term expectations (Dawson & McLean, 2013).

   In this chapter we highlight the tendency for narratives of change to take for granted an objective conception of time that largely ignores the more subjective elements brought to the fore by writers such as Bergson (1913) and Mead (see Simpson, 2014). As we shall discuss, there is a need to move away from a focus on chronological clock time towards less structured forms of story time (that incorporate objective and subjective time) to further theorization on change. In pursuing this objective, we commence by outlining the work of two eminent scholars in the field, namely, Yannis Gabriel (2000) and David Boje (2008). Their approaches are particularly pertinent as Gabriel (2004) works within a contained temporal frame with a recognisable BME, whereas Boje (1995) moves beyond the classical narrative form towards the less consolidated rough-living stories (2009) and what he terms as a bet on the future or antenarrative (2011). In his later work Boje (2012) also seeks to incorporate insights from quantum mechanics in his characterization of stories and change, and these can be contrasted with the more Aristotelean position of Gabriel (2000), who is interested in organizational stories (from a folklorist tradition) that have a fixed temporality with a plot and clear set of characters. After comparing these works we turn our attention to a series of articles from a special issue of *Organization* on storytelling and change. The close connection between storytelling research and theories of organizational change are discussed and the work of Pedersen (2009) is used to highlight the need to broaden our conceptions of time in developing more insightful change theories. The final section draws on three empirical studies concerned with temporal sensemaking and change that usefully illustrate how the multiple interlacing accounts of past, present, and future remain open with ongoing possibilities for renegotiation and reinterpretation. The chapter concludes by once again calling for further research, discussion, and debate on time if we are to further our insights into the place of stories in theorizing temporality and organizational change.

Storytelling in Organizations and Storytelling Organizations

Two eminent scholars in this field of study have produced two important books, one which is titled *Storytelling in Organizations* (Gabriel, 2000) and the other with a somewhat similar but importantly different title *Storytelling Organizations* (Boje, 2008). For Gabriel, stories are a subset of narratives and whereas all stories are narratives, not all narratives are stories. He argues that theories, statistics, reports, or documents that describe events and seek to present objective facts should not be treated as stories (nor for that matter should clichés) as stories interpret events, often distorting, omitting, and embellishing to engage audience emotions; they generate, sustain, destroy, and undermine meaning. Whereas they are crafted along particular lines, they do not obliterate the facts (Gabriel, 2000: 3–4). Drawing from the folklorist tradition, Gabriel is interested in the stories that arise in organizations from the personal experience of individuals (a form of living folklore) that, he argues, provides a useful lens into the nature of organizations. These stories are complete with a BME; they have characters with plots, and the story is told with narrative skill to entertain, engage, and persuade the listening audience (Gabriel, 2000: 22). In this sense, stories are seen to provide meaning and a sense of coherence to complex sets of events in enabling temporal connection and in reducing what Brown and Kreps (1993: 48) refer to as the 'equivocality (complexity, ambiguity, unpredictability) of organizational life'. The plot of a story provides movement over time from 'an original state of affairs, an action or an event, and the consequent state of affairs' (Czarniawska, 1998: 2). However for Gabriel, a good story is well timed and entertaining; it encourages repetition, but 'it does *not* invite factual verification' (2000: 23). His focus is on what he terms proper stories with actions, characters, and plots, not terse fragments, labels, clichés, platitudes, reports, or opinions that, according to Gabriel, simply obscure a proper story window into the rich tapestry of organizational life (2000: 29). He is critical of broader characterizations of stories and on the stance taken by Boje (2008), who argues that a few words can conjure up interpretative meanings and hence constitute a story. For Gabriel, viewing these types of accounts as organizational storytelling amounts to a form of narrative deskilling (2009: 20–21):

> Boje loses the very qualities that he cherishes in stories, performativity, memorableness, ingenuity, and symbolism. His terse stories amount to little more than delicate fragments of sense, communicating metonymically, as if they were product brands.

For Boje, storytelling in organizations is central to sensemaking but not just in a Weickian retrospective sense but also prospectively and in the ongoing present. This moves his interest in stories beyond the classic Aristotelian narratives with a linear time structure towards the simultaneity of storytelling (Boje, 1995) and prospective sensemaking in his bet on the future, stories that he terms 'antenarratives' (Boje, 2011). Boje (2001: 1) defines antenarrative as 'the fragmented, non-linear, incoherent, collective, unplotted, and pre-narrative speculation, a bet, a proper narrative can be constituted'. Unlike Gabriel's stories, with developmental plots and coherent linear structure, these 'before-stories' are more rhizomatic, non-linear, unfinalized, and fragmented. Although in his earlier work Boje places antenarratives along the arrow of time as future-oriented ways of sensemaking that can shape future outcomes (Boje, 2008: 13), in his later work that incorporates elements of quantum mechanics, he moves towards a more Baradian entangled 'spacetimemattering' view (Boje, 2012) but then moves back towards a more Einsteinian connected view of temporal and spatial relationships in using Bakhtin's (1981: 84) concept of chronotopes (literally, 'timespace') in an examination of Burger King's storytelling in space, time, and strategic context. From Boje's perspective coherent narratives built on retrospective sensemaking serve to control and regulate, whereas living stories in the present (as in simultaneous storytelling) disperse and challenge, providing alternative interpretations and ways of making sense of change, and antenarratives offer potential future options or possibilities through prospective sensemaking. In contrasting story to narrative Boje (2008: 7) notes:

> Story, in contrast to narrative (that is centering or about control) is more apt to be dispersive (unravelling coherence, asserting differences). Narrative cohesion seeks a grip on the emergent present, which story is re-dispersing. . . . The emergent present keeps changing. . . . We interact with others taking different pathways to make sense of it all. The act of storying usually leaves the explication to the listener's imagination, in act of co-construction, in an emergent assemblage sensemaking, across several (dialectical or dialogical) contexts.

Sequenced Time, Change, and Story Types in Organizations

Gabriel (2004) is critical of a lot of the research done into organizational stories that place too much emphasis on stories as repositories of knowledge and unquestionable accounts of human existence. Stories allow facts to be reinterpreted and can act as hegemonic discourses in oppressing groups as well as vehicles of sensemaking and contestation (2004: 19). Through poetic license the storyteller is able to embellish, omit, reshape, and build a story that engages the audience. Gabriel refers to this understanding between storyteller and audience as a narrative (psychological) contract in which the storyteller is able to suspend final judgement by the audience in constructing a story that is meaningful and verisimilar. As Gabriel states (2004: 19),

> Stories in and out of organizations are privileged among other discursive devices by unique combination of two qualities, those of having a plot at the same time as claiming to represent reality. Stories not only purport to relate to facts that happened, but also to discover in these facts a plot or a meaning, by claiming that facts do not merely happen but that they happen in accordance with the requirements of a plot. In short, stories are not 'just fictions' (although some, like 'jokes', may be fictions) nor are they mere chronologies or reports of events as they happened. Instead, they represent poetic elaborations of narrative material, aiming to communicate *facts as experience*, not facts as information (Benjamin, 1968). This accords the storyteller a unique narrative privilege, *poetic license*, which enables him or her to maintain an allegiance to the effectiveness of the story, even as he or she claims to be representing the truth.

Gabriel (2000) identifies a series of generic poetic modes in which primary types of stories comprise the comic, tragic, epic, and romantic, with secondary modes being characterized by humour, cock-up, tragicomedy, and epic-comic. In outlining the predicament, plot focus, poetic tropes, and emotions found within these story types (see Gabriel, 2000: 84–85), he argues that the strength and weakness of stories is how they can, through relatively simple plots, characters, and key motives, enable sensemaking of muddied, complex, ambiguous realities. In the collection of 377 stories from 126 interviews, four main types of stories were identified within organizations. First, comic stories provide a plot that is often interlaced with humour and mirth to amuse the listener, but these stories can also be disparaging of particular groups or individuals. Second, epic stories are usually about a hero or heroine who achieves great success or a noble victory (Kostera, 2002: 731). The listener is invited into the nostalgic mood of the tale, feeling pride or admiration for the hero/heroine. Third, tragic stories are tales where the protagonist is often positioned as a non-deserving victim, suffering misfortune and generating sympathy from the audience. Tragic stories invite collective identification among those who share the tragedy and often invite sorrow, pity, anger, and emotional support from the listeners. A key feature of the tragic tale, according to Gabriel (2000: 69), is that punishment, 'far from restoring justice, seems to reinforce injustice by being entirely incommensurable with the magnitude of the offence'. Fourth, romantic stories often involve entangled relations of love and romantic attachment. The power of love over adversity and 'acts of unsolicited kindness' are all characteristic of this type of story (Gabriel, 2000: 146).

The taxonomy put forward by Gabriel is not intended to be rigid but rather a heuristic device by which stories can be compared across organizational settings. Some stories also combine elements of different poetic modes to become hybrids or secondary types of stories such as gripes (personal injustices), traumas (deeper psychic injuries where protagonists claim to be 'scarred for life'), and practical jokes (often accompanied by disparagement towards the victim). Story categories are not 'pure', with subtle discursive devices often woven into the main story category; for example, tragic tales occasionally were laced with irony, and disparaging tales often invoked safety as a legitimating device to reinforce the sense of injustice inherent in these tales.

In all these story types that are found in organizations, there is a wholeness and linear structure that aligns with clock time and the Gregorian calendar (Gabriel, 2000: 239). The focus is on stories and storytelling in organizations and not on change per se or the way time is conceptualized. In this focus on storytelling in organizations (facts, fictions, and fantasies), Gabriel warns about treating these stories as simply texts without due recognition of the way they embellish and elaborate events and present 'wish-fulfilling fantasies' that arise from people's experiences of organizational life (2000: 241). These stories are seen as both fragile and special in providing cultural insights, often highlighting the untypical and exceptional enabling us to uncover what lies behind the routine and mundane. For Gabriel (2000: 239),

> Stories are narratives with plots and characters, generating emotion in narrator and audience through a poetic elaboration of symbolic material.

This material may be a product of story fantasy or experience, including an experience of earlier narratives. Story plots entail conflicts, predicaments, trials, coincidences, and crises that call for choices, decision, actions, and interactions, whose actual outcomes are often at odds with the characters' intentions and purposes.

These stories are narrated around issues that require change and movement in the decisions, choices, and actions that they call for. Chronology and objective time embed the stories with an identifiable past, present, and future and a linear causality that provides the temporal structure (BME with plot and characters). This linearity is tied to the inviolability of sequenced events that occur within a tensed notion of time where, for example, you cannot have a character seeking revenge before an original insult has occurred, nor can you have a punishment for a crime that will be committed later. There is an attribution of causal connection within plot lines that point to one incident as being responsible for another, and within organizations, these stories of change may be challenged by counter-narratives that question the order of events and propose an alternative sequence of causal events. In other words, what folkloric storytelling and Aristotelean theory of plot have in common is an emphasis that certain events happen in sequence and that this sequence cannot be violated.

Whereas there is a linear causality in this sequenced timing of events, the workings of time within these stories are often far from linear as witnessed by the original version of *Tender Is the Night* by F. Scott Fitzgerald, Homer's *The Odyssey* that starts on year nine of Odysseus's 10-year struggle to return home after the Trojan War, and Grimms' fairy tales that highlight a certain playfulness with time in the dramatic leaps, playbacks, and the simultaneous unfoldings of more than one plot line. From this folklorist perspective, sequenced event time predominates, and conventional temporality is not called into question, and yet there remains subtle and different conceptions of time, sometimes continuous, sometimes discontinuous, sometimes linear, and sometimes timeless, that extend beyond a simple characterization of Newtonian linear time. Boje (2006), however, maintains that there is a form of chronological containment within this perspective that we need to move beyond—or as he terms it—to set stories free from their narrative prison.

Unfinalized Time, Stories, and Change in Storytelling Organizations

Boje contrasts the linearity and coherence of modernist conceptions of narrative (Czarniawska, 1998; Gabriel, 2000) with the polyphony and unfinalized dynamic of storying in the here and now (Boje 2001; Collins & Rainwater, 2005). For Boje (2008: 1) narrative has served to present reality in an ordered fashion (a centripetal force), whereas stories are at times able to break out of this narrative order and offer a more diverse, fragmented, and muddled view of reality (a centrifugal force). He refers to a storytelling organization as a 'collective storytelling system in which the performance of stories is a key part of members' sensemaking and a means to allow them to supplement individual memories with institutional memory' (Boje, 1991: 106). For Boje, narrative has been shaped by modernity, in which the narrative plot cohesion is privileged and in which causally related episodes provide generalizations, whereas stories in the here and now interplay with the life-world. He is clearly against treating narrative and story as synonymous as it is the transformative dynamics from the interplay of story and narrative that changes organizations (2006: 3–4)

> when you realize story is not some whole text that is agreed-upon, told from beginning to end, as has been theorized in narrative research. Rather, a story released from narrative prison is dynamic, varies by context, can be quite a *terse* expression, where the hearer fills in blanks and silences with chunks of story line, context, and implication. . . . My early work (Boje, 1991, 1995) is . . . about . . . the struggle of official retrospective narratives of managerial control with counterstories, ones marginalized in official storytelling. . . . In what I call "*storytelling organizations*", stories and narratives are being challenged, reinterpreted, and revised by participants as they unfold in conversations. Collective storytelling occurs in which the performance of terse stories is key. . . . *Storytelling organizations* constitute tellers and listeners who become co-tellers and co-listeners.

Thus in contrast to Gabriel's (2000) completed stories, a key finding of Boje (1991: 112–113) is that 'people told their stories in bits and pieces, with excessive interruptions of story parts, with people talking over each other to share story fragments, and many aborted storytelling attempts'. Boje describes the stories he collected as 'terse' and acknowledges that in all his transcripts, hardly a single story bears repetition outside its home territory as a 'good story'. It is not surprising that Gabriel (2000: 18–19) is critical of this view and the claim by Boje that storytelling is the central sensemaking currency of human relationships within organizations. For Gabriel these stories are not proper narratives as they hardly ever feature as integrated pieces of narrative with a full plot and a complete case of characters (with a BME); instead, they exist in a state of continuous flux, fragments, and allusions as people contribute bits, often talking together. He prefers the term 'protostories' rather an antenarratives, which can be confusing, and although recognising that this is a veritable soup of fragments (half-spun tales, opinions, etc.), it is the vibrant stories (counter-narratives) that have more power and political potential to supplant and subvert the official narrative of change.

Boje (2008, 2012), in broadening the analysis of what constitutes a story, contests that stories differ from structured narratives, existing and operating in multiple and sometimes fragmentary forms that go beyond the retrospective. He argues that the focus in organization studies has been on retrospective sensemaking through an Aristotelian conception of a narrative that ignores prospective ways of sensemaking, whilst also giving less attention to retrospective narrative fragments and the here and now of storying (Boje, 2008: 1). In highlighting the need for more attention on prospective sensemaking, Boje develops the concept of antenarrative as a form of 'pre-narrative speculation', a bet on the future (Boje, 2001: 1). These future-oriented ways of sensemaking are dynamic and often change in the way they are told, written, or shown. Boje uses the example of Sam Walton (latterly of Wal-Mart, who died in 1992) to illustrate how he is used by Wal-Mart executives to present a story of Wal-Mart lowering costs to present a better life for all, which contrasts with the union perspective, which narrates a very different story around discriminatory practices and violations of labour standards (Boje, 2008: 14). As he states (2008: 15), 'Each is recasting elements of context into a forward-looking interpretation of Sam's way'.

In examining the present, Boje draws on a play by John Kriznac called *Tamara*, in which the actors are performing in a number of different rooms of a large mansion and the audience has to decide which room(s) they want to locate in or move between and/or which actors they wish to follow as they move around from room to room. In this way, the audience is not able to view all the performances as they occur but, rather, have to make sense from the sites in which they have been present. This simultaneous storytelling in multiple sites encourages dialogue between different members of the audience to ask about stories performed in places from which they were absent. Boje (1995) uses this insight to examine how storytelling operates within Disney and spotlights how researchers looking through one lens (stuck in one room) will be unable to make sense of the simultaneous storying that is occurring elsewhere (in other rooms) and advocates the need for more dynamic story-tracing methods.

In addition to the temporal dimension of retrospective and prospective sensemaking and the here-and-now storying, Boje (2008) claims that account needs to be given of the reflexive and transcendental nature of sensemaking. Moving beyond the reflexive dialectics of Hegel's thesis and antithesis or Ricoeur's (1984) identity of sameness and difference, Boje draws on the work of Bakhtin (1981: 2) to argue that whereas narrative is 'a monologic bid for order', stories are far more dialogical and seeks to elevate the place of stories in organization studies in examining the interplay between the control of narrative (order) and unfinalized nature of emergent story (disorder). As previously indicated, Boje (2006: 3) argues that we should set story free from the narrative prison that constrains our gaze to retrospective wholes (an Aristotelian/folklorist approach concerned with finalized retrospective narratives), with causally ordered sequencing of events, towards a storying turn concerned with unfinalized story variety making. Some of the constraints of a narrative prison are seen to comprise the following:

- The narrative needs coherence when life and stories of life are often muddled and incoherent.
- Narrative imposes linearity with a BME, whereas stories of lived experience are often partial and incomplete or to use Boje's words 'tersely told'.
- Narrative does not accommodate different stories occurring in different spaces.
- The oral story is seen to take precedence over written stories.
- Stories are often unfinished and ongoing, yet narrative requires wholeness and treats story as an objective, fixed entity.

These tendencies can present a type of collective organizational memory as a single rendition (managerialist with selective forgetting) rather than capturing the variety of collective memories that compete for recognition through emergent stories. For Boje (2008: 3), '*Emergent story* can be defined as absolute novelty, spontaneity, and improvisation, without past or future. Emergent stories are conceived in the here-and-now co-presence of social communicative intercourse'. As he goes on to explain (2008: 75),

> Emergent story begins in improvisation, quickly takes other forms of emergence as secret gossip-emergence jumps official channels to become rumour, and takes the rare turn of an emergence that is reforged into the narrative form of legend and myth. It is this dynamic quality of emergence, its morphing in to narrative form at differing paces in various groups spread across time and space that makes for dynamics of collective memory in storytelling organizations.

Boje argues against the tendency within narrative theory to view stories of past events as a stable form of collective memory in which stronger organizational cultures are seen to exhibit petrified stories that anchor and sustain this culture (Boje, 2008: 82). He points out how 'antenarratives of novel emergence' may restory collective memory and enable the silent voices to be heard:

> Organization history is oftentimes a few coherent living stories retold by a dominant power coalition. . . . Much of managerialist story research has focused on recirculating heroic stories of elite organization participants. Other heroes become dead stories. Stories of the little people have been marginalized, and get killed off. Managerialist story research services to further marginalize the less powerful tellers.
>
> (Boje, 2008: 242)

In his later work, Boje (2012) wrestles with the insights from quantum physics and tries to apply these ideas to his storytelling approach to organizations. He argues that change management is often conceived as a future end state that is predicted from making sense of historical patterns of activities (retrospective sensemaking) in a type of billiard-ball approach that utilizes a linear time model (Boje, 2012: 4). In his concept of antenarrative, Boje (2011) is concerned with what precedes narrative as well as what may become (a bet on the future through prospective sensemaking), and in this, there is a temporality of past, present, and future. Through then drawing on the work of Barad (2007), he engages with the notion of material-discursive entanglement through the dynamics of intra-activity in which observations or stories reconfigure the material-discursive world of which they are a part. The concepts of anteriority-antenarrative is used to capture the sense of the future beckoning the present (non-linear time) in the way the future may influence the present, and antecedent-antenarrative is used to accommodate the indeterminacy of possibilities ('now-ness potentialities'). This paradigm shift to quantum physics is seen to draw attention away from clock time towards 'an everydayness concept of time, a primordial sense of temporality and temporalization' (Boje, 2012: 13). But this notion is never fully unpacked; his concept of time remains ambiguous and unclear, especially in relation to the connection between the non-temporal indeterminacy and entanglement of subatomic behaviour and the temporality of change stories that in prospectively making sense of future possibilities gives new sense (stories) to what has occurred in the past in influencing choice making in the present. Time and temporality are identified as important, but the movement between tenseless and tensed notions of time in the translation from the quantum subatomic world to change management and storytelling remains hanging and unresolved.

Underlying contradictions, ambiguity, and some confusion are evident in the way concepts of time are identified as important and yet are not clearly clarified and articulated in the theorization that follows (see, e.g., Boje, 2012; Boje, Hayley, & Saylors, 2015). When the implicit conceptions of time and temporality are unmasked, significant ontological differences become evident between tensed and tenseless notions of emergence and reconstituted 'nows'. This once again highlights the importance of clarifying concepts of time in theorizing change and in reflecting on the temporal assumptions that underpin process philosophers who are critical of writers that conflate time with space and fail to maintain a distinction between external time with the way time is experienced within ourselves (Bergson, 1913; Deleuze, 1994; Heidegger, 1996).

Storytelling and Change: An Unfolding Story

In a special issue on storytelling and change in the journal *Organization*, Brown, Gabriel, and Gherardi (2009) draw attention to the heterogeneity and wide-ranging approaches that have emerged from the linguistic turn in organization studies that includes social constructionist, critical management studies and postmodern and realist perspectives that examine various aspects of identity, power, communication, knowledge, and sensemaking, arguing that there are no clear distinctions between storytelling and narratives. Unlike Boje (2006) they refer to narratives and stories interchangeably as vehicles that engage emotionally, are rife with meanings, often take a moral stance, and are integral to processes of change. They highlight the close connection between storytelling research and theories of organizational change, stating (2009: 325),

> Importantly, both have at their core notions of temporality, and are generally preoccupied with describing, understanding and explaining complicated processes in which multiple characters, agents, contexts and occurrences overlap and interweave—often in ways which are both uncertain and ambiguous (Humphreys & Brown, 2008). Whether stories are interpreted as constituting, mapping, encouraging, managing, upsetting, preventing or inviting change, they are an ever present feature of patterns of becoming, always evocative of actual futures and possible worlds. They are the means by which executives manage and the disaffected resist, they inhabit the boardroom and the unmanaged interstitial spaces in which those effected by power express their fantasies and their disquiet (Gabriel, 2000). Stories are often concomitantly, aids to memory and way of forgetting, diagnostic tools and distractions, means for social control and expressions of liberation, hegemonic and subversive. In all these ways, and others, stories are key to our conceptions, theories and research on change.

This collection provides useful insights into the storying process during times of change. For example, Sims, Huxham, and Beech (2009), although not explicitly concerned with time or temporality, show how audiences remember snippets of stories that are later reconstituted to serve their own purposes. Murgia and Poggio (2009) analyse the stories of eight men who have taken parental leave showing how stories not only support change but can also be used to maintain hegemonic practices and prevent change (in this case, the symbolic and dominant gender order between fathers and mothers). Driver (2009) adopts a Lacanian psychoanalytic perspective in analysing 40 stories of change that bring to the fore the power of storytelling, especially in providing opportunities for the storyteller to experience empowering and creative encounters. Beech, MacPhail, and Coupland (2009) spotlight the containment and anti-dialogic separation that can occur between storytellers in examining the stories that people tell when experiencing change. In their analysis of multiple stories, they discover a paradoxical tendency towards a singular, monological perspective and that even though there is an appearance of dialogue, these change stories are self-contained and separate from those that coexist around them. In each of these, the power of stories and storytellers to influence change is highlighted.

The polyphony of stories is further taken up by Whittle, Mueller, and Mangan (2009), who illustrate the multi-story nature of change processes in a qualitative case study of a UK public-private partnership. They identify competing narratives of change that challenge established identities through examining not only the larger narratives but also the smaller stories that people tell about themselves in ordinary conversational contexts. They argue that stories can be incomplete and precarious (in a similar vain to the work of Boje but with a focus on stories that compete and come into conflict), and in using Bruner's (1986) notion of character, they illustrate: 'not only the contestability of stories, and associated images of the self, but also the *temporal development* of such projections of the self—in our case from innocent victim and hero to (as re-cast by a senior manager) implied villain to (as later re-negotiated) heroic survivor' (Whittle et al., 2009: 439).

This study captures the multiple and contestable nature of stories in the recasting of characters over time (see also Dawson & Buchanan, 2012), and yet, there is a conventional temporality that underpins their analysis. In the work of Peirano-Vejo and Stablein (2009), temporality is central, especially in their analysis of stories and change. Their main concern centres on tensed notions of time in which the past, interpretations of the past, and interpretations of the future as uncharted territory influence the directions of change in the present. In their agricultural study based in Argentina, they analyse microprocesses of power in the sensemaking and sensegiving that occurs around narratives. Data collected from an institutional video, four in-depth interviews, and 21 interview transcripts are used to illustrate how old stories are told in new ways and how sensegivers have greater leverage in shaping change in the way that they deal with identity issues, knowledge, and time. The video is seen to offer a view of present change issues as the intersection between the past and present, essentially acting as a transition mechanism showing how the present (yesterday's future) is controllable. This in turn elevates the achievability of future change in showing how change, stability, and change can coexist. In other words, the uncertainty of the future is presented in a soothing and understandable way (2009: 451). In referring to the political tensions of the 1960s and 1970s, the authors illustrate how past conflicts are viewed retrospectively to bring attention to the ways that things settle down as time passes—as they note with regard to notions of the past (Peirano-Vejo & Stablein, 2009: 458),

> The past is a resource to support innovation rather than a barrier to change and a source of resistance. This will not be true for all organizations. For other organizations the past may be a resource for resistance to change, or the past may be forgotten, or the past may be irrelevant. A contribution which may be generalizable to other cases is a detailed attention to how time is constructed—which times are considered, which times are forgotten or silenced, which times are significant or insignificant.

Although the importance of time and temporality in stories that influence change is emphasised in this study, little attempt is made to unpack these concepts. They are largely taken as self-evident from the narratives and stories presented in the video and interviews. In contrast, Pedersen (2009) addresses concepts of time more directly, and in particular, she is critical of the tendency to overemphasise chronological time that is especially evident in traditional studies on organizational change. She argues for displacing chronological time (a tendency to examine time as a given empirical event during change) with the concept of 'chronotopes' (spotlighting how change is happening in a certain place and time) and the concept of 'shadows of time' (in presenting a new understanding of narrative time). For Pedersen, stories of organizational change present different stories of time. She uses Morson's (1994) 'shadows of time' to refer to temporal entanglement or tensed time in which the past, present, and future continually interweave; 'foreshadowing' foretells a hypothetical future in which the present centres on preparation (realisable possibilities), and 'sideshadowing' represents possibilities not taken in accepting a story as the only one possible (unrealised possibilities) (Pedersen, 2009: 393). Attention moves from the sensemaking that occurs around an event located in chronological time to the way events represent different understandings of time. Pedersen (2009) also uses Bakhtin's (1981) concept of chronotope to draw attention to the inseparability and interconnectedness of time and space (see also Boje, Hayley, & Saylors, 2015). The literary genre of the story are classified by the chronotopes of fairy tale, every day, biographic, idyll and carnival that are linked to part chonotopes (e.g., an encounter at the pub is used as an example of part chronotope of the every day). These chronotopes are seen to bring to the fore the time and place in which change stories happen and the choices for shaping change (she draws on Morson's comparison of the Greek romance, where there is no room for choice with the realist novel where choice is more pervasive).

In adopting a relational ontology, Pedersen (2009) seeks to explain time as both a narrative and theoretical concept. She argues that studies that address stories and change have taken four main lines of argument, namely: i) how stories and storytelling can support change initiatives; ii) how change is created through discourse and language; iii) understanding change and genre stories (e.g., Gabriel's taxonomy); iv) and the multi-voiced polyphony of stories and change (Pedersen, 2009: 390). Pedersen discards the first two and discusses the contribution of, first, the narrative genre approach in which different story archetypes (characterized by identifiable plots) may be used by different groups during change, creating conflicts that need to be resolved (Pedersen uses the example of Downing (1997) where managers are often seen to describe change through romantic myths, whereas those on the receiving end engage in tragic tales), and second, the polyphonic perspective in which change occurs from the many voices of individuals (2009: 391). She argues that with each of these there is an underlining chronological conception of time in which change occurs as a series of linear, time-based, empirical events with no attention given to time as a theoretical construct. This leads to an absence of analysis of how events represent different interpretations of time with an assumption that time is given and fixed. In summarizing her position Pedersen (2009: 390) states:

> The central argument of 'narrative time' is that time is not a pre-given chronological event, but a theoretical concept, that must be defined and thereby become something else than a chronological time event in a story. I define 'narrative time' as open time, that is, time can be defined in many different ways; as historical time, as living time, as foreshadows of time or as time bound to space.

In an ethnographic study of a rehabilitation ward in a Copenhagen hospital, Pedersen illustrates the relational and narrative conditions of time in the way that three different stories about the changes happening on the ward (consultant, social worker, and senior nurse) are usefully captured by chronotopes, sideshadows, and foreshadows that reflect different stories of time (Pedersen, 2009). These change stories are also used to highlight the importance of time and space as for Petersen (2009: 402–403) they 'are not translatable to other organizations or organizational levels [reflecting] the asymmetric understanding of time: the social worker is in the present, when students are arriving in the ward; the change consultant is in the future, and the senior nurse in the past telling about the unit'. From this perspective narrative time is seen to open new understanding and theoretical insight into the processes of organizational change moving away from chronological time events towards storytellers' temporal understandings. Pedersen concludes: 'One could argue that chronological time, which is used in most studies of organizational change, only allows sense-making in small separate units, while chronotopes and shadows of time open up stories of how time and space are intertwined' (2009: 404). In this approach, a useful contribution is made in highlighting how the temporalities of stories not only make sense of change but also give sense and shape to the changes they are describing (see also Buchanan & Dawson, 2007). Narrative time is seen to broaden sensemaking possibilities beyond an understanding of change as a time-sequenced series of events. It is to this area of sensemaking, time, and temporality that we now turn our attention.

Time, Temporal Sensemaking, and Interpretative Accounts

In addition to mainstream narrative researchers, there is a large body of work in organization studies on sensemaking (Brown, Colville, & Pye, 2015) that is concerned with interpretative accounts and storytelling (Reissner,

2008). Attention is given to the way various sensegiving devices influence and are influenced by the ongoing process of storying, in which past understandings (retrospective sensemaking) combine with 'future perfect thinking' (Weick, 1979: 198)—or as some would prefer prospective sensemaking (Wiebe, 2010)—that shape and are shaped by each other in making sense of the present and deciding on courses of present action to achieve future desired outcomes. In this temporal storying there is a complex interlacing and overlapping of individual and collective story fragments that assemble and disassemble in context over time. Individual and group accounts may be characterized as finalized or unfinalized stories that anticipate and evaluate the likelihood of possible futures. These prospective sensemaking stories draw from and may alter views of the past (reconstructing past accounts), and in the process of rethinking the past (through individual and collective sensemaking and sensegiving) the prospective views of possible futures may in turn shift and refocus individual and collective attentions all within a context where present happenings interweave shifting interpretations that may achieve some transitory stability when particular courses of action or decisions are made. In this sense, the temporal perspective releases time from the activity of timing the successive ordering of change (the chronological cage of change sequence), allowing multiple temporalities to emerge through stories that seek to make and give sense to experiences of change.

In examining these issues of temporality and storying, we focus here on three main studies that examine temporal interpretations and accounts: first, in strategy making (Kaplan & Orlikowski, 2013); second, among managers (Wiebe, 2010); and third, at the workplace (Dawson & McLean, 2013). Each of these studies draw out different temporal elements whilst they spotlight the importance of shifting interpretations over time in multiple, interlacing accounts of past, present, and future and how these remain 'open' for renegotiation and reinterpretation. Multiple competing views exist among individuals and groups within organizations, and these are seen to shift and change over time and in their interpretations of what really did happen (the past), of what is currently happening (the present), and what the future outcomes are most likely to be (the future). In short, the processes and implications of the dynamics of multiple temporal interpretations is the common theme that links these studies together.

In their study of strategy making, Kaplan and Orlikowski (2013) develop a model of temporal work that centres on the way different interpretations of the past, present, and future are reconciled in formulating strategies that are not only acceptable but are seen to represent a cohesive and plausible account worthy of action. This temporal shaping of strategic choice in the construction of strategies in the pursuit of future trajectories is also seen to shed insight on conflict and contestation that can inhibit change and promote organizational inertia. Far from being a rational technical process based on statistical forecasting techniques, they argue: 'Projections of the future are always entangled with views of the past and present, and temporal work is the means by which actors construct and reconstruct the connections among them' (2013: 1526). Their concept of temporal work arises from a practice lens (see Chapters 6 and 10) in which the authors distil insights into these processes from the practices managers engage with in trying to construct an acceptable account. The resolution of competing interpretations (past, present, and future), the resolving of tensions, and the further reconstruction of accounts if agreements break down are all seen as central to this dynamic, entangled process of strategy making.

Their model builds on Weick's (1995) concept of sensemaking as a rational retrospective process by which people reconstruct their past to justify and make sense of actions in the present (see also Weick, Sutcliffe, & Obstfeld, 2005). In organizations there may be agreement about the happening of certain events but not about the import or meaning of such events, and this is where multiple interpretations of what has happened can influence views on what might be achievable in the future (especially in relation to the actions worth taking in the present). The resolving of these interpretations and the potential reconstruction of past histories is seen to form an integral part of the collective sensemaking process. The authors also take a Weickian view on the future, which casts this as something that can only be understood retrospectively through the concept of 'future perfect thinking'. Like Dawson and McLean (2013), who argue that adherence to a retrospective lens is inappropriate when considering prospective sensemaking, the authors in support of Wiebe (2010) take an approach that accommodates the projective aspect of sensemaking. In emphasising the temporal embeddedness of agency, a distinction is made between the 'now' of the present and the present as a longer duration in which current concerns and interpretations are raised and discussed. In this they draw on the work of Emirbayer and Mische's (1998) treatise on agency, who forward this position:

> Theoretically, our central contribution is to begin to reconceptualise human agency as a temporally embedded process of social engagement, informed by the past (in its habitual aspect), but also oriented toward the future (as a capacity to imagine alternative possibilities) and toward the present (as a capacity to contextualize past habits and future projects within the contingencies of the moment). The agentic dimension of social action can only be captured in its full complexity, we argue, if it is analytically situated within the flow of time. More radically, we also argue that the structural contexts of action are themselves temporal as well as relational fields—multiple, overlapping *ways of ordering time* toward which social actors can assume different simultaneous agentic orientations. Since social actors are embedded within many such temporalities at once, they can be said to be oriented toward the past, the future, and the present at any given moment, although they may be primarily oriented toward one or another of these within any one emergent situation.
> (Emirbayer & Mische, 1998: 963–964)

In adopting this theoretical position, Kaplan and Orlikowski (2013) argue that interpretation of the past, present, and future all have equal standing in, for example, influencing senior managers' strategic choices and that plausible connections across these interpretation are necessary for action. Their main contribution is seen to arise from an empirical investigation into how competing interpretations are negotiated and resolved and how connections are made (Kaplan & Orlikowski, 2013: 967). Following five technology strategy projects within CommCorp, they examine a range of change strategies from incremental to mixed and more radical initiatives. Their data indicate that there were varied historical accounts, different interpretations of current concerns, and mixed views on the future and that these accounts were non-conflicting to conflicting, multiple, and interdependent. They characterize these processes (which they term 'temporal work') as reimagining the future, rethinking the past, and reconsidering present concerns, arguing that the more intense these processes were, then the more radical the change—represented by the strategy and not the technology. In other words, it is the construction of strategy rather than the characteristics of technology that shapes the nature of change in organizations (2013: 975–981).

In uncovering the dynamics of these processes, the authors chart a chronological map of breakdowns, decisions and settlements over time represented by months in the year (calendar time). They show how provisional agreements can break down following contextual shifts that call into question the plausibility of future projects, making them unacceptable and causing breakdowns that require further rethinking (past), reconsidering (present), and reimagining (future). This cycle of events is shown to continue over time until—in the case of eventual resolution—an end point is reached when interpretations connect to produce an account that is coherent, plausible, and acceptable, and it is at this stage that strategic decisions are made and actions taken (2013: 981–989). The authors conclude: 'An analysis of strategic change is, thus, incomplete without considering how actors negotiate and link their divergent interpretations of the past, present and future' (2013: 990). Whereas the study usefully highlights the dynamic process by which people interpret and reinterpret the present in view of their interpretations and reinterpretations of the past and future, and how differences need to be reconciled in constructing a collective account that is acceptable, it fails to address the implications of organizational reliance on linear, event, and cyclical time. The authors stress that the focus in organization studies has largely been on clock or event time, suggesting that they are offering something new and innovative in examining how actors make interpretative links over time; however, data are presented along a linear time frame (using the calendar) in which cycles of events occur (provisional settlement, decision, breakdown, temporal work, provisional settlement, etc.), and yet there is little further discussion. Nevertheless, along with the other studies to be discussed, there is clearly a shift towards a greater recognition of the importance of time and temporality in the generation and construction of collective accounts that shape change and decision making in organizations.

In discussing the concept of temporal sensemaking through examining managers' use of time to frame organizational change, Wiebe (2010) turns our attention towards the concept of prospective sensemaking not as a backward glance in a Weickian way but, rather, in the way that people actively configure the relationship of past, present, and future in making sense of their experiences of change. He argues that time is strangely absent from theories of organizational change that tend to view change as continuous or episodic and that clock time obfuscates rather than clarifies processes of change (2010: 214). There is seen to be a discrepancy between time as described, measured, and accounted for and time as it is lived. Taking a perspective of change as processes and events that continually emerge and shift within and outside planned programmes of change, Wiebe also builds on the work of Emirbayer and Mische (1998: 963) especially in his use of an interpretive stance to explore how managers use time to frame and make sense of the changes they experience. The concept of temporal sensemaking is used to situate managers within the flow of time in which they can configure, reconfigure, orient, and reorient past, present, and future. He notes how natural time in the forward flow of time, such as ageing, or in cycles, such as seasons or circadian rhythms, does not map onto our conscious temporal experiences, for example, in the way people reshape their pasts or project new futures to account for an emerging present. Following Mead (1932), Wiebe argues that people experience time as an essentially social process and that time is integral to consciousness responding with a type of temporal freedom (not being determined by natural time) to emerging and novel contexts.

In drawing on 21 interviews with managers involved in government-mandated change within a single health care organization, Wiebe identifies five constructed worlds that are used to illustrate the different temporal framings that mangers use in narrating their experiences of change. These narratives engage the narrator in temporal thinking in which the future and the past exist in the sensemaking of the present (i.e., it is not just retrospective). As a central cognitive activity, narrativizing engages with temporality in the five different constructions or 'worlds' of organizational change. First is a world of no change with a dominant temporality of the past, where views on the future, past, and present assert a sense of sameness and continuity. Second is a world of evolutionary change with a present temporal orientation; there is a sense in which real change might eventuate, but it is going to be a long time in the coming. Third is a world of discontinuous temporality (past within future perfect tense) in which a period of significant achievement is followed by a period of inaction ('hitting a wall'), causing uncertainty about the ability to establish new routines and not return to past behaviours. Fourth is a convoluted evolutionary world in which the process of change is uneven but continuous in that 'the past and the future are engaged with a continuously changing present' (Wiebe, 2010: 229). Fifth is a future-oriented world of unrelenting change in which ties with the past are broken. In other words, the sense of ceaseless upheaval and discontinuity present uncertain futures that require the discarding of old behaviours (2010: 230).

In these five worlds of organizational change, the temporality of past, present, and future are variously emphasised with continuity links being prevalent among those who orient to the past and present, whereas elements of discontinuity are evident among constructions that are more future oriented. Wiebe (2010: 235) claims that the way that these dissimilar managers' experiences—of what is essentially the same change—are constructed through different temporal framing provides considerable insight on the accomplishment and experience of change that would be invisible from a clock time perspective. He recommends that future research should extend their study from the individual worlds of change to the accomplishment or not of collective interpretations, as he concludes:

> The investigation of the interaction of temporal perspectives would illuminate how individual temporal constructions may become reconstituted, and how 'objects' within the change initiative may be used in that work of reconstitution. It may also provide insight into the temporal basis for conflicted groups.
>
> (Wiebe, 2010: 237)

In their examination of workplace change at a colliery in Australia, Dawson and McLean (2013) examine the storying process for understanding the collective sensemaking of employees during contested change. This study usefully extends the work of Wiebe (2010) and also builds on the notion of sensemaking being a prospective, and not just a retrospective cognitive process (Weick, 1979), and of making sense of actions already undertaken (enactment). Identity is central to their use of sensemaking in which the temporality of past, present, and future interlace in constructing stories that not only seek to make sense of what is going on but also bolster and reinforce a sense of collective identity—of what it means to be a miner—in the power-political dynamics of enforced change. Data are used from a longitudinal Australian-based study of miners' storied responses to managements' implementation of a performance appraisal system. It is shown how multiple complete and unfinalized stories emerge, compete, develop, and are called upon to reinforce, challenge, or reconstitute the place of the individual and group during times of contested change (Dawson & McLean, 2013: 199).

For Dawson and McLean (2013) sensemaking and sensegiving are ongoing social activities in which compelling stories may be used to provide the rationale for engaging in actions, and as such, stories are not just seen as communication devices but as power-political constructions that service ways of interpreting and making sense of their own and others' actions and behaviours. In the case of the underground workers of the colliery, identity-relevant stories extended beyond the language and performance of stories to the context, bodily practice, and material conditions of work that permeated the meaning making that occurred. In the relational interplay of temporal, contextual, and sensemaking processes, there were stories that were finalized constructions of the past with plot lines and characters that serviced forms of retrospective sensemaking, there were also stories that were partial and fragmented in imagining future scenarios and possible outcomes in forms of prospective sensemaking, and there were stories that reconstituted the past and anticipated futures in making sense of an ongoing present. In providing a temporal classification to locate some of these different types of stories and the storying process in changing organizations, Dawson and McLean identify four main groupings (see Figure 8.1).

As part of this contested change, miners engaged in storying to resist the identity threats from management in a form of discursive polyphony and dialogue in which they would continually reaffirm and reconstitute their collective identities. The storying process helped buttress the distinguishing collective features of what it means to be a miner and in this way stories were used to help others reaffirm their sensemaking—through giving sense to what was occurring—in steering collective sensemaking (see Gioia & Chittipeddi, 1991). Dawson and McLean (2013) detail a number of stories that spotlight how stories can act as a powerful discursive resource for resistance in the hegemonic struggle over collective identities (see also Brown & Humphreys, 2006; Humphreys & Brown, 2002) whilst recognising that their persuasive power is in turn influenced by existing authority structures and power relationships. They identify tensions between finalized stories that provide coherence and understanding to complex and ambiguous events in the form of a linear causal theorization (objective time), stories that capture lived time (as also illustrated by the work of Wiebe), and the non-linearity of subjective experience and stories that arise in the materiality and practices of working in the mine that conflict with the procedural discourse of management that seeks to subjugate and organize labour into a productive workforce. It is through the storying process that miners actively resist the new performance measures and temporal practices; there is no willing consent to the proposed time-measured changes, even though the historical legacy of clock time efficiency is part of the culture and operation of the mine.

This mining example also draws attention to nostalgia and affect arising from identity threats, and this mirrors some of the findings of an earlier study by Strangleman (1999) in the railway industry and Brown and Humphreys (2002) in a Turkish faculty of vocational education. As the latter state,

> Nostalgia, it is argued, is key to the understanding of the dynamics of individual and organizational identity-construction in several ways: it can be a means of maintaining a collective sense of socio-historic continuity, a source of resistance to hegemonic influence and a defence against anxiety. . . . It theorises nostalgia as giving access to a shared heritage of apparently authentic and identity-relevant values and beliefs, as an emotional support during periods of organizational change.
>
> (Brown & Humphreys, 2002: 141)

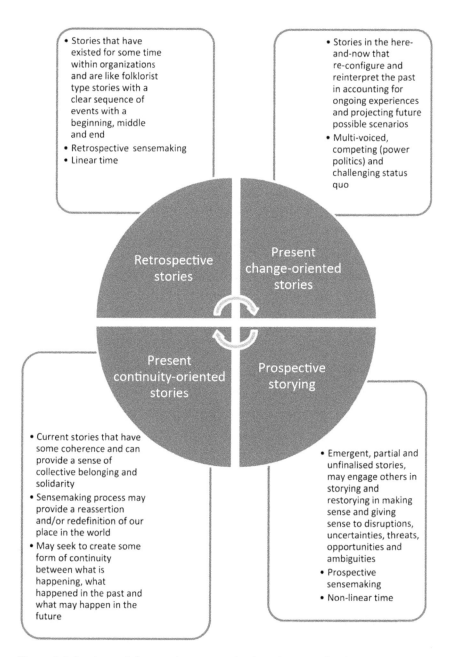

- Stories that have existed for some time within organizations and are like folklorist type stories with a clear sequence of events with a beginning, middle and end
- Retrospective sensemaking
- Linear time

- Stories in the here-and-now that re-configure and reinterpret the past in accounting for ongoing experiences and projecting future possible scenarios
- Multi-voiced, competing (power politics) and challenging status quo

Retrospective stories

Present change-oriented stories

Present continuity-oriented stories

Prospective storying

- Current stories that have some coherence and can provide a sense of collective belonging and solidarity
- Sensemaking process may provide a reassertion and/or redefinition of our place in the world
- May seek to create some form of continuity between what is happening, what happened in the past and what may happen in the future

- Emergent, partial and unfinalised stories, may engage others in storying and restorying in making sense and giving sense to disruptions, uncertainties, threats, opportunities and ambiguities
- Prospective sensemaking
- Non-linear time

Figure 8.1 Stories and the storying process in changing organizations

Source: Dawson & McLean, 2013: 203

Both studies draw on the work of Gabriel (1993: 121), who views nostalgia as a 'state arising out of present conditions as much as out of the past', and Strangleman also draws on Munro (1998), who identifies nostalgia as providing a sense of attachment through a heightened sense of belongingness (Strangleman, 1999: 727). He concludes that whereas nostalgia may provide memorial security for employees (through collective sensemaking), it can also be actively used by management to instill a sense of insecurity, noting,

> The past, recent or distant, becomes an object of manipulation in a far more active sense. A past that has been experienced as being positive can be rubbished or dismissed, replaced by a vision of the future that can barrow from another past, importantly one not experienced by the workforce themselves.
>
> (Strangleman, 1999: 742)

Both these studies usefully illustrate not only how the past informs present sensemaking through nostalgia but also the 'importance of nostalgia as a strategy of resistance' (Brown & Humphreys, 2002: 156) as well as an 'active tool in the hands of management' (Strangleman, 1999: 742). Times lived are not set but open to manipulation and political power plays in repositioning what was and in steering pathways to a possible future that not yet realized is presented as realizable to influence the sensemaking and sensegiving in the present.

Conclusion

> Narratives are ubiquitous symbols that are prevalent in all organizations. Also referred to as stories, scripts, myths, legends and sagas, narratives are accounts of events, usually developed chronologically and sequentially to indicate causality. . . . They are the vehicles through which organizational values and beliefs are produced, reproduced, and transformed. They shape organizational meanings through functioning as retrospective sensemaking, serving as premises of arguments and persuasive appeals, acting as implicit mechanisms of social control, and constituting frames of reference for interpreting organizational actions.
>
> (Putnam, Phillips, & Chapman, 1996: 386–387)

In the prescriptive change management literature, formal narratives of change are often constructed for identifying best practice guidelines that construct versions of change based around linear event sequences that present the organization as progressing through a series of stages. These accounts often present the organization and managerial champions of change in a positive light, especially when relaying 'successes' to external observers and wider media outlets. Not unlike the earlier planned change models discussed in Chapter 5, these narratives sanitise the change process in presenting data from which commentators can formulate neat linear prescriptions on how best to manage change. There is a narrative causality—whereby this led to this that caused this—in an uncritical acceptance of a Newtonian temporality in which the polyphony of change is ignored. The widespread acceptance and uptake of this consolidated narrative with temporal linear form in explaining and recounting change is problematic, and we have sought to highlight the implications of this for causal explanations (reinforced through collective sensemaking) and theorization.

In contrast, fine-grained contextual studies concerned with not only the formal accounts of change but with the living stories that emerge and compete during the change process draw attention to multi-vocality, polyphony, and the importance of multilevel interactions in the individual and collective sensemaking that is ongoing. Attention turns to the movement between rich, divergent narratives, in which the motives and actions of the main characters and the sequence of events combine in the construction of consolidated, plotted narratives, and the living, unfinalized stories that also emerge, providing multiple views through finely textured explanations of unfolding change processes. The former are often evident in post hoc rationalizations and formalized accounts of change, whereas the latter are particularly prevalent when change disrupts 'the way we do things around here' and people seek to make sense and give sense to what is going on—with these stories generally competing with more formal accounts. Narrative frictions arise as stories conflict as part of the political process of change and as stakeholders seek to steer the process in certain preferred directions. Power-political processes are played out in the management of meaning and collective understanding through the construction of compelling narratives that far from being neutral, seek to dominate, contest, resist, repudiate, and silence the competing narratives of others.

We have shown how some scholars give attention to different narrative genres, to the characterization of different types of stories (e.g., tragic, comic, and romantic), to stories in organizations as special narrative phenomena, and to emerging, unfinalized story fragments. The assumptions of time and temporality that underscore these perspectives have been critically evaluated with a focus on those that directly address issues of organizational change within the broader field of management studies. What is interesting in all these accounts is the importance of time and temporality as explicitly expressed or in providing an implicit, underlying frame for explaining narrative time and stories in making sense of change. Within completed, causally embedded narratives of change, time permeates through a conventional temporality with a BME, in which timing—in measuring and locating the successive ordering of change events—presents an objective, natural view of time in which the realities of change can be 'truthfully' depicted. From the perspective of lived time—time as subjectively experienced and recalled in stories of change—there is no clear beginning or end but multiple temporalities and differentiated timings in the unfinalized storying that is part of the ongoing processes of change. This dualism takes us back to long-standing debates between category oppositions, such as agency/structure and nature/culture, which are evident in the objective-subjective division. Whereas these categories can be useful in helping us analyse the world around us, they should not be seen as constituting reality. As we explained in our introductory chapter, the objective/subjective divide, whereas analytically useful, also limits understanding and misrepresents time in promoting a separatist ontology. We should also be careful not to impose a Manichean dualism in falsely contrasting a type of Newtonian-naïve-linear-conservative-simplistic-folkloric narrative perspective on the one side and a kind of polyphonic-polysemic-fragmentary-discontinuous-complex-sophisticated storying approach on the other. There is playfulness with time and the temporal flow in structured narratives, but the focus is with event sequences, plots, and characters often in a backward glance (completed retrospective narratives) rather than in the ongoing storying process that seeks to make and give sense prospectively. Storying in times of change is often critical to the contestation of the status quo through vibrant narratives that engage audiences and are highly plausible in the construction of compelling narratives that not only make sense of change but can shape the changes they are describing. As Dawson and Buchanan (2005: 862) conclude,

> When competing narratives discover or are permitted a voice, they can steal through the night on a counter-cultural crusade, exposing the shortcomings of 'official' accounts which may thereby be derailed. These competing narratives may also be informed by future expectations, and as a consequence be open to further modification and revision. The co-existence of multiple accounts of change, competing for the audience's attention and approval, provides insight, and is only deemed problematic in studies that seek to establish a singular 'authentic' account.

In the formal narrative account, there is an attempt to control interpretations, fix temporality, and finalize history, and yet the emerging stories around change compete, disrupt, and open up temporal perspectives. There is no separation or clear divide as our accommodation of conventional time shapes temporal norms that influence the way we see and make sense of what is occurring just as our subjective experiences as conveyed through living stories reconstitutes our temporal perspectives and informs the sense we give to change in the present, living past, and unfinalized futures. The various and competing stories that occur during times of change give attention to the plurality of temporal experiences that are shaped and re-storied in the context of existing power relations. To paraphrase Boje, it is time to set stories free from the prison of chronology, but it is also important to steer clear of any dichotomous framing whilst recognising that the representation of time in physical clocks and the language we use reinforce a sense that time exists and can be objectively measured as well as that the ways in which we understand and make social sense of time reinforces the idea of time being something essential to the nature of human consciousness. Elias (1993) advocates temporal, non-dichotomous framing as a way of lifting us out of the dualisms that dominate Western philosophical thinking and theorization (structuration theory by Giddens (1984) can be seen as one such attempt that highlights the difficulties, especially in moving from more abstract conceptualization to operationalization in empirically based research).

We contend that there is a need to move beyond a representation of time with space as well as a position in which objective time asserts a dominant and compelling narrative over lived subjective time towards non-dualistic considerations that accommodate multiple temporalities. Time as a concept that goes beyond a binary divide between an external (clock-oriented) and inner (conscious-oriented) world towards a rolling together, an interlacing with recurrent processual shaping in which time is not pinned down but opened.

References

Bakhtin, M. M. (1981). *The Dialogic Imagination*. Austin: Austin University of Texas Press.

Barad, K. (2007). *Meeting the Universe Halfway: Quantum Physics and the Entanglement of Matter and Meaning*. London: Duke University Press.

Beech, N., MacPhail, S. A., & Coupland, C. (2009). Anti-dialogic positioning in change stories: Bank robbers, saviours and peons. *Organization, 16*(3), 335–352. doi: 10.1177/1350508409102299

Benjamin, W. (1968). The storyteller: Reflections on the works of Nikolai Leskov. In H. Arendt (Ed.), *Walter Benjamin: Illuminations* (pp. 83–109). London: Jonathan Cape.

Bergson, H. (1913). *Time and Free Will: An Essay on the Immediate Data of Consciousness*. London: George Allen & Company.

Boje, D. M. (1991). The storytelling organization: a study of story performance in an office-supply firm. *Administrative Science Quarterly, 36*(1), 106–126.

Boje, D. M. (1995). Stories of the storytelling organization: A postmodern analysis of Disney as "*Tamara*-Land". *Academy of Management Journal, 38*(4), 997–1035.

Boje, D. M. (2001). *Narrative Methods for Organizational and Communication Research*. London: Sage.

Boje, D. M. (2006). Breaking out of narrative's prison: Improper story in storytelling organization. *Storytelling, Self, Society: An Interdisciplinary Journal of Storytelling Studies, 2*(2), 28–49.

Boje, D. M. (2008). *Storytelling Organizations*. London: Sage.

Boje, D. M. (2009). Forward by David Boje. In A. L. M. Adorisio (Ed.), *Storytelling in Organizations: From Theory to Empirical Research* (pp. x–xii). New York: Palgrave Macmillan.

Boje, D. M. (Ed.). (2011). *Storytelling and the Future of Organizations: An Antenarrative Handbook*. London: Routledge.

Boje, D. M. (2012). Reflections: What does quantum physics of storytelling mean for change management? *Journal of Change Management, 12*(3), 253–271.

Boje, D. M., Hayley, U., & Saylors, R. (2015). Antenarratives of organizational change: The microstoria of Burger King's storytelling in space, time and strategic context. *Human Relations, 69*(2), 1–28.

Brown, A. D., Colville, I., & Pye, A. (2015). Making sense of sensemaking in organization studies. *Organization Studies, 35*(2), 265–277.

Brown, A. D., Gabriel, Y., & Gherardi, S. (2009). Storytelling and change: An unfolding story. *Organization, 16*(3), 323–333.

Brown, A. D., & Humphreys, M. (2002). Nostalgia and the narrativization of identity: A Turkish case study. *British Journal of Management, 13*(2), 141–159.

Brown, A. D., & Humphreys, M. (2006). Organizational identity and place: A discursive exploration of hegemony and resistance. *Journal of Management Studies, 43*(2), 231–257.

Brown, M., & Kreps, G. L. (1993). Narrative analysis and organizational development. In S. L. Herndon & G. L. Kreps (Eds.), *Qualitative Research: Applications in Organizational Communication* (pp. 47–62). Creskill, NJ: Hampton Press.

Bruner, J. S. (1986). *Actual Minds, Possible Worlds.* Cambridge: Harvard University Press.

Buchanan, D. A., & Dawson, P. (2007). Discourse and audience: Organizational change as multi-story process. *Journal of Management Studies, 44*(5), 669–686.

Collins, D., & Rainwater, K. (2005). Managing change at Sears: A sideways look at a tale of corporate transformation. *Journal of Organizational Change Management, 18*(1), 16–30. doi: 10.1108/09534810510579823

Czarniawska, B. (1998). *A Narrative Approach to Organization Studies.* Thousand Oaks, CA: Sage.

Czarniawska, B., & Sevón, G. (Eds.). (1996). *Translating Organizational Change.* Berlin: Walter de Gruyter.

Dawson, P., & Buchanan, D. A. (2005). The way it really happened: Competing narratives in the political process of technological change. *Human Relations, 58*(7), 845–865. doi: 10.1177/0018726705057807

Dawson, P., & Buchanan, D. A. (2012). The way it really happened: Competing narratives in the political process of technological change. In S. Clegg & M. Haugaard (Eds.), *Power and Organizations* (pp. 845–864). London: Sage.

Dawson, P., & McLean, P. (2013). Miner's tales: Stories and the storying process for understanding the collective sensemaking of employees during contested change. *Group & Organization Management: An International Journal, 38*(2), 198–229.

Deleuze, G. (1994). *Difference and Repetition.* New York: Columbia University Press.

Downing, S. J. (1997). Learning the plot: Emotional momentum in search of dramatic logic. *Management Learning, 28*(1), 27–44. doi: 10.1177/1350507697281003

Driver, M. (2009). From loss to lack: Stories of organizational change as encounters with failed fantasies of self, work and organization. *Organization, 16*(3), 353–369. doi: 10.1177/1350508409102300

Elias, N. (1993). *Time: An Essay.* Oxford: Blackwell Publishing.

Emirbayer, M., & Mische, A. (1998). What is agency? *American Journal of Sociology, 103*(4), 962–1034.

Gabriel, Y. (1993). Organizational nostalgia: Reflections on 'the golden age'. In S. Fineman (Ed.), *Emotion in Organizations* (pp. 118–141). London: Sage.

Gabriel, Y. (2000). *Storytelling in Organizations: Facts, Fictions, and Fantasies.* Oxford: Oxford University Press.

Gabriel, Y. (Ed.). (2004). *Myths, Stories, and Organizations: Premodern Narratives for Our Times.* Oxford: Oxford University Press.

Giddens, A. (1984). *The Constitution of Society—Outline of the Theory of Structuration.* Cambridge: Polity Press.

Gioia, D. A., & Chittipeddi, K. (1991). Sensemaking and sensegiving in strategic change initiation. *Strategic Management Journal, 12*(6), 433–448.

Hayley, U., & Boje, D. M. (2014). Storytelling the internationalization of the multinational enterprise. *Journal of International Business Studies, 45*(9), 1115–1132.

Heidegger, M. (1996). *Being and Time* (J. Stambaugh, Trans.). Albany, NY: State University of New York Press.

Humphreys, M., & Brown, A. D. (2002). Narratives of organizational identity and identification: A case study of hegemony and resistance. *Organization Studies, 23*(3), 421–447. doi: 10.1177/0170840602233005

Humphreys, M., & Brown, A. D. (2008). An analysis of corporate social responsibility at credit line: A narrative approach. *Journal of Business Ethics, 80*, 403–418.

Kaplan, S., & Orlikowski, W. J. (2013). Temporal work in strategy making. *Organization Science, 24*(4), 965–995.

Kostera, M. (2002). Book review: Storytelling in organizations. *Human Relations, 55*(6), 728–734.

Mead, G. H. (1932/1980). *The Philosophy of the Present*. Chicago and London: The University of Chicago Press.

Morson, G. A. (1994). *Narrative and Freedom: The Shadows of Time*. New Haven, CT: Yale University Press.

Munro, R. (1998). Belonging to the move: Market rhetoric and the future as obligatory passage. *Sociological Review, 46*, 208–243.

Murgia, A., & Poggio, B. (2009). Challenging hegemonic masculinities: Men's stories on gender culture in organizations. *Organization, 16*(3), 407–423. doi: 10.1177/1350508409102303

Pedersen, A. R. (2009). Moving away from chronological time: Introducing the shadows of time and chronotopes as new understandings of 'narrative time'. *Organization, 16*(3), 389–406. doi: 10.1177/1350508409102302

Peirano-Vejo, M. E., & Stablein, R. E. (2009). Constituting change and stability: Sense-making stories in a farming organization. *Organization, 16*(3), 443–462. doi: 10.1177/1350508409102306

Putnam, L., Phillips, N., & Chapman, P. (1996). Metaphors of communication and organization. In S. R. Clegg, C. Hardy, & W. R. Nord (Eds.), *The Handbook of Organizational Studies* (pp. 375–408). London: Sage.

Reissner, S. C. (2008). *Narratives of Organisational Change and Learning: Making Sense of Testing Times*. Cheltenham: Edward Elgar.

Rhodes, C., & Brown, A. D. (2005). Narrative, organizations and research. *International Journal of Management Reviews, 7*(3), 167–188.

Ricoeur, P. (1984). *Time and Narrative* (K. Blamey & D. Pellauer, Trans.). Chicago: University of Chicago Press.

Simpson, B. (2014). George Herbert Mead. In J. Helin, T. Hernes, D. Hjorth, & R. Holt (Eds.), *Oxford Handbook of Process Philosophy and Organization Studies* (pp. 272–286). Oxford: Oxford University Press.

Sims, D., Huxham, C., & Beech, N. (2009). On telling stories but hearing snippets: Sense-taking from presentations of practice. *Organization, 16*(3), 371–388. doi: 10.1177/1350508409102301

Strangleman, T. (1999). The nostalgia of organisations and the organisation of nostalgia: Past and present in the contemporary railway industry. *Sociology, 33*(4), 725–746.

Weick, K. E. (1979). *The Social Psychology of Organizing*. Reading, MA: Addison-Wesley.

Weick, K. E. (1995). *Sensemaking in Organizations*. Thousand Oaks, CA: Sage.

Weick, K. E., Sutcliffe, K., & Obstfeld, D. (2005). Organizing and the process of sensemaking. *Organization Science, 16*(4), 409–421.

Whittle, A., Mueller, F., & Mangan, A. (2009). Storytelling and 'character': Victims, villains and heroes in a case of technological change. *Organization, 16*(3), 425–442. doi: 10.1177/1350508409102305

Wiebe, E. (2010). Temporal sensemaking: Managers' use of time to frame organizational change. In T. Hernes & S. Maitlis (Eds.), *Process, Sensemaking and Organizing* (pp. 213–241). Oxford: Oxford University Press.

9 Process Studies in Organizations
Digging in the Field

The next two chapters are dedicated to examining process perspectives on time in the field of organization studies and management. There has been a growing interest among organization scholars with processual and relational perspectives that move away from linear sequenced models for understanding change in organizations. Accompanying this shift there has been a movement away from using terms such as organization, change, and strategy to the more active verbs of organizing, changing, and strategizing, in which emergence, non-linearity, and notions of becoming start to take the fore in academic discussions and theoretical debates. In this first chapter our attention is given to processual research on organizational change and the empirical practice of studying change as it happens (longitudinal fieldwork studies) that requires the researcher to operationalize broader concepts and abstract ideas in study design, data collection, analysis, and write-up. The second process chapter examines the more abstract, theoretical, and conceptual debates around process organization studies. We suggest that many of the interesting questions, debates, and controversies lie at the intersection between broader theorization of changing and empirical engagement with people's experiences of ongoing change processes in organizations. We contend that even among process theorists (who draw on the insights from philosophers such as, Bergson, Whitehead, Mead, and James) and processual fieldworkers (who engage in detailed longitudinal studies of change), there is a lack of conceptual clarity around time and temporality, with a tendency to return to the long-standing debate between flux and fixity. Although we do not agree with the claim made by Weick and Quinn (1999: 363) that this 'may suggest a certain torpor in the intellectual life of scholars of change', it does suggest the need for greater attention to be given to time and temporality as it relates to the more abstract and empirically based process studies of changing organizations.

Early Studies on Workplace Change and the Building of a Process Perspective

Early process studies on workplace change include Dalton's (1959) study of the changing alliances, power plays, and the purposeful management of information by cliques in pursuit of advantages over others and Gouldner's

(1965) analysis of the dynamics of management-worker interaction and the influence of social processes during a succession of bargaining incidents. Roy's (1952) study on the process of quota restriction and goldbricking in a machine shop, conducted from November 1944 to August 1945, is a particularly good example. He illustrates the process by which operators met their quota for 'gravy jobs' then 'knocked off', adjusting the imposed disciplined time schedules of management and working towards their own time. Time was used to regulate and control expected output, but resistance to these imposed expectations occurred in a number of ways, including deliberately restricting output on jobs they considered 'stinkers'. In this way workers sought to manage their use of time outside the prescribed schedules to maintain earnings at a level that required less time effort than would be required under the formal regulations associated with jobs (i.e., the hourly production piecework rates). This entailed ensuring that the rates for 'gravy jobs' were not lost whilst engaging in work behaviours that would encourage the reconsideration of rates for 'stinkers'. As a fellow worker advised (Roy, 1952: 316), 'Don't let it go over $1.25 an hour, or the time-study man will be right down here!' As Elger indicates, many of these early empirical studies can be broadly placed within a processual school as they are concerned with transforming processes brought about through 'negotiations and interpretation among participants with diverse interests and resources' (Elger, 1975: 114). He argues how many of these early studies are too quickly ignored and misunderstood in the light of summaries and evaluations made at the time and since with little interest in reading the original work. For example, although the studies of Woodward (1980) are often used as the epitome of technological determinism (associated with contingency theory), he suggests that her case studies actually draw attention towards ongoing processes in which management ideology, established rhetorics, and political manoeuvring all serve to influence change outcomes. Similarly, in detailing the work of Burns and Stalker (1961), Elger (1975: 109) argues that whereas a systems typology is their starting point, 'they develop, in relation to a rich array of empirical materials, a processual analysis which treats actors' allegiances, perspectives and strategies as problematic features of organizational action'.

Undoubtedly structure, in terms of control, regulation, and clock time, are key elements running through much of this early work. Productivity and efficiency through time-regulated systems of control are central, but as Child (1972: 2) highlights in his critique of systems orthodoxy, studies were starting to draw attention to the process by which power holders make strategic choices. He highlights the dynamics of structure and agency, arguing that agency and choice are critical in the way that individuals and groups influence the environment (sociopolitical process) rather than simply being constrained (determined) by operational contingencies (Child, 1997: 44). In other words, these early fieldwork studies are processual in their focus on the way individuals and groups actively interpret and negotiate in shaping these processes over time in which outcomes are indeterminate.

Processual Studies on Strategy and Change in Organizations

From these early concerns with sociopolitical processes (Pettigrew, 1973), Pettigrew builds his particular processual approach in his longitudinal study of continuity and change at ICI (Pettigrew, 1985). In this study he views political process as evolving from individuals and groups; for example, interest groups may form and develop different rationalities that direct action and response (whereas a particular rationality may predominate at any one time, this is seen to be open to change). For Pettigrew (1985), change creates tension over the existing distribution of resources through threatening the position of some whilst opening up opportunities for others. As such, change stimulates power plays and heightened political activity. He notes how the greatest political energy is normally released when the decision to change is being made rather than during implementation, when constraints have already been set (Pettigrew, 1985: 43). He also demonstrates how strategic change is a continuous process with no clear beginning or end point and how it often emerges with deep-seated contextual, cultural, and political roots that support the establishment of a dominant ideology.

Pettigrew's watershed study in ICI usefully illustrates how strategic change processes are best understood in context and over time as continuity is often 'a good deal easier to see than change' (Pettigrew, 1985: 439). His research monograph demonstrates the limitations of theories that view change either as a single event or as a discrete series of episodes that can be decontextualized. In a comparative analysis of five cases of strategic change, the study illustrates how change as a continuous, incremental process (evolutionary) can be interspersed with radical periods of change (revolutionary). Major change initiatives are associated with significant changes in business market conditions (such as world economic recessions) in which managers develop active strategies that build on these circumstances to legitimate and justify the need for change. For Pettigrew 'change and continuity, process and structure, are inextricably linked' (1985: 1), and he argues that the intention is not simply to substitute a rational approach with a political process perspective but 'to explore some of the conditions in which mixtures of these occur' (1985: 24). He also notes how empirical findings and theoretical developments are generally 'method-bound' and how studies on organizational change have tended to adopt the planned stage model approach of OD. Pettigrew is highly critical of such approaches to change, which are seen to ignore the importance of *changing*. As he states (1985: 15),

> For as long as we continue to conduct research on change which is ahistorical, acontextual, and aprocessual, which continues to treat the change programme as the unit of analysis and regard change as an episode divorced from the immediate and more distant context in which it is embedded, then we will continue to develop inadequate descriptive

theories of change which are ill-composed guides for action. Indeed as I have implied already there is still a dearth of studies which can make statements about the how and why of change, about the processual dynamics of change, in short which go beyond the analysis of *change* and being to theorise about *changing*.

This call for using the terms 'organizing' and 'strategizing' (verbs) in preference to the terms 'organization' and 'strategy' (nouns) has been taken up by process organization theorists (Chia, 2013; Langley & Tsoukas, 2010) as they are seen to more usefully capture the dynamic nature of processes of change (see Pettigrew et al., 2003). In drawing on longitudinal contextual data (between 1975 and 1983, 134 people were interviewed), Pettigrew examines the interplay between internal contextual variables of culture, history, and political process with external business conditions as factors that maintain continuity or bring about change. In providing a holistic contextual analysis, the approach provides, first, a vertical analysis through examining factors such as external socioeconomic influences on internal group behaviour and, second, a horizontal analysis, for example, in studying changing organizations with a past, present, and future. In multilevel theory construction, attention is given to the way contextual variables in the vertical analysis link to those examined in horizontal analysis and to how processes both shape and constrain structures (Pettigrew, 1985: 37).

The five essential needs of processual analysis are seen to comprise, first, the need to study changes in their context, or what is referred to as 'embeddedness' (Pettigrew, 1997: 340); second, to study change over time and to identify the timing and sequencing of events; third, the need to recognise that context and action are always tangled together or, in Pettigrew's (1997: 341) words, 'context is not just a stimulus environment but a nested arrangement of structures and processes where the subjective interpretations of actors perceiving, learning, and remembering help shape process'; fourth, the need to identify patterns and interrelated links among a range of features; and fifth, the value of examining outcomes in comparative case settings to explore how context and process explain divergence in outcomes. These five assumptions of embeddedness, temporal interconnectedness, intertwining of context and action, holistic explanation, and the use of outcomes as a focus for processual analysis are seen to guide the researcher towards the case write-up as an 'analytical chronology' in which patterns in the data are identified and clarified (Pettigrew, 1997: 346). Emphasis is placed on comparative analysis with the goal of achieving broader thematic writing through 'meta level analysis and presentation'. The central aim is to weave an argument that constantly moves from the general to the particular in 'linking the theoretical and empirical findings across cases to wider bodies of literature' (Pettigrew, 1997: 346).

Underlying this explanation of fieldwork studies and processual analysis are a number of time-related features, both explicitly stated and implicit within broader concepts. Pettigrew clearly indicates that continuity is more in evidence than change during his 10-year study of ICI and that whereas shifts in context should be accommodated, the way routine practices and behaviours become embedded within organizations can serve to constrain change. In common with other change scholars, he argues change is conceptualized as a movement from current ways of doing things to some new, novel, or changed way of doing things. A conventional concept of time underpins this approach in which change represents movement to some new form over time and continuity represents things remaining the same over time. Pettigrew recognises the dynamics of continuous change and is here referring to patterns of similar practices and behaviours recurring over time as opposed to significant intervention and reconfiguring of the way things are done. In his notion of temporal interconnectedness, Pettigrew draws explicit attention to examining changing organizations not simply in relation to a 'now' moment but 'in flight' with a past, present, and future (Pettigrew, 1985). Culture, history, and political process are all seen to influence internal behaviour and strategizing; there is a temporality that cannot and should not be ignored. This horizontal temporal analysis is linked with a vertical analysis with external business and socioeconomic influences on internal behaviours in demonstrating how 'processes are both constrained by structures and shape structures . . . both in catching reality in flight and in embeddedness' (Pettigrew, 1985: 37).

In the intertwining of context and action, Pettigrew returns to the agency issues raised by Child (1972, 1997), arguing that context can both enable and constrain change; for example, contentment with the way things are, lack of commercial pressure, general absence of strategic thinking, and senior management leadership are all identified by Pettigrew as contextual factors constraining change. This intertwining is seen to continue over time in which the researcher needs to be contextually and analytically aware in identifying patterns and interrelated links that can be used to explain processes of change and continuity. The final focus on outcomes (and preferably comparative outcomes) stems from the need to more fully substantiate findings by exploring why the changing contextual conditions experienced by one organization compared to another produces similar or dissimilar outcomes. Once again conventional conceptions of time are used in examining the past, in delineating outcomes at a certain point of time (whilst recognising that change is continuous), and in accommodating projected and desired futures. Pettigrew has been concerned with the sociopolitical processes of strategic change through an holistic processual-contextualist approach in which the present can only be fully understood in the context of the past and the future. Conventional notions of time are used, and this maps onto a Westernized understanding of temporality (which as we shall see in the next chapter does not align with more abstract conceptions arising from more recent debates in process organization studies).

In his book *Organizational Change: A Processual Approach*, Dawson (1994) builds on research in industrial sociology and technology studies (see

Dawson, 1996) including the work of Whyte (1955; 1984), Child (1972), Friedman (1977), Pettigrew (1985), Rothwell and Zegveld (1985), and Clark, McLoughlin, Rose, and King (1988) as well as labour process theory (see, e.g., Knights & Willmott, 1988) in developing a process approach to change. This framework is empirically based on a series of in-depth longitudinal fieldwork studies. The focus is on examining processes of change as they unfold over time through spending long periods of time in the workplace observing, discussing, and interviewing employees at all hierarchical levels and spending time outside of the work setting in social situations. A range of change interventions were reported in the book, including the computerization of freight operations at British Rail; the reconfiguration of work arrangements at General Motors; and the introduction of just-in-time (JIT) management at Hewlett Packard. Since then, these and a host of other studies have been conducted (see, e.g., Daniel & Dawson, 2011; Dawson, 2003; Dawson & Palmer, 1995; Dawson, Sykes, McLean, Zanko, & Marciano, 2014; Dawson & Zanko, 2009; Farmer, Dawson, Thomson, & Tucker, 2007) and used in the further development and refinement of a processual perspective (Dawson, 2013, 2014a).

The perspective has developed from an early contextual concern with the influence of power and politics in shaping processes of change that sought to counter outcome approaches that posit change as determined by the impact of technology (technological determinism) (Dawson, 1994); towards an interest in the polyphony and multi-vocality of change in trying to capture, compare, and contrast not only the formal narratives of change but the contested stories and silenced voices (Dawson & Buchanan, 2012; Dawson & McLean, 2013) in, for example, viewing change as a multi-story process (Buchanan & Dawson, 2007) and in examining the way stories can present new pathways not previously considered (Dawson et al., 2014); and more recently, to a concern with time and temporality for theorizing change (Dawson, 2014a) and for engaging in longitudinal fieldwork studies of change in organizations (Dawson, 2013, 2014b). In an attempt to summarize this approach Dawson states:

> Processual research on change can be defined as the contextual, retrospective and real-time study of change as-it-happens over time through the observed, documented and lived experiences of people as they seek to make sense and give sense individually and collectively to decision and non-decision making activities, the actions and torpidity of others, the multiple stories that transform and compete over time, and the events and critical incidents that occur in expected and unexpected ways. The research is interested in the formal documented accounts, post hoc rationalizations and official versions of events, as well as in revealing the emergent, complex, muddied and unforeseen processes of change. It is interested in capturing attitudes and perceptions at all levels within the organization, from senior managers to operational employees

as well as various key stakeholders, such as consultants, change agents and trade-union officials. Fieldwork is intensive, detailed and longitudinal employing a range of data collection techniques to capture and analyse subjective experience, chronicle sequences of events, examine and interpret documented material, and observe behaviours and daily practices. The approach seeks to accommodate dominant narratives as well as the multiple conflicting stories and outlier or deviant views that co-exist and shift over time in trying to uncover the full range of experiences that includes the 'dominant' 'common', 'hidden' and 'silenced' voices on change

(Buchanan and Dawson, 2007: 681)

The process of change is conceptualized as a complex, ongoing dynamic in which three interrelated clusters are identified comprising the politics (internal and external), context (external and internal including culture and history), and the substance of change (which includes the content, scale, and scope of change). Each of these unbounded dynamic elements are seen to be in continual flux, ever changing as processes continue ad infinitum (time is implicitly conceptualized as ongoing). Essentially there is a continual interplay within and across these interrelated elements during ongoing processes of change. As with Pettigrew (1985) the temporal dimension to this approach is central; however as explained in the following section, more consideration is given to time and temporality, especially as it relates to the tensions between the practicalities of fieldwork studies and process theorization.

Time and the Practicalities of Doing Extended Fieldwork Studies

In considering the practicalities of doing extended case studies on processes of change, conventional notions of time (chronological, objective time) are used in the design and planning of processual fieldwork and in aligning activities with the requirements and needs of formal funding bodies. In collecting data and maintaining observation notes on incidents and key turning points, event time provides a useful organizing frame for locating and analysing data. In other words, time as an objective measurement can be used to document the intervals between activities, the duration of events, and the sequencing that occurs as change progresses forward in time. Recording events as they happen through observation enables the researcher to build up a sequence of what occurred in what order that may or may not align with formal documentation. Conventional time is also used in arranging familiarisation visits and scheduling observations and interviews to ensure that data are collected prior to the implementation of change and during implementation (the researcher may also plan for further observational work, follow-up interviews, and group discussions). Once the changes are complete, a further set of interviews and observations can be scheduled to take place. Following this type of format, data could be initially located under the general periods of before, during, and after change, comprising the following:

- The initial conception of a need to change
- The process of organizational change
- Operation of new work practices and procedures

These three general time frames provide useful starting points from which to begin a detailed examination of change. Although every major change program will have an organizationally defined BME, in practice it is not only difficult to identify the start and completion of change programs (e.g., there is often more than one organizational history of change, and these may be reconstructed over time) but also to explain the complex pathways and routes to establishing new operational processes. Therefore, in examining the complex dynamic processes of organizational change, there are considerable returns to be gained from developing a framework for data analyses. It is argued here that a useful way of tackling the problem of analysing complex change data is to construct data categories either around themes, groups of employees, time frames, or the various activities and tasks associated with change. For example, data categories for the activities associated with the establishment of new organizational arrangements may comprise system selection, identification of type of change, implementation, preparation and planning, and search and assessment. These tasks do not occur in a tidy linear fashion (change is a non-linear process) and will normally overlap, occur simultaneously, stop and start, and be part of the initial and later phases of major change programs. Nevertheless, they are useful for locating and sorting data on change that might otherwise be too complex to deal with systematically. Although at a more general level, there can be no definitive list of appropriate data categories, as these should be modified or revised to fit particular case examples and/or the characteristics of different change programs, task-oriented or thematic categories can provide a useful starting point for locating and analysing complex change data.

The research follows a natural flow of time from the beginning of a study to the final write-up of results that can be marked by dates on a calendar. In organizational settings, the measurement of time through the use of clocks, cycles of activities, and predictable and unpredictable events is all part of the work experience. Activities can be regularised, planned, and coordinated, meetings scheduled, and objectives set for defined periods of time. However, variations in individual and shared understanding of time occur across contexts and over time, and this is highlighted in close observational work through ongoing discussions and involvement where more subjective and less conventional modes of temporality emerge. This is most noticeable in the way that current interpretations of the world are influenced by changing interpretations of the past and expectations of the future. From this perspective, our understanding of time is not bounded by a particular moment but is part of a broader temporality in which the past, present, and future shape each other.

Conceptually our linear notion of time that is practically useful in organizing fieldwork does not accommodate a more process-oriented view of the world in which individuals and groups experience and make sense of change in organizations. The recall of the past is rarely uncontentious, with different groups and individuals reinterpreting key events in different ways (asynchronous subjective time) and with the consequent emergence of competing accounts that often seek to gain purchase and dominance (this is the way it really happened). The past is relived in the present just as expected future scenarios can influence our current understanding and sense of the world around us. These subjectivities of human experience all highlight the non-linearity of lived time and the importance of context to the processual approach. As such, interpreting the actions and events around people at work requires the researcher to construct a reading of the intersubjective meanings of actors involved in enactment. Change processes are experienced differently, and as such their temporal qualities as they are expressed through first-order concepts (thick descriptions) extend beyond any atomistic measurement of time, even prior to any attempt for second-order conceptualization (see Van Maanen, 1979: 540). This highlights the need for subjective concepts of time that can be used to explain the non-linearity of change processes as experienced by individuals and groups as well as drawing attention to the way that objective time is used by organizations not only to plan, measure, and evaluate change processes but also by processual researchers in structuring their fieldwork activities.

At the crux of these tensions is the need to schedule fieldwork whilst also engaging in research that enables sense to be made of emergent forms in recursive, non-linear processes that need to be examined to gain insight and understanding of people's lived experiences of change (e.g., to accommodate the fluidity, flux, and movement not only in forward dynamic momentum but also in the way in which the past is re-presented in the present to shape a future that has yet to happen). Chronological time thereby interlocks and overlaps with individual and social (collective) dimensions of time. It provides an important temporal perspective that enables the researcher to capture documented event time in being able to locate key events or critical turning points. Empirically there is value in this concept as it allows for categorization and analysis of the documented timing of events and the formal plans and justifications for change. Strategy, timelines, training schedules, purchasing of equipment, financial expectations, and the rationale and objectives of change may all be described in varying degrees of detail. Broader contextual data that are concerned with the lived experience and meanings ascribed to change processes are also required in which more subjective conceptions of time come into play. Temporality and how to interpret and present the dynamics of lived experience that consist of retrospective and prospective sensemaking (actors interpreting the present from an understanding of the past and expectations of the future) and that change over time (by actors as well as the researchers own interpretations of the interpretations of others) during the life of the research or through reflective ethnographic revisits (Burawoy, 2003) all draw attention to time as an integral issue in empirically based studies of organizations changing.

On issues of temporality and processual research, Tuttle (1997) usefully spotlights how temporal orientations can vary, for example, between the researcher and those being studied; whereas Orton (1997) calls attention to the need for improvisation whilst doing the research and issues of flexibility in being able to modify design intentions and to be open to multiple accounts in an ongoing iteration between theory and data. In a reflective piece on processual research, Pettigrew (2012: 1305) argues that temporality and embeddedness are reciprocal in that what has happened in the past will always influence the emerging future, highlighting how trying to understand the relationships among context, process, and outcomes will always be a major challenge for the process researcher (Pettigrew, 2012: 1315). In tackling these complex dynamics, Langley (1999) argues for the use of temporal bracketing to enable data to be temporally decomposed into successive adjacent periods. Under this technique, data can be analysed in phases to describe linear evolving patterns (temporal brackets generally unfold sequentially over time), whereas contextual data can also be analysed to examine mutual shaping processes, which Langley claims works well with dynamic, non-linear processual approaches (Langley, 1999: 703). She and her colleagues claim: 'The power of temporal bracketing actually lies principally in its capacity to enable the identification of specific theoretical mechanisms recurring over time' (Langley, Smallman, Tsoukas, & Van de Ven, 2013: 7). Buchanan and Denyer (2013) also advocate the benefits of temporal bracketing as a bridging strategy for processual research that supports explanations that are temporally sensitive. Essentially, the researcher needs to be able to deal with the paradox of time and the juxtapositions that arise between observed events, documents, and interviews at one period of time when compared and contrasted with data collected at different periods of time.

Dawson (2014b) puts forward a facilitating frame to encourage greater temporal awareness and the development of practices that deal with and manage conflicting concepts of time in use and to aid in the understanding of temporal merging both as it occurs in the data and as relayed in case study presentations. The three overlapping concepts advocated comprise, first, 'temporal awareness', which centres on foregrounding awareness of multiple conceptions of time and of the interplay of multiple temporalities whilst also being aware of self-conceptions of time and temporality as a field researcher and academic; second, 'temporal practices', which refers to the process by which the researcher builds and refines their own knowledge and experience in applying and using different conceptions of time throughout the research process; and third, 'temporal merging', which is used to refer to the interweaving of time and temporal conceptions, such as objective and subjective concepts of time, and to the way that past recollections and prospective futures can serve to shape human experience of the present.

These three concepts of temporal merging in being able to accommodate the entanglement of clock time, event time, and social time, temporal practices in being able to use different time conceptions without trying to resolve them during the collection and analyses of data, and temporal awareness in being able to accept the paradox of time in the use of a relational-temporal perspective provide a framework for dealing with the tensions that arise in moving from broader philosophical abstractions to operationalizing concepts in the pragmatics of engaging in longitudinal fieldwork studies and analysing data on changing organizations. On this issue of temporal understanding, Langley and Tsoukas argue that organizations should not be viewed as 'things made' but as processes 'in the making' (2010: 1). Their interest lies in the complex processes by which events take place or entities are constructed (the interactive processes of people at work that are continually reconstituted over time), in the unfolding of events and activities and in the interpretations and choices that people make over time (see also Mohr, 1982: 41–59), and on narrative understanding, where the emphasis is on context and temporality in examining plots, characters, and events in developing plausible explanations of occurrences (Langley & Tsoukas, 2010: 1–18). They argue that there is a need for process researchers to consider alternative templates (multiple narratives of explanation) that encourage a 'form of process theorizing that emphasizes meaning' and not just patterns.

Temporalities of Changing as a Multi-Story Process

In taking up the search for alternative templates in examining multiple narratives and process theorizing that emphasise meaning, Buchanan and Dawson (2007) draw attention to the way multiple meanings and interpretations of change are used to not only make sense and give sense to change but also to authenticate particular versions of change in reasserting power relationships and in seeking to legitimate decision-making processes. Dawson and Buchanan (2005, 2012) use the concept of multiple narratives in a critique of linear single accounts of change where clock time is linked to event sequences. In empirical illustrations of the power plays that occur as multiple versions of events that compete over time (the temporality of before, during, and after change), they highlight the multiple interpretive frames that are utilized in organizational struggles. Focus is given to the way stories are constructed to not only give sense to temporal process but also shape the processes they describe in certain preferred directions. The theory-laden nature of dominant narratives come to the fore when such sanitised accounts are taken up by management and used as knowledge to build linear recipes of success that exhibit causal links. In contrast to conventional time-sequenced research narratives that often seek to triangulate data in scripting an account of changes, Dawson and Buchanan (2005: 861–862) argue:

> There will always be a number of competing narratives of technology and change, each offering its own explanation of events and outcomes, framing a potentially unique, if local, theory of the technological change process. The temporal dimension to this process also draws our attention to predictive, real-time and retrospective narrations. The tendency has been to focus on narratives at a particular point in time rather than with a more processual analysis of narratives and their influence on change processes. As a vehicle of sensemaking, narratives of technological change are concerned with the way it is going to happen, and the way in which it is (or is not) happening, as well as the way it happened. Written before the fact, pre-implementation, such narratives project event sequences into the future, setting out the story which aims to lead to the desired individual, team, and corporate outcomes. Narratives thus have a peculiar form of causal power, which is temporally 'incorrect', in that current understanding of future events (the predictive narrative) is used as an instrument to bring out intended and preferred future consequences. Authoring a business case for new technology investment is a critical element in shaping that process and the direction of future events.

On this count Knights and Murray (1994), in adopting a political processual perspective, are critical of Pettigrew's (1985) ready acceptance of the strategies of management. They point out how practitioners often construct accounts that present their strategy for change as unnegotiable and inevitable given their account of, for example, the competitive risk of externalities that they characterize in a particular way. Managements' coherent and robust story is a power-infused construction that seeks to not only predict a necessary future but also to make that future a reality. As Dawson and Buchanan (2005) spotlight, change narratives are generally constructed with a particular audience in mind and often present linear time-sequenced accounts with inbuilt causality (we need to do this to solve this, then if we do this, we can achieve this) that shape organizational meanings through prospective and retrospective sensemaking devices with persuasive appeals (Putnam et al., 1996: 386–387). These accounts link antecedent (or antecedents) with action (or a sequence of events or a process) leading to a consequence (or pattern of action) and are theory-laden expressing causal relationships providing an explanation (Dawson & Buchanan, 2005: 850). They illustrate the value of exposing and unpacking simple, causal, time-sequenced accounts by using more temporally sensitive, process-contextual analysis (Langley, 1999; Pentland, 1999). They also illustrate the importance of retrospective accounts and the temporal shifting that can occur as these are modified, redefined, or replaced over time (Dawson and Buchanan, 2005: 862):

> After-the-event accounts are also important. The evaluations of technology projects may further influence strategic decision-making and are likely to reflect political processes in which certain 'voices' get heard, while others are silenced or hidden. Unless these accounts are proactively maintained, they are likely to be modified, redefined or replaced over time as other competing accounts emerge. When competing narratives discover or are permitted a voice, they can steal through the night on a counter-cultural crusade, exposing the shortcomings of 'official' accounts which may thereby be derailed. These competing narratives may also be informed by future expectations, and as a consequence be open to further modification and revision.

In building on this work and combining ideas from narrative and processual perspectives, Buchanan and Dawson (2007) set out to critically examine change as a multi-authored and multi-story process. Their main temporal interest is in the way retrospectives accounts and stories of the present (ongoing change) are themselves open to continuous modification and reconstruction as they seek to steer the processes they describe in telling stories constructed for a particular target audience. They identify four overlapping conflicts of interest that comprise, first, 'conflicts of attribution', where different explanations with embedded causality seek to gain legitimation as *the real* version of events, such as in public inquiries into disaster events that set out to present an accurate, coherent, and authoritative account that resolves the multi-vocal, conflicting, and fragmented versions that often arise from such incidents (see Brown, 2004: 96). Second are 'conflicts of assessment', both in terms of quantifiable metrics and subjective responses; for example, Buchanan (2000) illustrates how some of the evaluations of change at Leicester Royal Infirmary saw the initiative as a great success, whereas others deemed it a failure presenting conflicting financial cost-benefit figures to substantiate their claims. Third are 'conflicts of interpretation' between different stakeholder groups; Dawson and McLean (2013) provide a clear example of this between overground management and underground miners in their study of change at a colliery in Australia. Fourth are 'conflicts of audience' in which stories are reconstructed to meet the expectations of different audiences, and whereas these stories may conflict in narrative terms, they make sense politically.

In then drawing on Deetz's (1996) 'dimensions of contrast' in sources of ideas and concepts between, on the one dimension, the difference between those emerging from dialogue with respondents (local/emergent) or those arising from pre-established theoretical orientation (elite/*a priori*), to a second dimension, where the difference is between a focus on confirmation through research to improve our understanding of a dominant social discourse to one where the primary aim is to expose some of the problems and conflicts that need uncovering within the dominant discourse. Buchanan and Dawson (2007: 678–680) apply this frame to their conflicting accounts of change in capturing different orientations by researchers seeking to theorize and explain change processes. For example, an interpretive discourse moves away from single-event sequenced accounts as conflicts of assessment, attribution, audience, and interpretation are taken for granted, whereas a critical discourse is interested in exposing the way social practices and institutional structures create and sustain power differences, disenfranchising and silencing the voices of others who may attempt to resist such domination. In a dialogic or postmodern discourse, there is no single coherent reality or truth as the polyphony of change is part of the world we live in that is continually reconstituted through language, whereas in a normative or modern discourse, causal relations through systematic analysis are important in searching out the 'truth' of change (knowledge for further prediction, rationalization, and control) in which all conflicts are resolved in establishing the one accurate account. In developing their approach Buchanan and Dawson (2007: 680) argue 'that narratives of change are *discoursed*, articulated in a particular genre, and *audienced*, to influence a specific readership' (these genres for authoring research narratives are summarized in Table 9.1).

Critical and normative process theories are both interested in conventional clock time. For the normative genre, the calendar and clock provide a time frame codifying practical guidelines in event sequences, whereas for

Table 9.1 Genres and conflicting accounts

Genre	Status of conflicting accounts
Dialogic process theory frustrate truth statements	*Confirmatory*: display the polyvocal nature of social existence, reveal complexity, challenge status quo, confirm fragmentation and lack of coherence in accounts of 'reality'
Critical process theory embarrass power brokers	*Illustrative*: provide further evidence of conflict, struggle, and resistance, expose power differentials, give voice to the silenced and powerless, perpetuate the struggle
Interpretative process theory expose multiple realities	*Anticipated*: access lived experience and individual sensemaking; socially positioned accounts expose the social construction of organizational change phenomena
Normative process theory codify practical guidelines	*Irrelevant*: soft data, unhelpful, confusing, troublesome, unverifiable, uncodifiable, non-cumulative, interesting anecdote only, surgically removable by triangulation

Source: Buchanan and Dawson (2007: 680)

the critical genre, conventional time is used to regulate, control, and exploit labour and to sustain wealth inequalities and maintain unequal power relations in work and society. For the interpretative and dialogic process theorists, polyvocality and the subjective lived experience of time comes to the fore; attention turns to multiple realities and the idea of change as a socially constructed process that arises from the collaborative efforts that unfold over time as participants engage in conversations. For example, Jabri's (2012) dialogical approach adopts a process-relational perspective, arguing 'the need to drive change through an ongoing co-construction of meaning' (2012: 52). He uses Bakhtin's (1981, 1984, 1986) notion of utterances or meaning making through recursive discourses (some of which may resist and others promote change) that are seen to stimulate further conversations (responsive utterances) that can enable people to engage in dialogue (recursive discourses) in the co-construction of a shared understanding of different interpretations. The focus is on unfreezing a current state in changing towards some future desired state but not in a prescribed sequence, rather it is through the utterance of the word that is made meaningful through conversations that produces shared understanding and meaningful change through dialogue (2012: 256). In this there is an attempt to combine the more linear approach of Lewin with a process relational perspective, and yet some of the temporal contradictions that arise from this are not openly addressed, and to be critical, his attempt to counter the stability criticism with the concept of 'ice-topping' is rather incongruous and, one could argue, aprocessual. In contrast, Buchanan and Dawson (2007) and Dawson (2012) reject the linearity of the Lewinian approach and conclude in relation to their process perspective (Buchanan and Dawson, 2007: 681):

> The co-existence of multiple and conflicting narratives that are replaced, refined and rewritten to meet the shifting needs and expectations of different audiences, sits well with longitudinal processual studies. . . . Those multiple narratives do not simply provide a different lens from which to view lived experiences of change. They also reveal the iterative processes of sensegiving and sensemaking, demonstrating also how narrators (who may be both audience and co-authors of a number of stories over time) co-create narrative scripts that influence the understanding of and behaviour towards ongoing change.

This processual approach developed by Dawson (1994, 2003, 2012, 2014b) recognises the importance of conventional time in the development and implementation of schedules in managing change and in the construction of chronological change accounts, but it also sets out to incorporate the more subjective elements of time that arise in multiple ways, such as through the storying that occurs around contested change through to the multiple and reconstructed histories that shape decision-making processes and in the ways in which individuals and groups make and give sense to their experiences of change. For example, in a study on the uptake of a performance review system in an Australian colliery, Dawson and McLean (2013) examine the way that the miners used stories and storying to make sense and give sense to what was occurring at the mine. Miners reflected on their past experiences as miners (retrospective sensemaking) in sharing and co-constructing their collectives interpretations of what was happening in the present and in assessing what this was likely to mean for them as miners in the future (prospective sensemaking). There were also the very different stories of managers and those that presented a linear interpretation of change events (we did this, leading to this, which caused this to happen). The stories and the storying of change that Dawson and McLean (2013) observed used objective time (measurable and quantifiable time) as well as socially constructed forms of time (non-linear and qualitative in nature) in a variety of different ways:

> Empirically, we identify stories that are retrospective coherent stories, with plots and characters (Gabriel, 2000) stories that are partial, future-oriented and unfinalised (Boje, 2008); and stories of the 'here-and-now' that may seek to establish some form of continuity and/or challenge conventional ways of doing things (present stories that are change or continuity oriented). This framework draws attention to the way that stories and storying during times of change variously draw on elements from the past, present and anticipated future in seeking to make sense of what is occurring, and how stories are purposefully used to give sense to others in attempts to steer change and shape the process they may be describing. This storying process occurs in contexts in which prior relations and existing power dynamics may determine which voices get heard and who are silenced in the politics of change.
>
> (Dawson & McLean, 2013: 208)

Conclusion

In this chapter attention has been given to the more empirically based process studies that following Pettigrew's useful description, seek to examine 'reality in flight' through collecting longitudinal data on strategy and change in organizations. We commenced with an historical overview of some early studies interested in process within more structured accounts and then summarized the classic longitudinal study of ICI (Pettigrew, 1985), before examining more recent studies that develop the processual approach in studying change in organizations (Dawson, 2003, 2014a). The concepts of time and temporality used in processual fieldwork studies and how they translate into broader theoretical concerns were critically reviewed. Attention was given to the tensions of using conventional (external) clock time in fieldwork design and the study of change processes and in the collection and analysis of data that speaks to (internal) subjective and intersubjective conceptions of time and temporality in the experience and sensemaking that occurs during times of change. It was argued that a major weakness of mainstream management research has been the tendency to sidestep temporal and contextual elements, especially evident in variance theories that use conventional conceptions of time to identify causal relationships between dependent and independent variables in charting dominant trends and predicting the most probable future outcomes.

In contrast, processual researchers assume fluidity in examining the continual and multifaceted flow of processes in being concerned not only with identifying the dynamics of unfolding patterns but also in temporal interplays, the outlier and marginal, and the 'hidden' and 'silenced', where 'one is significant' (Dawson, 1997). They are interested in studying processes of changing, organizing, and strategizing and of observing and reporting on change as it happens, and in so doing, they are drawn towards a particular research methodology that seeks, among other things, to capture the temporal interconnectedness of processes through longitudinal research designs; engage with qualitative data in exploring meanings and subjectivities as well as documents and more formalized accounts in interpreting the scripting for particular audiences and the chronicling of key activities and events; and provide process data for reviewing conflicts and contradictions, such as conflicts of attribution, interpretation, assessment, and audience. The approach enables the presentation of either single, longitudinal, in-depth case studies or the development of a broader set of comparative case studies that can be used in the development of middle-range theory that seeks to explain the complex dynamics of changing. Organizational change is viewed as an ongoing and complex phenomena that is seen to generate multiple experiences, events, and unexpected interpretations in the continual shaping and reshaping of the meanings and outcomes of change for individuals and groups (Dawson, 1994).

In examining Dawson's (1994, 2003, 2012) processual perspective, the challenges of theorizing change as a non-linear process whilst empirically studying these process in a world dominated by conventional clock time were critically reviewed. Although this processual approach views change as a non-linear, complex, ongoing dynamic process with reversals, progressions, and overlapping processes in a type of corkscrew spiral image of time, it is also concerned with studying cycles of tasks and activities that repeat themselves over time but are unique within the changing context in which they occur—essentially differences and changes that exhibit recognizably similar characteristics—in more of a cyclical image of time. Event time is also important in marking out one-day events, formal launches, turning points, and critical incidents that become not only the milestones of linear representations of change but also provide a source for constructing stories in the sensemaking and sensegiving that surrounds ongoing change. On this count, whereas Dawson's (1994) processual perspective is highly critical of change theories that adhere to a simple linear perspective of clock or calendar time that separates event sequences in promoting stage models of change, in observing change through engagement in fieldwork studies, it is important to recognise the significance of this dominant time perspective to those managing and planning change. The notion of the arrow of time moving ever forward in a linear progression (straight-line image) that shapes decision making and activities is an integral part of changing that needs to be accommodated in data analyses and the presentation of findings. It is the way in which these various perspectives complement, merge, compete, and overlap in, for example, formal planning processes, in the subjective and intersubjective experiences of change, in fieldwork practices, and in the scripting of findings within particular genres that once again highlight the paradox and challenges of dealing with time and temporality in theorizing and studying organizational change.

On these difficult questions that surround time and temporality, the chapter draws attention to some of the current limitations of processual studies and to the problems of moving from more abstract theorization to empirically based studies that produce time-sensitive explanations. For example, in carrying out processual fieldwork, the concepts of temporal awareness, temporal practices, and temporal merging were identified as providing a useful facilitating frame (Dawson, 2014b). In building a processual approach that is sensitive to issues of time and temporality and to the apparently seamless transition by which individuals and groups move between conventional time regularised activities and subjective and intersubjective temporalities, some of the concepts and ideas from the narrative and storyist turn were identified as being useful in theorization. In particular, those that extend our temporal gaze towards polyvocality and the dynamic processes of sensemaking and sensegiving as well as enabling us to view change as a multi-story process (Buchanan & Dawson, 2007). Nevertheless, a key issue that remains is this gap between more abstract theorization that arises from philosophical debates on process organization studies and the operationalization of concepts in the practice of engaging in extended ethnographic case study research. In the chapter that follows, we turn our attention to these broader debates in process studies especially as they relate to our key concern on time, temporality, and organizational change.

References

Bakhtin, M. M. (1981). *The Dialogic Imagination.* Austin: University of Texas Press.
Bakhtin, M. M. (1984). *Problems of Dostoyevsky's Poetics.* Minneapolis: University of Minnesota Press.
Bakhtin, M. M. (1986). *Speech Genres and other Essays.* Austin: University of Texas Press.
Boje, D. M. (2008). *Storytelling Organizations.* London: Sage.
Brown, A. D. (2004). Authoritative sensemaking in a public inquiry report. *Organization Studies, 25*(1), 95–112.

190   *Organizational Change*

Buchanan, D. (2000). *The lived experience of high velocity change: a hospital case study*. Paper presented at the American Academy of Management Conference, Symposium on Strategy as Dynamic and Pluralistic, Toronto, Canada.

Buchanan, D. A., & Dawson, P. (2007). Discourse and audience: Organizational change as multi-story process. *Journal of Management Studies, 44*(5), 669–686.

Buchanan, D. A., & Denyer, D. (2013). Researching tomorrow's crisis: Methodological innovations and wider implications. *International Journal of Management Reviews, 15*(2), 205–224.

Burawoy, M. (2003). Revisits: An outline of a theory of reflexive ethnography. *American Sociological Review, 68*(5), 645–679.

Burns, T., & Stalker, G. M. (1961). *The Management of Innovation*. London: Tavistock.

Chia, R. (2013). Reflections: in praise of silent transformation – Allowing change through 'letting happen'. *Journal of Change Management*, 1–20.

Child, J. (1972). Organization structure, environment and performance: The role of strategic choice. *Sociology, 6*(1), 1–22.

Child, J. (1997). Strategic choice in the analysis of action, structure, organizations and environment: Retrospect and prospect. *Organization Studies, 18*(1), 43–76.

Clark, J., McLoughlin, I., Rose, H., & King, R. (1988). *The Process of Technological Change: New Technology and Social Choice in the Workplace*. Cambridge: Cambridge University Press.

Dalton, M. (1959). *Men Who Manage*. New York: Wiley.

Daniel, L., & Dawson, P. (2011). The sociology of innovation and new biotechnologies. *New Technology, Work and Employment, 26*(1), 1–16.

Dawson, P. (1994). *Organizational Change: A Processual Approach*. London: Paul Chapman Publishing.

Dawson, P. (1996). *Technology and Quality: Change in the Workplace*. London: International Thomson Business Press.

Dawson, P. (1997). In at the deep end: conducting processual research on organisational change. *Scandinavian Journal of Management, 13*(4), 389–405.

Dawson, P. (2003). *Reshaping Change: A Processual Perspective*. London: Routledge.

Dawson, P. (2012). The contribution of the processual approach to the theory and practice of organizational change. In D. M. Boje, B. Burnes, & J. Hassard (Eds.), *The Routledge Companion to Organizational Change* (pp. 119–132). London: Routledge.

Dawson, P. (2013). The use of time in the design, conduct and write-up of longitudinal processual case study research. In M. E. Hassett & E. Paavilainen-Mäntymäki (Eds.), *Handbook of Longitudinal Research Methods: Studying Organizations* (pp. 249–268). Cheltenham: Edward Elgar.

Dawson, P. (2014a). Reflections: On time, temporality and change in organizations. *Journal of Change Management, 14*(3), 285–308.

Dawson, P. (2014b). Temporal practices: Time and ethnographic research in changing organizations. *Journal of Organizational Ethnography, 3*(2), 130–151.

Dawson, P., & Buchanan, D. A. (2005). The way it really happened: Competing narratives in the political process of technological change. *Human Relations, 58*(7), 845–865. doi: 10.1177/0018726705057807

Dawson, P., & Buchanan, D. A. (2012). The way it really happened: Competing narratives in the political process of technological change. In S. Clegg & M. Haugaard (Eds.), *Power and Organizations* (pp. 845–864). London: Sage.

Dawson, P., & McLean, P. (2013). Miner's tales: Stories and the storying process for understanding the collective sensemaking of employees during contested change. *Group & Organization Management: An International Journal, 38*(2), 198–229.

Dawson, P., & Palmer, G. (1995). *Quality Management: The Theory and Practice of Implementing Change*. Melbourne: Longman.

Dawson, P., Sykes, C., McLean, P., Zanko, M., & Marciano, H. (2014). Stories affording new pathways in changing organizations. *Journal of Organizational Change Management, 27*(5), 819–838. doi: 101.1108/JOCM-12-2013-0245

Dawson, P., & Zanko, M. (2009). Cultural issues in organizational change: The case of the Australian Services Union. *Employment Relations Record, 9*(1), 19–41.

Deetz, S. (1996). Describing differences in approaches to organization science: rethinking Burrell and Morgan and their legacy. *Organization Science, 7*(2), 191–207.

Elger, A. (1975). Industrial organizations: A processual perspective. In J. McKinlay (Ed.), *Processing People: Cases in Organizational Behaviour* (pp. 91–149). New York: Hold, Rinehart and Winston.

Farmer, J., Dawson, P., Thomson, E., & Tucker, J. (2007). Rurality, remoteness and the change process: Evidence from a study of maternity services in the North of Scotland. *Health Services Management Research, 20*(1), 59–68.

Friedman, A. (1977). *Industry and Labour: Class Struggle at Work and Monopoly Capitalism.* London: MacMillan.

Gabriel, Y. (2000). *Storytelling in Organizations. Facts, Fictions, and Fantasies.* Oxford: Oxford University Press.

Gouldner, A. (1965). *Wildcat Strike.* New York: Free Press.

Jabri, M. (2012). *Managing Organizational Change: Process, Social Construction and Dialogue.* Basingstoke: Palgrave Macmillan.

Knights, D., & Murray, F. (1994). *Managers Divided: Organisation Politics and Information Technology Management.* Chichester: John Wiley & Sons.

Knights, D., & Willmott, H. (Eds.). (1988). *New Technology and the Labour Process.* Hampshire: MacMillan Press.

Langley, A. (1999). Strategies for theorizing from process data. *Academy of Management Review, 24*(4), 691–710.

Langley, A., Smallman, C., Tsoukas, H., & Van de Ven, A. H. (2013). Process studies of change in organization and management: Unveiling temporality, activity and flow. *Academy of Management Journal, 56*(1), 1–13.

Langley, A., & Tsoukas, H. (2010). Introducing "perspectives on process organization studies". In T. Hernes & S. Maitlis (Eds.), *Process, Sensemaking, and Organizing* (pp. 1–26). Oxford: Oxford University Press.

Mohr, L. B. (1982). *Explaining Organizational Behavior: The Limits and Possibilities of Theory and Research.* San Francisco: Jossey-Bass.

Orton, J. D. (1997). From inductive to iterative grounded theory: Zipping the gap between process theory and process data. *Scandinavian Journal of Management, 13*(4), 419–438.

Pentland, B. T. (1999). Building process theory with narrative: from description to explanation. *Academy of Management Review, 24*(4), 711–724.

Pettigrew, A. (1973). *The Politics of Organizational Decision-Making.* London: Tavistock.

Pettigrew, A. (1985). *The Awakening Giant: Continuity and Change in Imperial Chemical Industries.* Oxford: Basil Blackwell.

Pettigrew, A. (1997). What is processual analysis? *Scandinavian Journal of Management, 13*(4), 337–348.

Pettigrew, A. (2012). Context and action in the transformation of the firm: A reprise. *Journal of Management Studies, 49*(7), 1304–1328.

Pettigrew, A., Whittington, R., Melin, L., Sanchez-Runde, C., van den Bosch, F., Ruigrok, W., & Numagami, T. (Eds.). (2003). *Innovative Forms of Organizing: International Perspectives.* London: Sage.

Putnam, L., Phillips, N., & Chapman, P. (1996). Metaphors of communication and organization. In S. R. Clegg, C. Hardy, & W. R. Nord (Eds.), *The Handbook of Organizational Studies* (pp. 375–408). London: Sage.

Rothwell, R., & Zegveld, W. (1985). *Reindustrialization and Technology.* London: Routledge.

Roy, D. (1952). Quota restriction and goldbricking in a machine shop. *American Journal of Sociology, 57*(5), 427–442.

Tuttle, D. B. (1997). A classification system for understanding individual differences in temporal orientation among processual researchers and organizational informants. *Scandinavian Journal of Management, 13*(4), 349–366.

Van Maanen, J. (1979). The fact of fiction in organizational ethnography. *Administrative Science Quarterly, 24*(4), 539–550.

Weick, K. E., & Quinn, R. E. (1999). Organizational change and development. *Annual Review Psychology, 50*(1), 361–386.

Whyte, W. (1955). *Street Corner Society: The Social Structure of an Italian Slum* (2nd ed.). Chicago: University of Chicago Press.

Whyte, W. F. (1984). *Learning from the Field.* Newbury Park, CA: Sage.

Woodward, J. (1980). *Industrial Organization: Theory and Practice* (2nd ed.). Oxford: Oxford University Press.

10 Process Studies on Emergent Time in Organizing and Becoming

The previous chapter discussed processual research on organizational change and the empirical practice of studying 'reality in flight' through detailed longitudinal fieldwork studies. We discussed some of the challenges of collecting, analysing, and reporting data on the intertwining, complex relationships between organizational actors, their use of agency to affect strategy and politics, the affordance and constraints of organizational structures, and the shifting contexts of changing. Although the difficulties associated with capturing these unfolding dynamic processes are not new, what are often overlooked are the complex workings of time and temporal relations. The use of clock time in planning, implementing, and managing change processes, as well as in research designs and operations that collect processual data, intersect with more subjective notions of time both for those involved in the change and those researching the change. The intricate interweaving of time and temporal relations raise questions and controversies for researchers that have fueled the recent turn to process in organizational studies.

Over the past two decades, researchers have attempted to provide richer conceptualizations of processes and practices of emergent change (Burnes, 2013). In emergent change, time and temporal aspects come into play as the disjunctures and discontinuities of objective time are entangled with processes and temporal aspects in connections to past, present, and future practices. The aim of this chapter is to attend to some of these developing trajectories and to examine the more abstract, theoretical, and conceptual debates around time and temporality as they relate to emergent change and process organization studies. Interesting questions, debates, and controversies lie at the intersection between the theorization of change and empirical engagement with people's experiences of ongoing change in organizations. The movement among broader philosophical debates, theorization, and fieldwork studies often raises questions on the use and robustness of concepts (especially those not easily translatable). Concepts can become constrained by the historical and contextual conditions from which they emerge. The influence of Western culture and industrialization embedded in the accepted organizational studies discourse such as the pervasive, taken-for-granted assumptions about time reinforces the place of the clock and

Gregorian calendar in daily routines in our working lives. However, recent work contrasts the dominance of this view, emphasising alternative conceptions based on practice, process, and Eastern philosophical conceptions that not only challenge accepted assumptions but also provide new ideas for concept redevelopment and theorization.

In charting some of these developments in process and emergent approaches, we begin with some early studies that focus on the emergence of change in work practices that utilize implicit conceptions of temporality in promoting the need to understand change as a continuous process. We then show how later studies attempted to build on these notions of temporality in furthering our understanding of emergence and change. The development of these concepts and ideas can be categorized into several developing and overlapping trajectories. We begin with an examination of practice approaches to temporal work. This is followed by an elaboration of dimensions of temporal work as temporal orientation, awareness, and accommodation. We then turn attention to more radical views in which changing and becoming are not just processes but constitutive of reality. We illustrate how this turns away from a process approach that maintains some representational allegiance towards non-representational forms of process that have been informed on the one hand by elements of Eastern philosophical thought as well as by concepts originating in Western process thinking.

Time in Practice-Focussed Approaches to Emergent Change

The origin of the term 'emergent' in relation to viewing change in organizational studies is traceable to Mintzberg and Waters's (Mintzberg, 1979; Mintzberg & Waters, 1985) early work on strategy in which deliberate and emergent strategies are contrasted. As Orlikowski describes, 'Deliberate change is the realisation of a new pattern of organizing precisely as originally intended, emergent change is the realisation of a new pattern of organizing in the absence of explicit, a priori intentions' (1996: 65). Burnes's (2012: 133) more recent summary explains emergent change as non-linear and open-ended, messy, iterative, unpredictable, and temporally unfolding. These fundamental tenets of emergence are not well explained by conventional views of time and its measurement, where time is generally understood as linear, universal, and homogeneous. While the use and adoption of the emergent approach is traceable in a large and growing body of works in organizational studies, we have selected what we consider to be some of the important works in developing processual studies for closer examination of the uses of time and temporality (Feldman, 2000; Orlikowski, 1996, 2002; Tsoukas & Chia, 2002; Weick & Quinn, 1999).

In an early study of work practices, Orlikowski (1996) investigates the way that improvisation within practices leads to emergent change. She argues that the small, incremental changes that occur as actors adapt routines and practices in unforeseen ways can lead to transformational change (Orlikowski, 1996). In contrast with the then-dominant views of change that emphasise either the practices associated with planned change, the technological imperative to change, or the need for punctuated change following strategic drift, Orlikowski emphasises how actors routinely improvise, innovate, and adjust their situated work practices over time. Time remains in the background, but when it is discussed explicitly, it is linear and measurable or cyclical and iterative. On the one hand, she describes the project investigation as taking place over two years, thus locating the project against a nominal background timeline, and on the other hand, she emphasises that emergent change has neither beginning nor end, in other words, no actual timeline. The empirical study however homes in on the iterative and recursive performance of practices, and although not stated explicitly, they are underpinned temporally in the recursive enactment of ongoing improvisations. The more subtle and gradual but nevertheless transformational change, she suggests, is usefully illustrated using Escher's art in which the artist explains, through the passage of time, that 'a dynamic character is obtained by a succession of figures in which changes of form appear gradually' (Escher, 1948: 120, cited in Orlikowski, 1996).

Similarly, in her ethnomethodological examination of organizational routines, Feldman (2000) emphasises the importance of continuous endogenous change. Whereas routines are commonly understood as relatively stable, repeated, normative patterns of behaviour, she contests the idea of the stability of routines and 'locates the potential for change in the internal dynamics of the routine itself' (2000: 626). Routines in this view are 'ongoing emergent accomplishments, changing and becoming as actors adapt and calibrate their actions temporally with the affordances and breakdowns of material entities (Yanow & Tsoukas, 2009). In line with Orlikowski (1996), time is conceptualized using objective, linear timelines and unitary and abstract notions of clock time at the background macro level and cyclical and iterative at the microlevel of routines. Temporal practices relating to the changing routines are left in the background.

In Weick and Quinn's (1999) widely cited paper from the same era, time is discussed more explicitly with the rate or tempo of change as the main focus. Again, the contrast between episodic and continuous approaches to change is drawn, but instead of binarizing the positions, they suggest two views are not mutually exclusive and are related to the perspective of the observer. From the macro perspective the observer sees change as a relative flow of events and what appears to be repetition of practices and routines interspersed with episodes of distinctive change (1999: 362). In contrast, from the micro perspective, the observer sees change as reorganization, adaptation, and adjustment within practices. Appearing to the observer as relatively innocuous, albeit frequent and incremental, such adjustments are shown to be capable of altering structure and strategy. They conclude that change is not linear or an on-off phenomenon, and it is therefore more appropriate to use the term 'changing' rather than 'change' as the change process is not wholly dependent on management planning but unfolds emergently. Once again time is viewed as both linear at the synoptic level and cyclical in emergent practices. Although the authors advocate a process approach this has been criticized as being incongruous in the way that they adopt a 'bystander view' detached from ongoing processes (see Dawson, 2014a; Purser & Petranker, 2005). An imposed period of artificial immobility is created from which to view the change from a distance, and this has the effect of producing temporal misalignment or a past-centred or future-perfect version (Dawson, 2014a).

In summary, these three papers focusing on emergent change hold a view of time and temporality that is largely implicit except in relation to the pace or rate of change. Whereas spatial considerations and objective, linear notions of time dominate, we do see the beginning of a discussion of a more temporally oriented approach in the examination of the repetition of routines and practices. This work focusing on practices grew quickly in organization studies during the period of the early 2000s as scholars recognised the utility of the approach for studying organizations and work, and we turn to a brief examination in the following section.

Practice Approaches

Following the recent practice turn in social theory, practices are positioned as the primary form of social analysis (Schatzki, Knorr Cetina, & von Savigny, 2001). In this view, social order within society occurs through the complex nexus of interconnected practices. Whereas there is not one accepted definition or understanding of practice, it is broadly accepted by practice scholars as an 'embodied, materially mediated array of human activity centrally organized around shared practical understanding' (Schatzki, 2002: 2). A wide range of practice approaches have been developed (see, e.g., Feldman & Orlikowski, 2011; Gherardi, 2001; Reckwitz, 2002), and it is not possible to detail them all in this work. However, in the area of organizational studies, Davide Nicolini (2012) provides an excellent introduction and comprehensive overview (for a detailed account of the development of philosophical approaches to practice including Science and Technology Studies [STS] explicating the work of Pickering, Haraway, Turner, Latour, Law, and Woolgar, see also the work of Joseph Rouse, 1987, 1996, 2007).

Theodore Schatzki's (Schatzki, 1996, 2001, 2002, 2010; Schatzki et al., 2001) work has been drawn upon widely by scholars in their use of practice in organization studies. Schatzki (1996: 89) points to the performative enactment and dispersion of practices across time and space, suggesting they are 'temporally unfolding and spatially dispersed nexus of doings and sayings'. He sees practices as having constituting features, or what he terms 'organization' (Schatzki 1996, 2002) and suggests this organization is comprised of practical understandings, rules, and orientations towards specific ends in what he calls 'teleo-affective structuring'. He also emphasises that practices are located within, and shaped by, specific material arrangements, an area taken up more strongly in the work of Orlikowski (2007, 2010), who as discussed in Chapter 6 draws upon the work of Barad (2007) in emphasising the sociomateriality of practices. Barad (2007) has a strong view of process in her view of the ongoing intra-active becoming of practices in contrast to the view of Schatzki (1996, 2002), who sees practices (and reality) as comprised of substances and entities that become.

In a similar, yet contrasting, phenomenological approach drawing on Heidegger (1962), MacIntyre (1981), and Wittgenstein (1963), practices are described by Yanow and Tsoukas (2009) as 'organized human activities regulated by goals and standards' (2009: 1347). They go on to propose that practices have three constituting features: '[first] cooperative activity bounded by rules, and extended in time; [second] a set of "internal goods": outcomes that cannot be achieved in any other way but through participating in the practice . . . and [third] attempting to achieve the standards of excellence operative in the practice at that time' (Yanow & Tsoukas, 2009: 1347). As well as the constituting features, they emphasise the importance of practitioners, through repetition over time, making increasingly refined, language-based distinctions to describe the calibration and recalibration of practice performance (Yanow & Tsoukas, 2009). Some examples of everyday practices include cooking, gardening, or playing football, whereas examples of professional business practices might include recruitment, auditing, or marketing. Practices in this view are more than routines or habitualized actions. Following Dreyfus and Dreyfus (2000), Yanow and Tsoukas show that learning or entry into a practice requires competent performance of a series of activities to an accepted normative standard; they suggest: 'Unless one accepts the authority of both the standards of the practice into which one has entered and the judgments of acknowledged masters of that practice, one will never be accepted into that practice' (Yanow & Tsoukas, 2009: 1347). Mastery of a practice is achieved as essential skills are embodied and expertise is articulated readily across different contexts and with increasingly refined, language-based distinctions (Yanow & Tsoukas, 2009).

Thus in relation to time and temporality, practices are performed over periods of time and are temporally constructed. The performance of a practice is oriented toward a future end, and on this count, Schatzki (1996, 2002) uses the term 'tele-affectivity' to describe the future affective commitment of the practitioner towards a given end, whereas Rouse (2007: 533) suggests that practices are 'constitutive performances to issues and stakes whose definitive resolution is always prospective' and that 'normativity is an interactive orientation toward a future encompassing present circumstances within its past'. Although practices are oriented towards the achievement of what is at stake and/or issues, the past is also present in practices in embodied actions. Learning a practice is achieved by *practicing* through drilling or repeating sequences of actions until they are embodied. Habituated, embodied responses acquired in the past may then be repeated fluently to normative standards in the present. A practice is thus an event in the present that is inseparable from habitualized knowing in practice with an orientation to achieving what is at stake in the performance of the practice.

Based on these works, a group of researchers examined time and temporality more explicitly in a trajectory that emphasises temporal practices. In this approach, emergent change is examined imminently drawing on actors' temporal experience and practices as they unfold. In an early paper exploring these ideas, Orlikowski and Yates (2002) examine 'time as an enacted phenomenon'. Unlike the papers emanating from the same period discussed earlier here, the authors explicitly discuss temporality in the performance of what they term 'temporal structuring' of organizing practices (2002: 684). They develop the notion of temporal structuring as a means of identifying how time is used to structure social practices. They suggest that earlier discussions of time in organizational studies tend to position time in one of two ways: either as objective time based on notions of clock time and Newton's absolute time or, alternatively, as subjective time where time is constructed based on the experience of events. A similar divide is said to have existed from ancient times such as the Greek distinction between *chronos*, or serial time measured in chronometers, and *kairos*, the human time of opportunity, purpose, and intention (2002: 686). To move beyond what they see as limited views, Orlikowski and Yates (2002) develop the term 'temporal structuring', drawing on Schatzki's (1996) practice theory. They cite the benefits of this practice-based view of studying time—that is time as it is used—in collapsing and bringing to the fore unhelpful binary divisions such as the universal and particular, linear or cyclical views of time, or closed- and open-ended temporal orientations (Orlikowski and Yates, 2002: 689–692). Their study shows that by moving the unit of analysis to social practices and attending to temporal structuring, the use of binaries becomes obsolete as practices combine and integrate universal, particular, linear, and cyclical dimensions in the creation and adaptation of temporal structures.

In more recent papers temporal practice is further extended. Kaplan and Orlikowski (2013) explore the idea of 'temporal work' in strategy as practice in organizational change. They show that the practice of strategy is dependent on what they term 'temporal work', where organizational actors negotiate interpretations in shared sensemaking practices to align future strategic decision making with narratives of the past. Sensemaking of past trends, current analogies, and present concerns are negotiated to fit with future strategy. Such work is consistent with a growing body of work exploring sensemaking and temporality (Wiebe, 2010). They show that this may mean reworking narratives of the past to make them consistent with the future. For example, they show how one organization, in its need to formulate strategy for organizational survival and in the midst of 'breakdown', changed its conception of the past by reviewing its corporate history. The reinterpretation was from 'a portrayal of CommCorp's history as a company that developed transformational technologies rather than the more widely held image of CommCorp as an optical technology company' (Kaplan & Orlikowski, 2013: 977). In this view, sensemaking as discussed in Chapter 8 (Weick, 1995; Wiebe, 2010) is central to temporal work, and time and temporal considerations move beyond common conceptions used in studies of organization where time is conceived as linear or cyclical, a sequence or synchronization, rate and pace of change, or temporal structuring (Kaplan & Orlikowski, 2013: 990). Change emerges in response to ongoing temporal work as Kaplan and Orlikowski (2013: 991) explain: 'Actors may act to change the situation by reinterpreting the past, and responding differently to present concerns, and envisioning the future in innovative ways'. They conclude that temporal work performed in the midst of change opens the future by unlocking the future from the constraints of the past articulated in organizational history.

A further aspect of the practice trajectory of emergent change focuses on the notion of 'timespace' in practice and its influence. Hydle (2015) draws on the Heideggerian concept of timespace that is used by Schatzki (2010) to examine temporal and spatial practices in the context of strategy. In this view, spatial and temporal dimensions are not objective. The concepts of spatiality and temporality as used by Heidegger are space and time as they are bound up with Dasein. Temporality and spatiality come together at the level of activities that are defined as 'intentional and voluntary events with temporal-spatial aspects' (Hydle, 2015: 645). In turn, activities are linked to form practices that, following Schatzki (1996), are the performance of 'doings and sayings'. Activities are related in different ways across timespace, and Schatzki (2010) suggests these relations occur in three concepts of commonality, sharing, and orchestration. She provides the following illustration:

> When several people from two different organizations physically meet, they share a common spatiality, a common temporality in the present (being in the meeting room), an orchestrated past (not being involved in the project together) and a shared future (with a motivation to land a successful project together). Temporality therefore embraces common presents (with ends and purposes of discussing the project), orchestrated pasts (different reasons to be involved in the project meeting) and shared futures (being involved in a project from two different organizations without having established a normal way of cooperating)
>
> (Hydle, 2015: 646)

Temporal Orientation, Awareness, and Accommodation

Writing from a different trajectory based on what he terms a 'processual approach', Dawson (2014a) argues that in much of the organizational change literature, time is confused and misunderstood. He examines the conceptualizations of time and temporality in some common approaches to organizational change, arguing that conceptualizations of time and temporality are best understood as woven together in organizational processes. Both subjective temporal experiences associated with the sensemaking of change (retrospectively and prospectively) as well as in institutionalized forms of time used by change agents in scheduling various activities chronologically (Dawson, 2014a: 302). He concludes that paradox and contradiction are inevitable and may be unresolvable. He advocates an increasing temporal awareness both by researchers as studies of change are undertaken and by theorists in developing concepts of change. He suggests the need to engage in multiple temporalities and suggests three concepts to assist temporal orientation, temporal awareness, and temporal accommodation (Dawson, 2014a).

First, in temporal orientation he suggests that two dominant human orientations are materiality, with an objective conception of time and sociality with a subjective and temporal orientation (Dawson, 2014a). He suggests that in organizational change, most approaches have a combination of both sociality and materiality and therefore ought to have conceptions of time that encompass both of these orientations. In temporal awareness, issues of concern relate to the extent to which time and temporality remain in the background or foreground and how researchers and managers conceive of time and temporality in organizational change. He cautions that there is no universal or one true concept of time and therefore advocates openness to different viewpoints. Finally, temporal accommodation relates to the ways different conceptions of time are accommodated and used in research practice, arriving at findings and theory development (Dawson, 2014a: 304).

Dawson (2014b) develops these ideas further in explicitly examining time and temporality in relation to ethnographic methods and in forwarding the concept of temporal merging to refer to the interweaving of objective and subjective concepts of time and to the way that the past and prospective futures shape human experience of the present. He argues that the conundrum around competing concepts of time can challenge the field researcher and that juxtapositions can inadvertently lead to a sojourn of resolution where there is a need to accept the paradox of time in the use of a relational-temporal perspective in opening up opportunities for greater insights in carrying out ethnographic studies on changing organizations (2014: 148). As he concludes:

> Time is central in making sense of the complexes of occasions and of the interaction of emergent forms in recursive non-linear processes . . . overlaying a relational-temporality with a processual approach enables theoretical insight into the attraction and persistence of rational stage models of change as well as explaining the dynamic indeterminacy of ongoing human experiences in changing organizations.
>
> (Dawson, 2014b: 147)

Contrasting Western and Chinese Perspectives

By turning to Eastern philosophical and theoretical approaches, a contrasting view of reality is evident in the often unquestioned and dominant views held in the West. Such contrasts become evident in relation to the theorizing of time and temporality and change. An early example is in the work of Marshak (1993), who to explore the assumptions underpinning the phenomenon of change in two cultural settings, contrasted the OD approach exemplified in Kurt Lewin's model with a Confucian or Chinese model. His method identified 'candidate assumptions' in the literature of discussing both approaches; he developed a series of key dimensions of the models that he then used to draw contrasts between the two (Marshak, 1993). The construction of this perhaps overly simplistic, binarized representation does serve to provide a contrast of the salient and generalized differences between Western and Chinese approaches to change; nonetheless, time and temporality are not the main focus and therefore remain in the background. The key assumptions of Lewin's OD view of change are listed as: linear, progressive, goal oriented, based on disequilibrium, planned, and unusual. In contrast, Marshak (1993) lists the assumptions of the Chinese model of change as cyclical, processional, journey oriented, maintaining equilibrium and harmony and finally change as usual and expected and the way of the universe or dao.

In Lewin's approach, implicit clock time and Newton's notion of absolute time provide the timeline on which the intended change is plotted. Lewin was strongly committed to action cycles as part of OD, which rely on more cyclical views of time. In contrast, Marshak (1993) posits the Chinese view of change as bound to cycles of ongoing change, balance, and mutual constitution through the dominance of the concept of *yin yang*. In this view, stability and being are not prioritized, and change is not viewed against the background of objective time, for becoming and change flow from within the dao. About a decade later Chia takes up this contrast more deeply in his work on strategy and change (see, e.g., Chia, 2003, 2010, 2014).

The Time of Silent Transformation

In exploring Eastern approaches, Chia (2002, 2003, 2010, 2014) presents conceptions of change, time, and temporality that contrast with naturalized Western notions. As he comments,

> In the East the idea of a ceaselessly fluxing, relentlessly changing, and self-transforming reality is readily accepted as a given and finds numerous expressions in the classic ancient Chinese texts including the I Ching . . . and in the . . . writings of Lao Tzu and Chuang Tzu, both of whom insisted on the fecundity and primacy of a pro-generative, emergent, and undifferentiated 'Tao' as the ultimate basis of reality.
>
> (2010: 119)

In his later work, Chia (2010, 2014) draws strongly on the work of the French philosopher and sinologist Francois Jullien and his 'oblique' approach to change, including allowing things to happen and to unfold naturally instead of trying to force reality into shape, as in many Western 'heroic' approaches. Changing reality is not something that can be brought under control but must be allowed to realise its own potential—the 'propensity of things' (Chia, 2014: 2). He suggests embracing changefulness as a way of thinking and understanding reality. He identifies this as an emergent approach:

> Eschews rapid, disruptive and dramatic interventions such as down-sizing, layoffs or divestment in favour of the gradual incremental development of human resources and the building of internal organizational capabilities. The emergent perspective is a bottom up approach to change and views outcomes as the cumulative and often 'piecemeal' adaptive actions taken in-situ by organizational members in learning how to cope with the exigencies of organizational situations
>
> (2014: 4)

Chia's (2014) work on 'letting change happen' is strongly influenced by the work of Jullien in his work titled *The Silent Transformation*. To begin with, Jullien (2011) introduces the term 'transformation' to mean the sorts of changes that occur in ageing or in the changing seasons, not the cyclical movement but the imperceptibility of gradual transformation. He suggests that although this type of change process forms part of life's common experience, due to its imperceptibility, it is seldom discussed and not just because it is 'too progressive and continuous to be apparent to our eyes, but also because everything within us ages' (2011: 2); it is the totality of the person that ages and escapes our perception. Jullien uses the term 'silent' in contrast to 'invisible' or 'imperceptible' to describe the process, arguing that it is more telling, operating 'without warning' or 'attracting attention' (2011: 3). This transformation is total to the point that as we look at old photographs, we hardly recognise the images. Jullien (2011) finds this process anomalous and overlooked in the West with the dominant conceptions of being and time infused into language structures that eliminate 'the becoming' evident in the silent transformation. In contrast, in Chinese conceptions, Jullien (2011) shows how transformation is understood and communicated by the use of different language structures that do not distinguish time as a separate entity or category. Instead, movement and becoming are seen to occur naturally through yin and yang within entities—old is contained in young and so forth. He goes on to discuss what he sees as a Chinese traditional view of time (Jullien, 2011: 100–115), arguing that the Western tradition of understanding time as an abstraction detached from the descriptions of changes to being that deflects our understanding and deceives us. He suggests that such a view of time or *chronos* is 'hegemonic and enigmatic' and does not serve a positive purpose in helping us to understand the becoming of reality at all (2011: 101). He poses the question:

> Is Time not that characteristic of a dramatic fiction we have invented in order to give a false name and a face to what we are unable to think, and to make it play a great, and undoubtedly widespread, explanatory role, one from which a more painstaking attention to silent transformations would have excused us?
>
> (Jullien, 2011: 101)

In this view, the accepted conception of abstract time developed in Western science and philosophy is shown to be unreal and of limited use in adequately explaining changing reality. He argues that the Chinese traditional view of change had no concept of time before coming into contact with Western culture. Instead, the Chinese speak of a number of concepts that attend to transformation more closely. The notion of season (*shi*) is the moment-occasion 'which through its variation measures the life of things, induces our activities and serves as a framework for ritual. . . . The term is profoundly anchored in a qualitative circumstantial meaning' (2011: 101). A second term used is 'duration' (*jiu*), 'which proceeds from the alternation of such moments and is paired with space' (2011: 101). If this idea of silent transformation is applied to organizational change, it does not mean that there is passivity on the part of the actors or managers. As Jullien indicates, the notion of *shi* is a means of managing reality without direct human action on events, and with care and diligence, the wise manager uses the propensity of things—the agency in the event—to achieve silent transformation.

Jullien discusses the origins of the Western and Eastern views and suggests three reasons for the development of these very different time conceptions (the Western notion of time is not articulated in the Chinese vocabulary [2011: 102]). First, Western views of time relate to the development of concepts originating in physics in which when an object is in motion, time (as a measurement of intervals) is used to account for the displacement and movement of that object, whereas in China the notion of *yin yang* emphasises correlation and ongoing becoming. Second, in Western metaphysics that opposes time to eternity, the notion of eternal being contrasts human being and existence in time. In contrast in China the notion of eternity did not exist, but the term 'without end' or the inexhaustible' served to distinguish the idea of perpetuity with extinction (Jullien, 2011: 104). Finally, in the West, European languages conjugate verbs that divide time morphologically into past, present, and future, and the passing of time is movement from one tense to another (2011: 104). In contrast the Chinese do not conjugate and linguistically distinguish changes in time not with three but with two terms, namely, going away and coming here (*Guo wang jin lai*), where 'the past is endlessly going away and the present is endlessly coming here' (2011: 104). This differs from many conceptions of change that locate formal notions of objective, Newtonian time as the background in which entities are seen to change; where here, temporal change is not explicit but is encapsulated in discussions of the transformation that occur within the notion of becoming. This conception of time is similar to that of McTaggart (1908) and others discussed in Chapter 2, who hold the view that objective time does not exist but is an illusion.

Process Organization Studies and Debates on Time and Temporality

In a fourth trajectory that is traceable to Tsoukas and Chia's (2002) earlier paper, the authors radically extend Western approaches to processual change in the uptake of concepts from process philosophy. Tsoukas and Chia (2002) suggest that whereas many works identify emergent change and signal its importance for progressing notions of how change occurs in organizations at the microlevel, they do not go far enough in reconceptualizing ongoing change. They propose an ontological repositioning of the debate by extending the premise that change is not only ongoing but that change is all there is; they move from being to becoming as the ontological starting point both for change and organizing. They argue for the adoption of this radical process view in supporting more adequate conceptualizing of both organizations and change. This view is underpinned by concepts derived from process philosophers who emphasise the ontological priority of change, temporality, and becoming and the conceptual limitations of representational epistemologies and concepts for discussing change (Rescher, 1996). They show that if change is what occurs as an entity moves over time from a stable point T^1 to a second point T^2, then complex and paradoxical issues arise that obfuscate what appear to be relatively simple treatments. For if the discussion of change attends to what occurs to the phenomena or the differences that occur between T^1 and T^2, then the change itself has escaped unobserved. Even if each increment is examined in ever reducing sizes, as in Zeno's paradox, the focus is still on stable, albeit in-between, representations of the phenomenon (Tsoukas & Chia, 2002: 570). They argue that the way that conceptual orders and cognitive processes work in representational orders is through stabilizing, that is, fixing temporal movement in stable concepts or representations that produce a substance ontology that contrasts with their suggested process ontology. To support this radical move to process in which 'everything is in a constant state of flux', organizations are viewed as constantly becoming while appearing as ongoing, apparently stabilized accomplishments (Tsoukas & Chia, 2002). Interestingly, the important temporal relations that structure the recursive performance of practices and their improvisation are not discussed. Time in this move from incrementalism is seen to flow, a view consistent with a more radical process approach; however, it remains implicit and linear and only touches on the richer, subjective notions of time associated with process philosophy.

In his reflective piece in the journal *Organization Studies* around the same time, Chia (2002) attempts to rethink process and change in organizational analysis based on a move from the Newtonian conceptions of absolute time (represented by clock time), noting that 'process theorists' rediscovery of actual time . . . enable us to make important adjustments in our thinking about the nature of movement, process and change'. He draws upon Bergson's notion of *durée* that is qualitatively different to clock time, and his description warrants quotation in full, as he states,

> For Bergson, real universal time is indivisible and has its origin in our consciousness of duration. Bergson insisted that public clock time is a 'counterfeit' representation of lived experience produced by the conversation of temporal experiences into discrete and measurable instantaneous moments. According to him, real time is inextricably linked to our consciousness and involves the continuous progress of the past as it gnaws into the future and swells as it advances, leaving its bite, or the mark of its tooth, on all things. It is this 'ballooning' metaphor of time that is overlooked when we begin to theorize on process and change
> (Chia, 2002: 864)

Such a view makes explicit the subjective experience of time or temporal consciousness as included in the locus of all change and organizing.

Conclusion

In this chapter we have presented a discussion of time and temporality as it relates to emergent approaches to change. We identified four trajectories that comprised, first, approaches with an endogenous focus that attend to microlevel routines and practices that show emergent change to be ongoing in the iterative and innovative performance of the routines and practices. Routines and practices are shown to be ongoing emergent accomplishments; however, time remains as the background timeline, and temporality is not discussed explicitly. In focusing attention on the practice turn, time and temporal practices become more explicit as practices are not bound to dualist representations and are temporally oriented as events in the present, inseparable from habitualized, knowing in practice orientated to achieving what is at stake in the performance of the practice. In a second trajectory, conceptualizations of time and temporality are considered to be best understood as woven together in organizational processes. Here the emphasis is on the need to engage in multiple temporalities, and temporal orientation, temporal awareness, and temporal accommodation are discussed as concepts that orient this engagement (Dawson, 2014b). A third trajectory that draws on Eastern conceptions of change provides a strong contrast with dominant Western conceptions discussed in earlier chapters. Here the notions of silent transformation and the innate propensity of things to change are shown to be imperceptible and silent yet inexorable. In this view, temporal change is not explicit but is encapsulated in discussions of the transformation that occur within the notion of becoming. In the final trajectory there is a move to go beyond representational views in more radical adoption of process-thinking views. Here change and becoming are considered to be the ontological stage on which the becoming of organizations is performed, yet although time is seen to flow, it remains implicit and hidden. Each of these trajectories contributes to an enhanced view of time and temporality. We therefore conclude that each trajectory can contribute to richer conceptualizations of time and temporality that are necessary for a more adequate understanding of emerging change in organizations.

These trajectories usefully illustrate developments in our understanding of emergent change in the use and refinement of concepts that emphasises change through adaptation and innovation at the microlevel of routines and practices as well as more radical departure to a process ontology in which change is everything and should not be reduced to objects, structures, or an organization (that exists with boundaries) as using such a representational epistemology ultimately obfuscates change as a process. As the scholarly work discussed here makes clear, there is a move from time as a reification that sits implicitly in the background with an implicit, objective, temporal orientation exhibiting limited temporal awareness in what are largely representational approaches toward processual studies that engage with representations as experienced by people at work. A broader temporal orientation is adopted in seeking to accommodate the more material objective conceptions of time with the more social subjective conceptions. The improvised performance of practices over time is discussed along with more abstract philosophical views of process that views change and becoming as an ontology in which temporal orientation moves away from the 'counterfeit' representation of clock time to conscious extra-spatial time with a temporal awareness that is inextricably linked to the consciousness of duration.

Once again the issue of dualism and the use of representational and non-representational approaches to studying the process of change in organization arise. On one end of this continuum, we could characterize the world as being represented by language and structured by clock time (what from a process perspective would be seen as a counterfeit reality), and at the non-representational end, there would be a displacement of entities of enduring hegemonic relations and authority structures with changing and becoming being all there is. At the two extremes we move from an objective, external world view to a more subjective, internal being that is part of consciousness. The problem arises when we seek to study change processes in organizations (with enduring power relations, orders, and structures), accommodate the subjective and intersubjective experiences of time, and also maintain and develop a process perspective that extends beyond binary divisions in the multiplicity of changing and the multiplicity of times. In many ways the contradictions that arise in using process perspectives for studying organizational change mirror the contradictions of time—an issue we continually return to—and one that is taken up by Hernes (2014) in the chapter that follows (who returns to a type of structuration in tackling dualism and the relation between process and structure). Within the trajectories discussed in this chapter, there is a growing recognition of time and temporality, and yet there remains both a tendency to sidestep the paradox of time and an unresolved tension in the negation of time as represented by the clock in a process ontology that rejects structured time.

Taken as a whole these trajectories signal a move from implicit to explicit conceptions of time and temporality in the growing uptake of process views of organization. In its early conceptions research in emergent change focussed on contrasts between planned and emergent change. Time was mainly considered in relation to timelines based on notions of absolute time, objectivized clock times that although important, were not considered part and parcel of the practices of change itself. However, as demonstrated in the work discussed in this chapter, there has been a refocussing of research towards the more recursive performance of practice in which temporal relations have become more visible, and in this, recursive change to routines and practice necessitated temporal considerations to improve past practice for the future. As research attention turned to the performance of practices, more adequate process theorizations have developed that are congruent with and adequate to the phenomena under investigation. What is clear is that temporality can no longer be ignored either as a conceptual dimension of the phenomenon under investigation or in the practices used in the investigation itself. These developments in a process approach to organization studies and, more particularly, organizational change set the scene for the next chapter in which these recent turns in process approaches are further discussed and extended in drawing on the work of Bergson and Deleuze.

References

Barad, K. (2007). *Meeting the Universe Halfway: Quantum Physics and the Entanglement of Matter and Meaning*. Durham, NC: Duke University Press.

Burnes, B. (2012). Understanding the emergent approach to change. In D. Boje, B. Burnes, & J. Hassard (Eds.), *The Routledge Companion to Organizational Change* (pp. 133–145). London and New York: Routledge.

Burnes, B. (2013). A critical review of organizational development. In H. Leonard, R. Lewis, A. Freedman, & J. Passmore (Eds.), *The Wiley-Blackwell Handbook of the Psychology of Leadership, Change and Organizational Development*. Chichester: Wiley-Blackwell.

Chia, R. (2002). Essai: Time, duration and simultaneity: Rethinking process and change in organizational analysis. *Organization Studies, 23*(6), 863–868.

Chia, R. (2003). From knowledge creation to the perfection of action: Tao, Basho and pure experience as the ultimate ground of knowing. *Human Relations, 56*(3), 953–981.

Chia, R. (2010). Rediscovering becoming: Insights from an oriental perspective of process organization studies. In T. Hernes & S. Maitlis (Eds.), *Process, Sensemaking and Organizing* (pp. 112–139). London: Sage.

Chia, R. (2014). Reflections: In praise of silent transformation—allowing change through letting happen. *Journal of Change Management, 14*(1), 8–27.

Dawson, P. (2014a). Reflections: On time temporality and change in organizations. *Journal of Change Management, 14*(3), 285–308.

Dawson, P. (2014b). Temporal practices: Time and ethnographic research in changing organizations. *Journal of Organizational Ethnography, 3*(2), 130–151.

Dreyfus, L. H., & Dreyfus, S. E. (2000). *Mind over Machine*. New York: Free Press.

Feldman, M. (2000). Organizational routines as a source of continuous change. *Organization Science, 11*(6), 611–629.

Feldman, M., & Orlikowski, W. J. (2011). Theorizing practice and practicing theory. *Organization Science, 22*(5), 1240–1253.

Gherardi, S. (2001). From organizational learning to practice-based knowing. *Human Relations, 54*(1), 131–139.

Heidegger, M. (1962). *Being and Time* (J. M. E. Robinson, Trans.). New York: Harper Collins.

Hernes, T. (2014). *A Process Theory of Organizations*. Oxford: Oxford University Press.

Hydle, K. M. (2015). Temporal and spatial dimensions of strategizing. *Organization Studies, 36*(5), 643–663.

Jullien, F. (2011). *The Silent Transformation*. Calcutta: Seagull.

Kaplan, S., & Orlikowski, W. (2013). Temporal work in strategy making. *Organization Science, 24*(44), 965–995.

MacIntyre, A. (1981). *After Virtue: A Study in Moral Theory*. London: Gerald Duckworth & Co Ltd.

Marshak, R. (1993). Lewin meets Confucius: A review of the OD model of change. *Journal of Applied Behavioral Science, 29*(4), 393–415.

McTaggart, E. (1908). The unreality of time. *Mind, New Series, 17*(68), 457–474.

Mintzberg, H. (1979). An emerging strategy of "direct" research. *Administrative Science Quarterly, 24*(4), 582–589.

Mintzberg, H., & Waters, J. (1985). Of strategies, deliberate and emergent. *Strategic Management Journal, 6*(3), 257–272.

Nicolini, D. (2012). *Practice Theory, Work, and Organization: An Introduction*. Oxford: Oxford University Press.

Orlikowski, W. (1996). Improvising organizational transformation over time: A situated change perspective. *Information Systems Research, 7*(1), 63–92.

Orlikowski, W. (2002). Knowing in practice: Enacting a collective capability in distributed organizing. *Organization Science, 13*(3), 249–273.

Orlikowski, W. (2007). Sociomaterial practices: Exploring technology at work. *Organization Studies, 28*(9), 1435–1448.

Orlikowski, W. (2010). The sociomateriality of organisational life: Considering technology in management research. *Cambridge Journal of Economics, 34*(1), 125–141.

Orlikowski, W., & Yates, J. (2002). It's about time: Temporal structuring in organizations. *Organization Science, 13*(6), 684–700.

Purser, R., & Petranker, J. (2005). Unfreezing the future: Exploring the dynamic of time in organizational change. *Journal of Applied Behavioral Science, 41*(2), 182–203.

Reckwitz, A. (2002). Toward a theory of social practices. *European Journal of Social Theory, 5*(2), 243–263.

Rescher, N. (1996). *Process Metaphysics: An Introduction to Process Philosophy.* Albany, NY: State University of New York.

Rouse, J. (1987). *Knowledge and Power: Toward a Political Philosophy of Science.* Ithaca and London: Cornell University Press.

Rouse, J. (1996). *Engaging Science: How to Understand Its Practices Philosophically.* New York: Cornell University Press.

Rouse, J. (2007). *Practice Theory.* Retrieved from http://wesscholar.wesleyan.edu/div1facpubs/43

Schatzki, T. (1996). *Social Practices: A Wittgensteinian Approach to Human Activity and the Social.* New York: Cambridge University Press.

Schatzki, T. (2001). Introduction: Practice theory. In T. Schatzki, K. Knorr Cetina, & E. Von Savigny (Eds.), *The Practice Turn in Contemporary Theory* (pp. 1–14). Oxon: Routledge.

Schatzki, T. (2002). *The Site of the Social: A Philosophical Account of Social Life and Change.* Pennsylvania: Pennsylvania State University Press.

Schatzki, T. (2010). *The Timespace of Human Activity: On Performance, Society, and History as Indeterminate Teleological Events.* Plymouth, UK: Lexington Books.

Schatzki, T., Knorr Cetina, K., & von Savigny, E. (Eds.). (2001). *The Practice Turn in Contemporary Theory.* New York: Routledge.

Tsoukas, H., & Chia, R. (2002). On organizational becoming: Rethinking organizational change. *Organization Science, 13*(5) (September–October 2002), 567–582.

Weick, K. (1995). *Sensemaking in Organizations.* Thousand Oaks: Sage.

Weick, K., & Quinn, R. (1999). Organizational change and development. *Annual Review of Psychology, 50*(1), 361–386.

Wiebe, E. (2010). Temporal sensemaking: Managers' use of time to frame organizational change. In T. Hernes & S. Maitlis (Eds.), *Process, Sensemaking and Organizing* (pp. 213–241). Oxford: Oxford University Press.

Wittgenstein, L. (1963). *Philosophical Investigations* (G. E. M. Anscombe, Trans.). Oxford: Blackwell.

Yanow, D., & Tsoukas, H. (2009). What is reflection-in-action? A phenomenological account. *Journal of Management Studies, 46*(8), 1339–1364.

11 Processes in the Making

Living Presents and the Multiplicity of Times

Time is not only the regulative force of life as we know it (as Darwin claimed), it is the very motor of the universe as a whole (as Bergson implied), as well as the principle of life to come, life that overcomes itself (as Nietzsche affirmed)

(Grosz, 2004: 245)

Introduction

In this chapter we seek to extend existing concepts of time and temporality in developing processual approaches for understanding organizational change. As discussed in our previous chapters, process scholars in organization studies have increasingly turned to the ideas of Western process thinkers such as Whitehead, Mead, Bergson, and Schutz in attempting to more adequately conceptualize process approaches to organizational theory and practice. These approaches have engaged more deeply with the concepts of time and temporality as illustrated by the notable work of Hernes (2014) in his book *A Process Theory of Organizations*, which as the title suggests, attempts to build a comprehensive theory of process. This work and some of the originating ideas of Bergson provide a useful way forward, particularly when seen in conjunction with Deleuze's (1994) work on time and the insightful commentaries provided by Buchanan (2000, 2008), Grosz (2004) and Williams (2011). In the first section of this chapter, we unpack some of the key concepts and ideas that Hernes (2014) presents that echo some of our earlier discussion of ANT (see Chapter 6). In the second section, we aim to extend this recent work on process by drawing on some of the philosophical thinking from the work of Bergson (2010), Deleuze (1994), and Grosz (2004).

The Process Turn in Organization Studies

There has been an increase in support for a process turn in organization studies (Langley & Tsoukas, 2010; 2016). A growing number of scholars who often opt for action verbs, such as organizing, strategizing, changing, as opposed to the more static and conventional use of nouns, such as organization, strategy, and change, are engaging in various forms of process studies that examine the complex underlying processes that comprise entities and events (Langley, Smallman, Tsoukas, & Van de Ven, 2013; Langley & Tsoukas, 2010). Following on from philosophers such as Bergson (1911/1998), Mead (1932/1980), and Whitehead (1929), they draw on process ontology in which the world is seen to be continuously reconstituted through ongoing processes (Rescher, 1996). Although patterns of activities are recognised, scholars taking up this perspective often refer back to the classic dictum taken from the Greek philosopher Heraclitus that 'you could not step twice into the same river; for other waters are ever flowing on to you', quoted in the dialogue by Plato titled *Cratylus* (see Sedley, 2003: 23). Within this more dynamic concept of changing, there is a relational component that rejects the ontology of separateness where things are seen to exist in and of themselves (independently of other things) (Tsoukas & Chia, 2002). This approach advocates that everything that is only exists in relation to other things (Langley & Tsoukas, 2010). As such, it is these complex interactions and the ways in which sense is made of emergent forms in recursive non-linear processes that are examined to gain insight and understanding of peoples' lived experiences of change.

In his recent work, Hernes (2014) builds on these earlier ideas in an attempt at a full-blown process theory of organization. The work develops a theory of organization in a synthesis of the work of process thinkers: Whitehead, Bergson, Heidegger, Deleuze, Mead, Schutz, and others. In the opening sections he clarifies the position taken:

> When I use the expression 'organizational life' I do not mean 'life in organizations'. What I mean by organizational life is the ongoing process of making, remaking, unmaking, and relating of organizational actors of all sorts: humans, technologies, concepts, groups, and the like, into meaningful wholes. These meaningful wholes can be a Twitter community, an emerging interest group, an entrepreneur with an idea, a think tank, a fashion show, sporadic interactions among scattered actors around a concept, or the spread of a technology, as well as any form of formalized organization or institution. Meaningful wholes are not entities as such, but may be temporarily experienced as entities
>
> (Hernes, 2014: viii)

He positions the book as a piece that engages with the role of time and temporality in the making of actors in examining notions of continuity and change as well as the meaning and relationship of past, present, and future. At the outset, he identifies the importance of understanding how individuals, groups, organizations, technologies, and markets deal with being in time and how interactions between diverse entities give shape to and reshape meaning over time and enable agency. He argues that 'the slippery slope of time' requires temporal distinctions to be made to more fully understand how organizations happen over time. He is critical of process approaches in organization that accept objective notions of time and merely plot organizational activities on a timeline then call this a processual study, when all they are doing is reducing process to measured sequences of clock time.

Hernes (2014: ix) draws on Heidegger, maintaining that 'time creates temporality' in which he refers to 'the carving out of temporal existence (present, past, and future) from the passing of time'. This carving of temporality occurs through ongoing tangled relations, and although agency is important, this is not seen to come from our usual understanding of human action, that is, the purposeful engagement of people in acts that seek to bring about a desired outcome, solve a problem, or prevent something undesirable from happening; rather, there are tangled relations (actors are not separate and distinct) in which organizational actors arise from the process of acting rather than vice versa. In this sense, agency permeates into the flow of life; it forever touches the continually reconstituted tangledness of being over time, but it is not directly discernible as a distinct act other than in our own false constructions of identifiable forms of agency arising from human action. Order arises from the flow of life and not from the actions of people in the building of structures and systems for regulating socioeconomic behaviour. Connections with his earlier work using ANT (Latour, 1991; 2005) are evident in the adoption of a more distributed notion of agency with other living and nonliving entities that all form part of related and interrelated assemblages. Hernes (2008, 2014) uses the concept of 'tangledness' to convey processes of becoming among entangled actors that are not separate and distinct but part of the fluidity of day-to-day organizational life.

His ideas on the relation between process and structure extend earlier work, for example, that by Tsoukas and Chia (2002). His argument is as follows: If process is all there is and everything is in a state of constant flux, then a major problem is how to distinguish any entities and how to discuss change if nothing is stable. In contrast, he argues that structure and stability do exist but not as ontological forms. He suggests that structure is only the appearance of stabilization and that it is always mutually constituted with and in action—a type of structuration. In this way, change and process are made meaningful as they provide a way of viewing entities that are experienced as stable and are subject to temporality.

Temporality in Organizations: Living Presents, Events, and Meaning Structures

Hernes (2014) develops a conceptual framework based on the concepts of the living present, events, clusters of events, and meaning structures and their articulations. The notion of the 'living present' is a term used by Deleuze

(1996), although Hernes's (2014) view of the living present is quite different from that of Deleuze (1996). A number of points are salient. First, the living present locates the past and future as dimensions of the present, not as separate ontological entities; the present is dynamic and has a form of agency in that it shapes the past and potential futures. Second, and in contrast to Deleuze (1994), Hernes (2014) argues that the living present is the present experienced only by human actors and not only as individuals but with the possibility of co-presence. Following Schütz (1972, 1973), he introduces the idea that living presents have a 'we' dimension where the experience of the present is shared and may involve the interactions between individuals and their shared experience of the present. Third, the living present is experienced time. Hernes (2014) draws on Whitehead and Bergson's distinction between the present as experienced and the experience of the present conceptualized, which Whitehead terms as the 'specious present'. The specious present is the present consciously reflected on and is not the direct experience of the present, for once the present has been conceptualized, it has passed. Bergson (1908/2010) identifies a distinction between *durée* or 'pure passing of time' or 'real time' and 'reflection', that is, spatial thinking and therefore of a different order or kind than *durée*. This distinction is very important for Hernes's (2014) idea of the living present, as the experience of the flow of the moments in the present without reflection and his subsequent development of the notion of the 'event'.

A second key concept for Hernes (2014) is that of 'events' that are presents that have passed and been reflected upon—they occur at a particular past moment and have a spatial form and context—they occur in specific spaces or locations. Events have agency in the form of their lineages to past and future potential and their overlap with other events. They open possibilities based on living presents to shape the past and to establish propensities for the future. Events can coalesce as they are framed together in retrospective and prospective sensemaking in ordering the becoming of entities and processes. In 'drawing on Whitehead's (1920) atomistic view of events', Hernes (2014: 95) considers that event formations are structured in 'manifolds:'

What characterizes a manifold beyond having different forms or elements is that elements are woven together in a continuum that has no endpoints, rather like planes that intersect and self-intersect. In mechanics a manifold appears as tubes spreading like a fan out from a central point, allowing liquid or gas to reach several spatially dispersed points simultaneously. The image of a mechanical manifold is already very different from imagery of a line. When points are seen temporally, that is, as events rather than spatially, that is, as points in space, it means that multiple events both in the past and future are affected by what takes place in the present event.

Manifolds exist in what he terms neighbourhoods and are constituted in three different relationships: continuity, connectedness, and convergence (2014: 96). Thus events arising out of the reflective structuring of living presents are foundational and lead him to develop the third strand of his conceptual framework in the concept of 'meaning structures', a term built on the works of Heidegger and Schutz in which entities like processes become through ongoing meaning making that he calls 'noun-making', thus extending Weick's (1995) concept of verb making. Hernes (2014: 106) uses a number of examples to illustrate, such as

> A dairy plant produces milk, the milk is a material object in its crude form in the sense that it was extracted, transported, refined and traded. But it may take on the qualities of a sign when it is referred to in conversation or translated into various schemas, diagrams, statistics etc. that is when milk encounters other actors at organizational presents, which turn into events. At another level of signification it becomes a symbol, such as when it comes to symbolize, life, reproduction, nature, or purity as it encounters actors at other presents that turn into events.

Meaning structures are produced by actors in performance of various practices and actions, although these do not exist external to the performance of meaningful actions but can structure social interactions. He links the notion of meaning structures to that of articulation, a concept drawn from the sociologist Strauss (1988) that he finds useful in conceptualizing meaning structures in ways that do not return meaning to representation. Articulation is the way that meaning structures are connected to different actors and seems to relate (although Hernes does not say so) to the ANT notion of translation. He suggests five modes of articulation: intersubjective, practical, textual, material, and tacit. Each of these modes of articulation supports the movement and connections of meaning structures, actors, and entities in their becoming (Hernes, 2014: 125). Becoming is not restricted to things becoming different but relates to the temporal connections made by the articulation of meaning structures. These connections may be in the form of remaking the meaning of the past in line with present meaning structures and in anticipation of future potential. In drawing the strands of his argument together, he proposes that 'it is this spatio-temporal ordering that may be taken as "the organization", which consists of conceptual, human, or material elements forming interconnected wholes' (2014: 105).

Along with the increasing body of work on process organization studies (see, e.g., Helin, Hernes, Hjorth, & Holt, 2014; Hernes, 2008, 2014; Hernes & Schultz, 2015; Hernes, Simpson, & Soderland, 2013), Hernes provides a useful contribution not only in providing much more detailed explications and fine-grained analyses of process theory but also in revisiting time and reconceptualizing temporality. He does not sidestep the problem of moving from a world characterized by representational language in the everyday to a process ontology in which there is a fluidity and tangledness to organizational life. There is an interconnectedness of being in the flow of time where the living present is not experienced separately but remains intimately part of the past and future, and in this, there is a form of agency in the way that the dynamic present shapes both the past and potential futures. This view on temporality is useful as is the notion of the present as experienced and the present as conceptualized experience, but for us, there remains a concern about the absence of political time as agency for future potential as well as a pervasive instrument of dominance and power (an issue we shall return to later).

Extending Conceptualizations on the Multiplicity of Time: Deleuze

In extending some of the ideas already presented, especially the notion of a living present, and building on our discussion of a processual approach in Chapters 9 and 10, we turn to Deleuze (1994), whose work has had limited use in organizational studies particularly outside the later work with Guattari (1987). Several key concepts from his work are the focus of our attention here with the aim of broadening our understanding of time and temporality and furthering theorization on organizational change. But first we provide a brief overview of his background and approach.

Deleuze: His Work and Method

Deleuze has often been labelled a post-structuralist, a tag that centres discourse as the central mediating mechanism between thought and reality; however, he considered himself as a metaphysician with his central concern ontology (Kristensen, Lodrup-Hjorth, & Sorensen, 2014). Although the use of metaphysics is strongly rejected by many contemporary thinkers, Deleuze considered it a creative opportunity to discover what could be if we are enabled to think differently (Kristensen et al., 2014). His early works are largely commentaries on a select group of philosophers, for example, Hume, Kant, Spinoza, Leibniz, the Stoics, Bergson, and Foucault, from whose work he re-created concepts in rather novel and controversial ways to explicate his own views. Not surprisingly, in his later work with Guattari (Deleuze & Guattari, 1987), they advocate the idea of the development of concepts as the defining task of philosophy (Buchanan, 2000).

In what follows, we present a number of concepts drawn from the work of Deleuze as Buchanan (2000: 48) explains for Deleuze: 'Concepts are not what philosophers think about, but what they think with'. In discussing these concepts that are all used by Deleuze as tools to explicate the notion of difference as it is in itself, we want to propose not just another temporal philosophy but to underscore the notion that starting from an ontology that privileges difference extends the concepts of temporality and their uses in studying organizational change. However in seeking to be Deleuzian in our approach by employing his concepts for use in this work, it is important to emphasise here a second central tenet of Deleuze's philosophy, namely, that it is actively anti-representational (Buchanan, 2000, 2008; Hughes, 2012; Williams, 2013). As Buchanan (2000: 3) insists, citing Deleuze's 'unvarnished admiration' for the work of Melville, 'Every writer writes two books, Melville says, one for which we need only ink, and another which is inscribed in blood and anguish on our soul' (2000: 3). Deleuze seeks throughout his work to elucidate the inadequacies of representational thinking and the limitations of the expressionist move in which the expression and 'its signifiers are adequate expressions of its signifieds' (2000: 3). In Deleuze's work, we therefore find a useful foundation not in seeking to slavishly follow him or his many commentators but to develop an eclectic approach consistent with the multiple times at work in processual understandings of organizational change. In so doing, we adopt a performative, processual approach that does not privilege one best way of time or temporal orientation. In attempting to use a Deleuzian approach, we do not explicate his view of time as the only way but show that his approach, consistent with his ontology of difference, worked for him and his purposes.

Difference and Repetition

Deleuze's key undertaking in his opus magnum *Difference and Repetition* is to develop a comprehensive philosophical system based on difference and multiplicity. It is this work that we are mainly focusing on in this chapter in which he draws together many of the concepts he explored in the early commentaries to create and develop his central philosophical concept of difference as the ontological starting point. This philosophy returns to the starting point of Platonic ontology and the centrality of the notion of being and the related ideas of identity and presence that provide the ground for most of Western philosophy (Williams, 2013). Deleuze (1994) takes a different position and sets out to develop an idea of becoming and being that centres on the concept of difference. In this approach he uses difference not as a comparison with that identified in another being that has presence, nor as something as it relates to the pure form of a thing or its idea, but difference as something that distinguishes itself (Deleuze, 1994). To make this clear he goes back to critique the notion of being and its relationship to substance as explicated by Plato and Aristotle. Through drawing on a wide range of philosophical concepts, Deleuze (1994) builds his notion of difference in itself (pure difference), which he contends has not been adequately discussed or developed elsewhere. This notion of pure difference is not in contrast to forms of identity, such as comparison or resemblance, but as it is in itself. This nuanced concept can be a little difficult to grasp given the common link of identity and presence to representations (through language and experiences) that are strongly embedded in our Western ways of thinking.

Western thought and language are imbued with notions developed by Plato and expanded on by Aristotle that privilege identity and representation as the ontological beginning—reality or being is structured and represented in knowable orders and categories built around genera.

Deleuze's (1994) discussion of repetition similarly presents a novel interpretation of the meaning of the term. He interprets repetition as the return of the different, not the return of the same. He develops his line of argument with the idea that repetition is not resemblance or reducible to sameness but that it actually relies on difference. For something to repeat, there must be something different about that which repeats for it to be repetition. This seems paradoxical at first but is clear if an example is used. He draws on Hume's idea that the object of repetition may not be noticeably different but that the experience of the thing as it comes later in time is different as it is experienced by the observer. Further, as the connections between the thing or event are constantly becoming, the thing itself is never the same.

The radical approach to difference and repetition is at odds with most other views of time and temporality, with the exception of Bergson discussed in earlier chapters. Elizabeth Grosz (2004) in her book *The Nick of Time* demonstrates the utility of Bergson's view of difference encapsulated in the work of Deleuze through employing a form of eclecticism similar to the Deleuzian method. She explicates an ontology emphasising difference, duration and becoming, in her particular emphasis on bodies and gender. In developing a feminist politic, with strong traces of the influence of the work of Luce Iragary, the work connects the ideas of three thinkers who are seldom considered as bedfellows but who have all emphasised the evolution of time and bodies in very difference way,: namely, Darwin, Nietzsche, and Bergson.

In a feminist critique, Grosz (2004: 160) argues that Bergson presents a view of time (building on ideas found in Darwin and Nietzsche) in which the past (male dominance) does not swallow up the future but is returned to open the future (offering potential for gender equality). She identifies the Bergsonian distinction between differences of degree and differences of kind (Grosz, 2004) as the central tenet of the idea of duration. Bergson's work on difference is seen to be central to the later development of the metaphysics of difference in Deleuze's philosophy. Differences in degree relate to matter and the external world being quantitative, homogeneous, and connected to space, whereas differences of kind relate to consciousness and sensation, which are qualitative: 'They differ from themselves in duration' in the experience of time (2004: 159).

Syntheses of Time

Deleuze's (1994) work on time forms a central component of his process philosophy as his three syntheses of time are inextricably linked to the genesis and reconceptions of difference and repetition (Deleuze, 1994;

Williams, 2012). James Williams (2012, 2013) has written extensively about Deleuze's work on time and shows that Deleuze's philosophy of time entails 'difference as becoming', where difference is not identified with any theory of presence or identity. Williams suggests that the development of his concept of time enables him to 'ground his process philosophy without linking to a prior metaphysical system or identity or to locate on an empirical basis' (2011: 2). Deleuze identifies three syntheses of time that are irreducible to one another but 'form a network of asymmetrical formal and singular processes' (2011: 3). He defines synthesis either active or passive as processes that produce multiple times (2011: 3). Asymmetry implies the irreversibility of time:

> In turn, this is a first clue as to the radical nature of Deleuze's philosophy of time: it is inherently anti-conservative and anti-reactionary due to its inbuilt and unavoidable asymmetries of time. There is no represented original to go back to. There is no eternal realm to escape to in the future, where time stands still. Every process is multiple, irreducible. . . . There is no way back and no way up and out.
>
> (Williams, 2011: 4)

Williams suggests that for Deleuze, the notion of singularities is contrasted to the general features often associated with discussions of time, such as things occurring in the present, past, or future. The occurrence of the singularities of individual processes at work is what produces different or multiple times (2011: 4). Such singularities are said to be formal in that they describe types of processes, for example, those determining the past as a dimension of the present; however, within that frame, 'singular processes determine their own times' (2011: 5). He concludes that for Deleuze, time is irreducibly multiple and complex (2011: 5). The syntheses are irreducible to one another or to an overarching unity. Williams (2011) suggests that for Deleuze, past, present, and future are not separate parts of time but are dimensions of one another. 'All of these times interact and interlock, but . . . they do not submit to any external or internal order that can reduce the multiplicity of times to a single set of laws, patterns or probabilities' (2011: 11).

Passive Synthesis

The concept of synthesis underpins and is central to the development of his understanding of time. Williams goes so far as to say that

> Deleuze's account of the structure of reality depends on arguments for the necessity and universality of synthesis. In this synthesis all living things develop expectancy based on the passive inclusion of past repetitions in

anticipation of the future. We only acquire habits by synthesizing earlier members of a series in later ones. We only acquire representations in memory and language by synthesizing earlier memories that are themselves synthesis of experiences.

(Williams, 2013: 14)

He argues that the key syntheses that occur in the development of time are passive and not the province of human agency—all living things are open to syntheses (Williams, 2013). Likewise, Buchanan (2008) agrees that the concept of passive synthesis underpins Deleuze's (1994) work, influencing his idea of the unconscious and desire that dominate his later work with Guattari (1987). Buchanan (2008) argues that for Deleuze, the use of passive synthesis enables him to discuss the vexing question of 'how can the mind constitute itself without first of all having an idea of itself?' (2008: 52). In contrast to Hegel and Kant, who posit spirit and mind respectively as the prior categories on which to address the issue, Deleuze's (1994) solution is 'to posit at a foundational level a set of passive syntheses that are constitutive without being active' (2008: 52). Buchanan (2008) unpacks his argument that the synthesis is passive, citing Deleuze (1994): 'It is not carried out by the mind, but occurs *in* the mind which contemplates, prior to all memory and reflection'. In the following passage, Buchanan (2008: 52–53) succinctly shows the connections between the central ideas of passive synthesis, expectation, and contraction that underpin Deleuze's argument in relation to the originary status of time:

> Deleuze writes, 'we must regard habit as the foundation from which all other psychic phenomena derive.' (DR78/107). The passive synthesis of habit 'constitutes the habit of living, our expectation that "it" will continue'. (DR, 74/101). Habits are the 'presents' (moments of pure lived time) the imagination seizes from the flow of time, without ever ceasing to be temporal. . . . Habit is used in a pre-subjective sense. It doesn't refer to the habits, good or bad, of a fully formed subject, like smoking or reading the Sunday papers in bed. It is not something 'I' do. It belongs rather to the order of the formation of the organism itself, at its most elementary. The capacity to contract a habit is in this respect the most basic prerequisite of the organism. Habit is a mode of contraction. Contraction for Deleuze is the synthetic basis of all life forms, describing literally how they come into being. At the level of organic synthesis: 'We are made of contracted water, earth light and air—not merely prior to recognition or representation of these, but prior to their being sensed. Every organism in its receptive and perceptual elements, but also in its viscera, is a sum of contractions, of retentions and expectations.'
>
> (DR73/100)

It is in the contractions in the passive synthesis that the becoming of being and difference occur and, as Williams (2011, 2013) shows, that time originates.

The First Synthesis of Time: The Living Present

In the first synthesis, Deleuze (1994) discusses how this passive synthesis is not the product of human conscious action but is the result of a contraction of present moments in the repetition of an action or a habit. Here the action occurs based on learned responses over time that become repeatable without conscious thought or memory. The synthesis is passive and based on repetition. Time is produced as a living present, a concept that he develops based on Bergson's discussion of how living organisms responding to stimuli first pause prior to acting. The pause is a contraction, a living response. Deleuze takes up this idea in his view of the living present in which the past and future only exist as dimensions of the present.

In the second synthesis of time, he develops the idea that for the present to pass, there must be something that occurs to move the present on to be a past present. He suggests that memory moves from the living present to what he calls the pure past, which includes all past presents but not as discrete events. Memory of particular events is different to the pure past. In this synthesis the present and future are dimensions of the past. Difference is possible in that it is the difference between all possible past events—it is not the difference of the events from one another but that all events in time are essentially different. The third synthesis of time 'depends upon the notion of pure difference' or novelty as constituted in singularities (Williams, 2012: 15). Singularities provide cuts in the flow of time so that the past and present are divided by each singular event. Singularities then are cuts or caesura that divide time. In this synthesis the future is central, and the past and present are dimensions of the future. Deleuze is strongly influenced here by the idea of the return of the different, an idea drawn and developed from the work of Nietzsche.

Virtual and Actual

As discussed, Deleuze (1994) develops a formal or transcendental concept of difference that refers to difference not in or between things but difference in its pure form. To develop this idea, he introduces the distinction between the actual and the virtual existence of things. The actual relates to the categories of the thing in terms of genera, including its qualities and extension in space. Things differ categorically. In contrast, virtuality relates to the becomings of the thing and its relations to everything else—actual and potential things. The virtual is experienced consciously in what he calls, following Nietzsche, 'intensities' that are the potentials and relations that relate to a particular thing—the flow of ideas, affects, and relations that arise. He shows how these virtual becomings or intensities are equally a part of 'reality' along with actual things. Things are made up of actual and virtual becomings and are not fixed by present boundaries. The fixity by which we regard things is an illusion as all things are becoming. As Williams (2013: 13) says, 'He is committed to the reality of things that are neither actual nor identifiable'. Intensities, he suggests, are necessary to make life significant and are singular in that they are experienced differently by 'individuals'. Here the term 'individuals' exceeds humans: 'An individual is a thing where thought takes place' (2013: 6). Grosz also draws the contrast between the actual and the virtual as found both in the work of Bergson and Deleuze but also in the work of Darwin and Nietzsche in which the future remains indeterminate and open as she says (2004: 251–252):

> The virtual exists only in time. Objects in space carry all they require of the past within themselves as their present. They are actual manifest. The past subsists in the present only for living beings or for open systems: it is only for living beings that history is significant, that the past can modify the future and the future the past, providing possibilities that the present hasn't contained. The virtual is the condition of being otherwise than what something is at the moment, its capacity for self-modification, elaboration, overcoming. It is thus the very possibility of the cultural, the political, the conceptual. The virtual is another name for the inherence of the past in the present, for the capacity to become other. . . . The virtual is the resonance of potential that ladens the present as more than itself, that disrupts the continuity of the present, to open up a nick or crack, the untimely, the unexpected, that welcomes the new, whether a new organism, organ, or function a new strategy, a new sensation, or a new technological invention.

She suggests that freedom is the capacity of the body to act based on knowledge of the past to create something new in the present or future. This delayed response to stimulus by living things is linked to the capacity for choice based on needs, desires, and so forth that creates the virtual in the face of the actual. The object creates a virtual interval: 'The cerebral interval is filled with affective, body memories (or habit memory) and pure recollections (duration)' (Grosz, 2004: 169). She shows temporal understandings and practices emphasising the contrast between the actual and the virtual as the central component of her feminist politic:

> The past is never fixed, completely known, transparent and unalterable, it remains open and is 'never exhausted in its virtualities' it is always open to another historical reading or interpretation. Thus history is controversial and volatile 'not simply tied to getting the facts of the past sorted out and agreed on. 'It is about the production of *conceivable*

futures, the future understood not as that which is simply contained in the present, but rather, as what diverges from the present, what produces a new future, one uncontained by and unpredicted from within the past'.

(2004: 255)

She concludes that 'sensations, feelings, affects always transform themselves over time' (2004: 161–162).

In viewing time and temporality in organizational change from the perspective of an ontology of difference, new horizons are glimpsed, for in contrast to approaches that are founded on the notion of being as a univocal expression that privileges identity, which leads to the continuation and return of the same, difference is all there is—not just difference of degree but differences in kind. In relation to change in organizations, every repetition of the same (routines and practices) is different by virtue of the concept of repetition as the repetition of difference. The repetition of actions as habitual— the contractions of what might be termed muscle memory within certain habits and memorized, physical actions—are always different, even though to all intents and purposes they may appear the same. Duration as difference of kind means that the experience of a routine or practice is always singular and unique. As discussed in Chapter 10, change as a result of the repetition of routines and practices is thus an example of repetition that is different, thus it is perhaps not surprising that such change can be transformational (Orlikowski, 2002). The potential for change of the actual into something wholly new is opened by linking the idea of repetition to the concept of the virtual in which the potentials and relations of a thing and its relations to everything else open up the future through recognition of the reality of things 'that are neither actual or identifiable' (Williams, 2013).

The political implications of this approach are explicated by Grosz (2004) in that a certain view of the past may be riddled with challenges, but the past may also be rewritten in the light of the virtual, the openness, and indeterminacy of the future. In terms of organizational change, what has been may well repeat but will necessarily be different. Multiple, competing views and temporal orientations will at times inevitably align or collide with important ramifications for organizations and their actors. In this we are reminded of the early processual studies of Buchanan and Badham (1999), Dawson (1994), and Pettigrew (1985) that reject apolitical accounts of organizational change by explicitly demonstrating the centrality of political alignments in understanding and enacting organizational change. As discussed in Chapter 7, power and politics are ubiquitous, enacted either directly in forms of coercion or through disciplining mechanisms in micro-relations and webs of power utilizing subjugation, acquiescence, and consent smoothed out in discourse, production, and hegemony. A multiplicity of times as explicated by Deleuze provides a conceptual framework that makes sense of how a politically homogenized past can be reviewed and disrupted, opening virtual space for the becoming of the different. Politics, as Grosz (2004) reminds us, is an opportunity for the becoming of the untimely 'nick of time' and not merely the negative return of the same. Thus temporality is linked to agency and becoming not through the power or agency of individual subjects but as those implicated in passive synthesis and assemblages.

Conclusion

In tracing the development of the process turn in organization studies, we can see a major contribution to the development of understanding time and temporality in organizations. The detailed and tightly constructed arguments based on the works of Whitehead, Mead, and Schutz in the development of this temporal structure of organization in Hernes (2014) and the concept of the living present and the multiplicity of temporalities presented by Deleuze (1994) are useful. Also the ontology of difference aligns well with a process view of organizational change that is ongoing, complex, dynamic, and forever changing. In this work attending to organizational change, we see useful associations to our own approach in seeking to explicate richer and more adequate explanations of time and temporality in studies of organization. The fluidity of tangledness and the network of relations evident in the work of Hernes usefully speak to the collapse of linear time and displace any notion of time as a singular concept and movement as something that is ultimately linked with space. There is an interconnectedness that is not limited by space or clock time but a part of a past and future that flow in a living present. This inseparability combined with a sense of agency in which indeterminacy is not outside of our living influence resonates well with some of our own processual ideas (although we feel the need for more engagement with power). The uniqueness and difference that are a part of change is an intimate part of a Deluezian position and one that we also adhere to. Change is not just found in change, but it is found in routines and habitual actions; there is no return of same but only the return of difference. Change is essential to being and existence; it is part of the everyday found in the workplace, in the home, and in our dreams. For us this return of difference is not just to be found in the internal consciousness of being but also in the external world in which structures and agencies are represented through language. There may be silent transformations, but these are still transformation—different, unique, and forever changing. Our own processual perspective accords well with these views and are areas that we hope to further develop in our potentialities for the future in our living present (whilst only being too aware that these words are written in ink and are limited whilst our internal dialogues draw blood of soulful anguish for the words that we were unable to find but continue look for in our continuing journey). In short, there are useful contributions from these works that move us forward in our understanding of time and temporality, but there are also limitations.

For us a major limitation in much of this work is the tendency to move outside of lived experience and to ignore the inequalities evident in work and society, the power differential among individuals and group, the wealth disparities that create divisions that need to be represented and tackled, and the often degrading and painful experiences of those on the receiving end of change. In all of these ongoing discussions about process in the recent turn to process in organization studies, there is little (if any) explicit consideration of power and politics. This in our view is a major deficit as, along with Clegg and Haugaard (2013), we consider power and politics to be central to understanding organizations, change processes, and temporality. In drawing on insights from Grosz (2005) and taking a Deleuzian orientation to concept development and theorization, we suggest that a return to a processual framework for understanding change that takes power and politics as central, as exemplified by the polyphony of change narratives and the political process of change as a multi-story process.

Similarly, in seeking to explicate views of complex organizational change, we are reminded by Mol and Law that complexity is where 'things relate but don't add up' and that 'events occur but not within the processes of linear time' (2002: 1). The propensity to simplify, homogenize, and classify are both necessary and problematic, for as Mol and Law (2002: 1) go on to say, 'The world is complex and that it shouldn't be tamed too much—certainly not to the point where simplification becomes an impediment to understanding'.

Organizational change is often tied to the discrete or sequential unfolding of events and the agency enacted in such events. However, the overlapping of multiple times in 'asymmetrical and singular processes' and passive syntheses explicated by Deleuze open the possibility for a multiplicity of times where multiplicity is 'about coexistences at a single moment' (Mol & Law, 2002)—an account of organizational change located not only in linear, cyclical times or time created in events along the arrow of time but also in asymmetrical and singular processes and multiplicities saturated with the virtual.

References

Bergson, H. (1911/1998). *Creative Evolution.* New York: Dover.
Bergson, H. (1908/2010). *Matter and Memory* (N. Paul & W. Palmer, Trans.). Overland Park, Kansas: Digireads.com Publishing.
Buchanan, D. A., & Badham, R. J. (1999). *Power, Politics, and Organizational Change: Winning the Turf Game.* London Sage Publications.
Buchanan, I. (2000). *Deleuzism: A Metacommentary.* Durham: Duke University Press.
Buchanan, I. (2008). *Deleuze and Guattari's Anti-Oedipus.* London: Continuum International Publishing Group.
Clegg, S. R., & Haugaard, M. (Eds.). (2013). *The SAGE Handbook of Power.* London: Sage.
Dawson, P. (1994). *Organizational Change: A Processual Approach.* London: Paul Chapman Publishing.
Deleuze, G. (1994). *Difference and Repetition* (P. Patton, Trans.). New York: Columbia University Press.
Deleuze, G., & Guattari, F. (1987). *A Thousand Plateaus: Capitalism and Schizophrenia.* Minneapolis: University of Minnesota Press.

Grosz, E. (2004). *The Nick of Time: Politics, Evolution and the Untimely*. Durham and London: Duke University Press.

Grosz, E. (2005). *Time Travels: Feminism, Nature, Power*. Crows Nest, NSW: Allan & Unwin.

Heidegger, M. (1962). *Being and Time* (J. M. E. Robinson, Trans.). New York: Harper Collins.

Helin, J., Hernes, T., Hjorth, D., & Holt, R. (2014). Process is how process does. In J. Helin, T. Hernes, D. Hjorth, & R. Holt (Eds.), *The Oxford Handbook of Process Philosophy and Organization Studies* (pp. 1–16). Oxford: Oxford University Press.

Helin, J., Hernes, T., Hjorth, D., & Holt, R. (Eds.) (2014). *The Oxford Handbook of Process Philosophy and Organization Studies*. Oxford: Oxford University Press.

Hernes, T. (2008). *Understanding Organization as Process: Theory for a Tangled World*. London and New York: Routledge.

Hernes, T. (2014). *A Process Theory of Organization*. Oxford: Oxford University Press.

Hernes, T., & Schultz, M. (2015). *Organizational Time*. Paper presented at the Seventh International Process Symposium, Kos, Greece.

Hernes, T., Simpson, B., & Soderland, J. (2013). Managing and temporality. *Scandinavian Journal of Management, 29*(1), 1–6.

Hughes, J. (2012). *Deleuze's Difference and Repetition*. London: Continuum International Publishing Group.

Kristensen, A., Lodrup-Hjorth, T., & Sorensen, B. (2014). Gilles Deleuze. In J. Helin, T. Hernes, D. Hjorth, & R. Holt (Eds.), *The Oxford Handbook of Process Philosophy and Organization Studies* (pp. 499–514). Oxford: Oxford University Press.

Langley, A., Smallman, C., Tsoukas, H., & Van de Ven, A. (2013). Process studies of change in organization and management: Unveiling temporality, activity and flow. *Academy of Management Journal, 56*(1), 1–13.

Langley, A., & Tsoukas, H. (2010). Introducing perspectives on process organization studies. In T. Hernes & S. Maitlis (Eds.), *Process, Sensemaking, and Organization* (pp. 1–26). Oxford: Oxford University Press.

Langley, A., & Tsoukas, H. (Eds.). (2016). *The Sage Handbook of Process Organization Studies*. London: Sage.

Latour, B. (1991). Technology is society made durable. In J. Law (Ed.), *A Sociology of Monsters: Essays on Power, Technology and Domination* (pp. 101–131). London: Routledge.

Latour, B. (2007). *Reassembling the Social: An Introduction to Actor-Network-Theory*. Oxford: Oxford University Press.

Mead, G. H. (1932/1980). *The Philosophy of the Present*. Chicago and London: The University of Chicago Press.

Mol, A., & Law, J. (2002). Complexities an introduction. In A. Mol & J. Law (Eds.), *Complexities: Social Studies of Knowledge Practices* (pp. 1–22). Durham and London: Duke University Press.

Orlikowski, W. (2002). Knowing in practice: Enacting a collective capability in distributed organizing. *Organization Science, 13*(3), 249–273.

Pettigrew, A. (1985). *The Awakening Giant: Continuity and Change in Imperial Chemical Industries*. Oxford: Basil Blackwell

Rescher, N. (1996). *Process Metaphysics: An Introduction to Process Philosophy*. Albany, NY: State University of New York.

Schütz, A. (1972). *Phenomenology of the Social World*. Evanston, IL: Northwestern University Press.

Schütz, A. (1973). *The Structures of the Life World: Volume 1*. Evanston, IL: Northwestern University Press.

Sedley, D. (2003). *Plato's Cratylus*. Cambridge: Cambridge University Press.

Strauss, A. (1988). The articulation of project work: An organizational process. *The Sociological Quarterly, 29*(2), 163–178.

Tsoukas, H., & Chia, R. (2002). On organizational becoming: Rethinking organizational change. *Organization Science, 13*(5) (September–October 2002), 567–582.

Weick, K. (1995). *Sensemaking in Organizations*. Thousand Oaks: Sage.

Whitehead, A. N. (1929). *Process and Reality: An Essay in Cosmology*. New York: Free Press.

Williams, J. (2011). *Gilles Deleuze's Philosophy of Time*. Edinburgh: Edinburgh University Press.

Williams, J. (2012). *Gilles Deleuze's Philosophy of Time*. Edinburgh: Edinburgh University Press.

Williams, J. (2013). *Gilles Deleuze's Difference and Repetition: A Critical Introduction and Guide*. Edinburgh: Edinburgh University Press.

12 Conclusion

Although our sojourn has been necessarily broad, our aim has been to extract out and explain central polemical discussions and to unveil and debate rather than to resolve ongoing issues and concerns. Our main focus has been on time, temporality, and organizational change, and we have continually emphasised the surprising absence of time in concept development and theorization, even though temporality is implicated in the models and frameworks that seek to describe, predict, guide, or explain organizational change. In exploring different conceptions of time in science, sociology, psychology, philosophy, and organization studies, we identified the tendency to divide objective concepts of time from time as subjectively experienced, and we spotlighted the pervasiveness within change theorization—either explicitly but more often implicitly—to use a Newtonian concept of linear time. We contend that this is problematic as too much attention has been placed on the objective dimensions of time in theoretical explanations, and this is a major current weakness in much of the mainstream change management literature. Surprisingly, in related fields, such as change and technology, storytelling, and sensemaking, there has also been an absence of time that has largely gone unnoticed (even within major reviews). Whereas we examined some scholarly work that addressed time and temporality in organizations, these were thinly spread and rather sporadic. To put it bluntly, the organizational studies and management literature are marked by a general silence on temporality and the various uses made of time in, for example, the process of conducting organizational research on change from design, fieldwork, analysis, concept development, and theorization.

As our broad and extensive review has highlighted, objective forms of time dominate the literature with the more subjective experiential dimensions either being ignored or downplayed. We strongly advocate the need to counter this inclination in presenting a more thorough examination of subjective time. In considering the relationship between objective and subjective time, caution should be given to simple divisional representations (as being separate and identifiable elements) as attention should also be given to viewing time and temporal relations as being mutually constitutive (relational), as well as the need to consider multiple temporalities in a more time-sensitive approach to the study and theorization of complex processes of organizational change.

In reflecting on our own perspective, there are many areas that we wish to explore further in continuing to develop our approach. We have outlined our current position in adopting a processual ontology with a sociological orientation in which power and politics, culture and context, sociomateriality and multiple temporalities are all used to inform our understanding. In our grounded research, longitudinal contextual studies are used to collect empirical data within organizations over time. We observe and attempt to explain complex, non-linear processes of change associated with both planned and unplanned change initiatives that take place within organizations with established hierarchies and enduring social relationships in which individuals and groups make and give sense to what is occurring and respond in a variety of different ways and variously engage and disengage with the power-political processes of change. Orientation issues in studying time and how it relates to processes of change in organizations and broader scientific and philosophical concerns have been an issue that we have sought to explore. Whereas the importance of a critical reflective methodology and a representational epistemology have been manifest in our own fieldwork studies and in our systematic examination and academic evaluations of the work of others (as well as being important to studying people in organizations who make and give sense to processes of change representationally through language, symbols, non-verbal forms of communication, etc.), we have also been aware of the limits of language in capturing some of the nuanced ideas and concepts of time. This issue of language and the problem of representationalism have been addressed in the literature, and it is one that we briefly return to in our final section (interestingly Barad's work—that adopts agential realism—highlights the contortions of language required in explaining a performative posthumanist perspective that adopts a diffractive methodology and a relational ontology).

Historically, there have been many beliefs, methods, and artefacts linked to concepts and reconfigurations of time that illustrate the multiple, heterogeneous, and dynamic character of time. Yet whereas there is an innate feeling that we understand time, it remains outside of our senses, invisible but ever present in pasts that we recollect and in futures that we anticipate. With every breath taken our thoughts seem to easily accept the notion of the progressive flow of time in the passing of moments and events in our lives. There is a sense in which we are constantly aware of duration, a duration that has a past and a time yet to be; there is an intuitive sense of temporality. But our sense of temporality has also been shown to be culturally influenced;, for example, for some cultures there is a temporality of a past and present and, for others, a temporality of a past, present, and future (Jones & Brown, 2005; Levine, 2006). There is nevertheless an intuitive understanding of time that extends beyond the 'now' of the present into a history and context that reconfirms (and at times questions) our place in existence. Broader questions arise around our timely existence on, for example, whether we exist in time or whether time exists in us. Is our perception of the present extending into a temporality of experience a part of an external reality, an aspect of internal consciousness, sociologically determined, or a complex entanglement? These and a multitude of other questions have been raised in this book and continue to stimulate controversies and debates on time.

In this final chapter we do not seek to summarize all that has gone before but to open up further discussion, academic conversation, and scholarly debate on time, temporality, and organizational chapter around four issues that are pertinent to the conclusion of this book, namely:

1. The paradox of time
2. The institutionalization of clock time and the privileging of objective time over subjective time
3. The implications of science, philosophy, and social science debates on time for concept development and theorization in organization studies
4. The need to take a more critical stance in broader conceptualizations of time and temporality in the further development of organizational change theories

But first, we consider the subtitle of this book, namely, the arrow of time and the 'reality' and 'illusion' of temporality.

Bending the Arrow(s) of Time

The arrow of time captures notions of progress, of life cycles, and of seasonal rhythms in the unidirectional movement of a universe that is expanding. Entropy—central to the arrow of time—provides a scientific underpinning to the notion that time flows forward and that we are part of the forward movement as disorder increases or stays the same. From this perspective, there is a general acceptance of linear, homogenous time and a ready adoption of time-metering devices that reinforces Newtonian time through the clock and Gregorian calendar. This concept of the arrow of time originated from the British astronomer Arthur Eddington in 1927, who although recognising that time reversal was theoretically possible, advocated that time within the universe moved only in one direction (the forward movement of time), and this is how we, as people, experience time on earth. Although in practical terms we engage in a present, we observe through our own eyes events that have already happened (to put it simply by the time light reaches us for us to see the movement of those around us, the event has already occurred). In terms of the expansion of the universe and the increasing disorder that occurs, the direction of time is seen to flow forward. This builds on the second law of thermodynamics, where entropy (randomness) always increases (or remains the same) at a later time. This scientific position supports the irreversibility of time that is reinforced by the fact that there have been no scientific studies that have proven the practical possibility of people being able to go against the arrow of time and travel back in time (this remains in the realm of science fiction).

Even though we are aware of relativity from Einstein's concept of space-time, this Newtonian determinacy of an external absolute time that moves ever forward has provided a useful conceptualization and starting point for scholars to counterpoise and develop their own theories on time and temporality. In his book *A Brief History of Time*, Hawking (2011), drawing on elements from Newton, Kant and Einstein, puts forward the idea of three arrows of time. The first refers to the arrow of time as commonly conceived and is referred to as the 'thermodynamic arrow' in which entropy increases or remains the same. The second he terms as the 'cosmological', arrow which refers to the forward direction of time in which the universe expands rather than contracts. But the third arrow, titled the 'psychological arrow', sets out to capture our experiences and feelings of how time passes and includes memories of the past but not of the future. For Hawking, the thermodynamic and psychological arrows will always point in the same direction as we remember events in the same movement of time that entropy takes; that is, we can remember the past (which has occurred) but not the future (which has not occurred).[1] In this Hawking does not incorporate the work of social psychologists, such as Zimbardo and Boyd (Zimbardo & Boyd, 2010), who forward the concept of a five-frame time perspective that includes future orientation (see Chapter 3) and, as such, has been criticized for an oversimplification of the social and psychological dimensions of time.

A more appropriate psychological arrow of time that incorporates the work of Zimbardo and colleagues would contain a fivefold frame representing temporality in the way our relationship to time affects psychological health and our sense of a meaningful present and possibilities for the future. Under this psychological arrow people can become trapped in a past, forever reliving critical moments or nightmare events that prevent them from engaging in the present or preferring to remember the good times and wishing to remain in memorial time; others may live for potential futures and defer gratification in the present to work towards something for themselves or perhaps significant attachments, such as other family members; yet others may simply live for the now in hedonistic pleasures or become fatalistic in feeling a lack of agency or potential to shape their own destinies. This psychological arrow building on the work of Zimbardo (Zimbardo & Boyd, 1999, 2010) is more temporal than the one suggested by Hawking as it accommodates time not as experienced in a past towards a present but as comprising heterogeneous and relived experiences of past, present, and future.

In drawing on the work of Durkheim (1915), Elias (1993), Levine (2006), and Marx (1930) it is possible to add a fourth arrow to this typology, namely the 'social arrow' of time that takes into account the way concepts of time are shaped by historical, material, contextual, cultural, and political processes. For example, Durkheim viewed time as being socially determined—a social fact *sui generis* (peculiar in their characteristics)—being used by people in society for social purposes in the pursuit of individual, collective, and institutional goals. From this sociological perspective, time shapes behaviour and exerts power over our beliefs and understanding, constraining and enabling the way people act and think in relation to not only time per se but also other social and temporal phenomena. In his *Elementary Forms of Religious Life* Durkheim (1915) highlights the importance of culture and context in shaping social conceptions and the way people experience and make sense of the world. For Durkheim (1915), time cannot be explained by our psychological makeup, nor should it be seen as simply an external absolute or a derivative of individual consciousness, rather it is social and collective in character, reflecting the nature of society, and as such, the bending and reconfiguration of this social arrow of time is part of broader social changes. As Elias reflects, our perceptions of time are shaped historically through intergenerational learning, the building of knowledge, and the development of concepts in which time 'is not an occurrence directly accessible to sense-perception' (1993: 102) but is a human-made symbol of relationships 'always in flux, always having become . . . and always evolving' (1993: 132), noting,

> One will remember that the moon—which has almost disappeared as a timing device from the life of urbanized citizens of industrial nation-states, who suffer from the pressure of time without understanding it—was once a messenger which allowed people at more of less regular intervals to institute breaks in their social life.
>
> (Elias, 1993: 200)

In bending the social arrow of time, we can question the close association of movement with progress in our social use of time—we may be building societies that are regressive in terms of ideals of freedom, democracy, meritocracy, and so forth—and yet the political economy of global capitalism continually reasserts a view of time as progress. It then becomes an easy step to equate organizational change initiatives as representative of progress regardless of the consequences of change for those on the receiving end (a fairly endemic problem in the mainstream change management literature, we would suggest).

In some of these arrows of time, there remains a notion of forward movement, a link with an external world where time can be measured by the passing of days, hours, minutes, and seconds—there is an arrow of progressive time. In others, the arrow is better represented by a bending in the arrow of time (or in some cases bendings in the arrows of time), and yet, there remains an essential link with time and temporality as comprising a present, past, and future. In yet others, the arrow is a boundary only formed in cutting into a boundaryless, entangled world; it is a creation in performativity, an agential cut. Once again we return to dualism, the paradox of time, and the age-old questions about the existence of time and whether temporality is 'living' or 'dead' beyond a present that is now.

Living the Arrow of Time: The Power of Time's Temporality

In organization studies and sociological accounts of work, employment, and society, there is greater attention given to social aspects and the importance of the subjective and intersubjective (Shutz, 1982) in which the dominance of clock time to shared, lived-through time in the Western world supports the general acceptance and internalization of these more linear concepts of time (Adam, 2004). They permit and overflow to our thinking and influence the way we approach, study, and theorize. For example, from a critical management perspective, clock time is seen as a social construct that reflects power relations in pulling people away from natural rhythms and flows to a time that is objectified so that it can be measured, controlled, regulated, and divided (Willmott, 1995). As we outlined in Chapters 4 and 7 clock time has become the dominant time in the Western world and is integral, almost as seamless part of everyday activities both in work and nonwork activities. The institutionalization of clock time has resulted in a tendency for temporal understanding to remain rooted in the Gregorian calendar and atomic clock with studies and theorization linked to a chronological conception of time. Foucault (1979) aptly captures the power and control embedded in the uptake of new time regimes that adopt objective, precise measures in his discussion of disciplinary time:

> Time measured and paid must also be a time without impurities of defects; a time of good quality, throughout which the body is constantly applied to mental virtues of disciplinary time. . . . A sort of anatomo-chronological schema of behaviour is defined. The act is broken down into its elements; the position of the body, limbs, articulations is defined; to each movement are assigned a direction, an aptitude, a duration; their order of succession is prescribed. Time penetrates the body and with it all the meticulous control of power.
>
> (Foucault, 1979: 151–152)

Living in a shared social world where history, context, and culture shape the social dimension of time, our understanding of time arises as part of lived-through, intersubjective experiences. The world in which we reside is socially constructed and one in which we become aware of our birth and inevitable death whilst recognising that the world in which we exist is inherently unequal and will continue long after we are gone. In this sense, all human experience is social and political, but whereas we may internalize clock time and others may construct our life history through the lens of objective time, we nevertheless experience life and meaning subjectively and intersubjectively within an ongoing present in which time is shaped and reshaped. In this regard, a number of social scientists (Boje & Durant, 2006; Schütz, 1972) and philosophers (Bergson, 1913; Heidegger, 1996) bring us back to the importance of consciousness, intersubjectivity, and meaning making in which the non-linear heterogeneity of time is emphasised. Temporality takes centre stage in the way we make sense and give sense to an ongoing present through drawing on a past and future that are never fixed but open to continual reinterpretation as we reconfigure our place in the world, even as the study of people in organizations continually brings us back to the dominance of clock time in the shared, lived-through experience of work.

At the level of consciousness, Bergson (1913) draws our attention to the variability of time through our experiences of *durée* (duration); Heidegger (1996) through his concept of Dasein (being in the world) highlights mutually defining temporality in our awareness of our origin (birth) and the inevitability of our end (death)—this awareness infuses our being in the world; whilst Deleuze (1994) articulates the three modalities of time through the living present (habitual time), memorial time (memories of past experiences), and future time (the eternal return of difference). In examining the relationship between the objective and subjective, Schütz uses the notion of pre-predicative, pre-phenomenal time to capture Bergson's *durée* (the continuous flow of indistinct, unstructured, qualitative consciousness within our internal world) and predicative and phenomenal time, which are likened to attention to the external world in which we recompose and make multiple connections through reflective consciousness. Time and meaning are given to lived experience through our reflective gaze rather than meaning being an intrinsic feature of experience (Muzzetto, 2006: 10). In other words, in the inner world of *durée* consciousness flows with the flux of experience in which we remain unaware, and it is only when we turn our attention to those experiences and make them part of our reflective thinking that we provide meaning. The present also acquires meaning from our capacity to reflect on the consequences of our actions (a product of intentionality) in anticipation of the future. Schütz refers to the synthesis between the outer quantitative, spatialized time and inner qualitative time as being characterized by what he calls a 'vivid present', which is tied both to the future and the past. However he notes how the vivid present of our 'self' is inaccessible insofar as 'self-consciousness can only be experienced *modo praeterito*, in the past tense' (Schütz, 1962: 173). As Muzzetto (2005: 25) concludes,

> Time enters directly, constitutively, in the construction of meaning. Meaning is a function of lived-though time, which changes at every instant, and at every instant assumes a meaning different from any other, necessarily unique, and unrepeatable, Thus Schütz gives scientific substances to the existential principle of the uniqueness and unrepeatability of all human life. . . . The present is the time that plays a strategic role in the construction both of the reality of the everyday life-world and of the reality and identify of the Self. . . . It is in the *working*, hence in the present, that one experiences the external world and its resistance. It is

again in the present that the working Self experiences the unification of present, past and future.

This movement between objective (external) and subjective (internal) time is well illustrated in in our examination of narrative time and storytelling (Boje, 2008; Gabriel, 2000). In examining narratives with a clear BME, and protostories or antenarratives (a bet on the future), we compared and contrasted the linearity and coherence of modernist conceptions of narrative (Czarniawska, 1998; Gabriel, 2000) with the polyphony and unfinalized dynamic of storying in the here and now (Boje, 2001; Collins & Rainwater, 2005). Moving beyond a reflective gaze where the past is seen to provide a backcloth for understanding present experiences, stories that anticipated possible futures in prospective sensemaking were also identified. Although the temporal flow in structured narratives did not always align with a chronological sequence (a certain playfulness with time remained), the completed retrospective narratives comprised plots, characters, and event sequences that contrasted with the ongoing storying process among individual and groups around change initiatives that also sought to make and give sense prospectively. These stories in times of change are often highly political in seeking to influence the sensemaking of audiences in presenting compelling narratives that not only seek to make sense of change but also aim to shape the changes they are describing. Interestingly, the arrow of time embedded in narrative structures unravels in the storying during times of change where the past, present, and future are continuously reconfigured not as a neutral movement but as a highly political power-laden, contested process. There is an indeterminacy that goes beyond any attempts by management to plan and control that warrants political activity in processes of becoming to transform and revise a future that is yet to be—a narrative bending of time. As Hernes extrapolates on the flow of time and temporality,

> The flow of time gives rise to ordering attempts, which in turn give rise to organizations. This I believe, is a feature of the world in which we find ourselves, where an idea in one part of the world, a piece of regulation in another, technology in the third, production in the fourth, and finance in the fifth may come together momentarily and set in motion an assembly of events and elements, which precariously yet vigorously reproduces itself from a growing past which continually change for a different future. It is this sense of movement that traditional organization theory has withheld from organizational life. It is time to put it back where it belongs.
>
> (2014: X)

Hernes's interest rests on the way people carve out their temporal existence—in relation to a continually reconstituted present, past, and future—and how dispersed agencies interact in ways that generate agency and meaning. From this perspective, time as lived experience is far more complex, emergent, and dynamic than commonly represented in more positivistic studies. Change and becoming are central to our experience of reality in which succession of events, thoughts, and words all present possibilities for relationships between phenomena in temporal connections. These temporal relations encapsulate our conception and understanding of time, and this relational view is not cemented into clock time but open, free flowing, and contextual. There is no fixed order of events in our lived experience of time, only in the documented histories that use calendars and clocks to present a fixed chronology of events. Unlike the relativity of time in physics that describes the way objective clock time slows down when moving at speeds close to the speed of light, relational time is referring to the different ways in which people can simultaneously experience time within their subjective life-worlds. As such, time is not simply seen as a moment in the present, something that we all experience together; rather it is unique, temporal, and indeterminate. There is a difference in the way we use and interpret the past and project to the future in an ongoing, reconstituted present that is not separate but part of a larger temporal whole.

We contend that opening temporal boundaries offers opportunities for widening our understanding in the ways that we make sense of time, not as simply a time-reckoning system, or a chronological marker of sequenced events, but as stories of lived experience in which time is open, non-linear, and varied. In the movement between singular notions of time bounded by precise measures of intervals and linear temporality towards an understanding of multiple time concepts with merging temporalities, we become more aware not only of the importance of subjective time but also of the regulatory and power-laden use of objective measures that standardize, control, and coordinate our lives. The arrow of time is not fixed but open for change; there is flux and movement and opportunities for new possibilities of becoming, but these possibilities are contextual, temporal, and political, enabled and constrained by power-laden stories that tell us how life is.

Openings

In recapping on our own position, we do not see that there is any way forward in trying to resolve the paradox of time. On the contrary, we contend that any resolution of the paradox of time would present time as something other than it is (a representational whole captured by language that is aprocessual and ahistorical). Nevertheless, we do see value in engaging with time as a paradox (a paradox that warrants examination and discussion, not resolution). Likewise with temporality, in which combinations of the past, present, and future can be presented in a number of different ways (e.g., structured narratives provide illustrations of casual-temporal embeddedness), each can shed light on understanding processes of change in organizations. From our perspective, there is no one all-encompassing temporality but multiple temporalities, and whereas we propose a particular processual framework (outlined in the previous chapter), we maintain the need for further process developments in theorizing change.

The Paradox of Time's Temporalities

As we have argued throughout this book, time is not something open to our sense perception, nor is it a thing that can be fully conceptualized. We can talk of time as a dynamic compound concept, of multiple times and temporalities that merge, separate, and reconfigure, and we can link time with many scholastic endeavours including: scientific theories of the universe (e.g., space-time); with quantum theories and the existence and nonexistence of particles (e.g., quantum time); with contexts and cultures (e.g., social time); with realist, external, now moments (e.g., unreal time); with moments internal and heterogeneous (e.g., pure time duration); and with being and existence (e.g., primordial time). Yet time remains a conundrum, a puzzle that has challenged scholars throughout the ages, and although these debates have stimulated many ideas, concepts, and theories, they have not resolved the paradox of time. Whereas Elias (1993) refers to these endeavours as nothing but a wild goose chase, we contend that considerable knowledge and understanding has been achieved by the scientists, social scientists, and philosophers in the process of thought experiments, of critical reflection, of abstract theorizing, and on debates on the existence and nonexistence of time. There is also a great deal to be achieved from continuing scholarly attention to this unresolvable paradox, *time*.

In moving away from any resolution or closure, attention turns to openings and to expanding our understanding of time and temporality in revisiting organizational change theories and their development. In the case of science, we showed how Newton's concept of absolute time was challenged by Einstein's notion of relativity and how current developments in quantum mechanics are calling into question the applicability of this macro explanation of time and the universe at the microscopic level. In philosophy, we illustrated different aspects of subjective time in relation to, for example, Heidegger's (1996) sense of primordial time, Bergson's (1913) view of pure duration (extra-spatial time), and Deleuze's (1994) three modalities of time. All these approaches counter a more Kantian position on the illusion of time and highlight the importance of subjective, lived experience, consciousness, and temporality. We have consistently argued that there is no simple division or binary divide between objective and subjective time as the two intermix and intertwine, and yet, these generally remain separated with an emphasis on objective time in the purposeful management of work practices and the establishment of systems of control. We also suggest that whereas this dualism does not represent a constitution of reality, the concepts are useful in examining change interventions in organizations, especially in the imposition of control and new performance management systems based on clock time conceptions.

Institutionalized Time and the Privileging of Objective Time Over Subjective Time

Current conceptions of time that dominate are closely linked with the rise of commerce and new forms of work organization following industrialization (Rose, 1978). Time is money, and efficiency (as measured time) is the bastion of advanced capitalism. Whereas the subjective is degraded and relegated to the periphery, hard economic reality is seen to continually return attention to numbers, amounts, size of budgets, affordability, and efficiency. Time other than that which can be measured is of no economic concern; the narrative of chronological clock time dominates and pervades all aspects of life in Westernized capitalist economies. It becomes an economic variable of exchange value that is not to be wasted but to be used wisely—a time-coordinated society where clock time is used in attempts to control the present and the future and to regulate precisely a world where punctuality is extoled as a key virtue, a world where we experience time through digital smartphones, computers, clocks, and electronic diaries linked to emails and other devices and software developments. These representations of time in clocks cannot be ignored and are essential elements to the way we live and make sense of our lives, but they should not be seen to be time. To step out of these constraints requires us to not only recognise the subjective dimensions to time but also the constructed and imposed disciplinary time regimes that equate with something objective, real, and absolute. As such, the subjective qualities of time are no less important and, we would argue, an aspect that has been too easily overlooked by management and organization scholars.

Throughout our exposition of time we have highlighted how objective forms of time have been elevated and institutionalized and how the concepts of objective and subjective time are meaningful to others and can provide a useful lens for understanding workplace behaviours. However, they also draw attention to the privileging that has occurred with more positivistic, objective notions of time dominating theorization in the modelling of change. This privileging has resulted in an undue neglect of subjective time in studying processes of change in organizations. There is clearly a need to counter this bias, both in empirical fieldwork studies and in theorization and concept development. A central aim of this book has been to counterbalance this absence by bringing subjective time to the fore in our discussions of temporality and organizational change and to open up dialogues rather than impose any definitive view on time, temporality, and organizational change. For us, there is a temporality to human existence in which events going to be and being made are recalled as past events then are continually changing as new events going to be and being made became more pasts that differ in their place and configuration of processes of change that continue ad infinitum. To take licence from Bergson (2010: 82), we can only ever *practically* perceive the past as by the time our consciousness considers the present, it is already past but not in any isolated, dead sense as the past *gnaws* into the future in the present before it becomes lived experience.

Thus there is a need to go beyond this simple binary divide towards a more differential understanding of times and temporalities, but in so doing, we need to ensure that we do not lose sight of our focus on processes of change in organizations and consequently that we do not decontextualize time and present concepts that are apolitical and aprocessual. Time interweaves through our lives in society; is forever changing, heterogeneous, and multiple; and in our view, does not exist as something distinct and separate but is integral to being and existence. Thus, whilst we call for openings, we should be aware of the tendency for closure, to downplay subjectivities, and to focus on time as precisely measured intervals.

The Science and Social Science of Time

Unlike matter and our human engagement with physical objects, we cannot observe time. It is not a tactile substance; time remains out of reach even as we experience the very physical process of ageing. The perennial question returns: If we cannot see, hear, touch, or smell time, how can time be said to exist? This in turn takes us back to our opening chapter and the well-quoted confessions of St Augustine (2002). Yet as shown in earlier chapters, social time has strong representations in society through historical, cultural, and contextual developments in notions of time from the early links with nature and seasonal fluctuations in cycles of activities and events through to cultic beliefs and religious orders, to the enlightenment, non-secular explanations and the development of industry and commerce.

Ironically, whereas Newtonian time has become institutionalized in the Western world and is manifest in clock time and the Gregorian calendar that is a mainstay to a digitalized, networked, global, industrial world in which representational, objective time dominates, scientific time has moved beyond Newtonian conceptions of time and Einstein's relative notions of space-time. We not only need to draw on the work of philosophers (such as Bergson, 1913; Deleuze, 1994; Grosz, 2004; Heidegger, 1996) but also that of social scientists (e.g., Adam, 2004; Elias, 1993; Wajcman, 2008) in bringing time and temporality to the fore in our study and theorization on change. As Wajcman (2015: 3–4) points out, 'It is simply impossible to disentangle our notion of time from our embodied habitual involvement with the socio-material world. We make the world together with technology and so it is with time'.

Yet, there remains considerable debate around the notion of time as something absolute and external and the way time is experienced internally through human consciousness. Phenomenological approaches are concerned with time as experienced in which temporal flow is relative and ever changing and not something that can be conceptualized or standardized in absolute terms. Departure into human consciousness and being in existence takes us into philosophical debates in which subjectivities take precedence over any notion of an independent objective world, for example, as in Bergson's concept of durée as well as in the way experiences of time past and time yet to come can change contextually.

Even though conventional clock time is unable to deal with macro and micro extremes, in for example, explaining our observation of phenomena occurring light years away in which we need to introduce the concept of relative time, or in the quantum entanglement of particles in which time is more of an emergent, non-linear phenomenon, it remains central to the gravitational world of our everyday existence in which the normal laws of science hold sway. But debates on time and temporality continue, and whilst there is an interesting intertwining of ideas across the sciences and social sciences, for example, the current interest in quantum mechanics for organization studies (see Barad, 2007; Boje, 2012; Leonardi, 2013), time remains largely implicit in the use of these ideas for theory development, even within the change management literature, where studies that seek to provide explanations of movement and transition are derivative of concepts of time.

Taking a More Critical Stance Towards Time and Temporality

In developing a more critical stance towards time and temporality, we advocate making explicit the place of time in theory and concept development and to consider issues of temporal merging in the way that individuals and groups accommodate different conceptions of time in giving and making sense of their experiences of change in organizations (e.g., the interplay and interpenetration of objective/subjective time, chronological/kairotic time, external/internal awareness, and time consciousness). This suggests an extension of sensemaking as a backward glance (Weick, 1995), as a way in which through the interplay of action and interpretation, people make plausible sense retrospectively (Weick, Sutcliffe, & Obstfeld, 2005) to a process that also incorporates future perspectives and expectations (Wiebe, 2010). Whereas the divisional constructs that predominate reinforce a more clearly delineated, separatist world, we argue that through the interplay and coexistence of time conceptions and the way in which these are mutually constituted in everyday life, a useful starting point is to approach time as a multiple and compound concept whilst recognising the importance of divisions to underpinning time assumptions and explanations in organization studies. This enables accommodation of paradox (multiple and competing conceptions), enabling a more critical focus on those who use singular, reduced, and reified concepts in theoretical explanations, especially those that focus on objective dimensions of time in developing models that claim to master, control, and predict change. Even within frameworks that have been less prescriptive, attention is on either objective or subjective forms of time—with a predominant emphasis on clock time-based explanations that neglect relational and subjective aspects. There is therefore a need to counter this tendency in a more thorough examination of time in management research, and debates in organizational studies provide an ideal forum for such developments.

Note

1. Although Hawking (2011) originally extrapolated from this theory that once the universe started to collapse, the arrows of time would reverse, he has since reconsidered this position, agreeing that according to existing theories of quantum mechanics and relativity, there is no support for the notion that the universe would have to contract backwards in time (see discussion on Hawking's imaginary time in Chapter 2). Bending is possible (i.e., Einstein's theory of relativity through gravitational time dilation where there is a bending of space-time) but not reversing, as one cannot physically return to an early time in one's life. Hawking has further developed his thinking on time in working with Penrose (2011), arguing that all moments in time simultaneously coexist (see also the section on dualism in this chapter).

References

Adam, B. (2004). *Time*. Cambridge: Polity Press.
Augustine, A. (2002). *Confessions*. London: Penguin Books.
Barad, K. (2007). *Meeting the Universe Halfway: Quantum Physics and the Entanglement of Matter and Meaning*. London: Duke University Press.
Bergson, H. (1913). *Time and Free Will: An Essay on the Immediate Data of Consciousness*. London: George Allen & Company.
Bergson, H. (2010). *Matter and Memory* (N. Paul & W. Palmer, Trans.). Overland Park, Kansas: Digireads.com Publishing.
Boje, D. M. (2008). *Storytelling Organizations*. London: Sage.
Boje, D. M. (2012). Reflections: What does quantum physics of storytelling mean for change management? *Journal of Change Management, 12*(3), 253–271. doi: 10.1080/14697017.2011.609330
Boje, D. M., & Durant, R. A. (2006). Free stories! *TAMARA: Journal of Critical Postmodern Organization Science, 5*(3/4), 19–37. Retrieved from http://search.ebscohost.com/login.aspx?direct=true&db=buh&AN=24327334&site=bsi-live
Collins, D., & Rainwater, K. (2005). Managing change at sears: A sideways look at a tale of corporate transformation. *Journal of Organizational Change Management, 18*(1), 16–30. doi: 10.1108/09534810510579823. Retrieved from http://search.ebscohost.com/login.aspx?direct=true&db=buh&AN=16618736&site=bsi-live
Czarniawska, B. (1998). *A Narrative Approach to Organization Studies*. Thousand Oaks, CA: Sage.
Deleuze, G. (1994). *Difference and Repetition*. New York: Columbia University Press.
Durkheim, E. (1915). *Elementary Forms of Religious Life*. London: George Allen & Unwin.
Eddington, A. (1928). *The Nature of the Physical World*. Cambridge: Cambridge University Press.
Elias, N. (1993). *Time: An Essay*. Oxford: Blackwell Publishing.
Foucault, M. (1979). *Discipline and Punish: The Birth of the Prison*. Harmondsworth: Penguin.
Gabriel, Y. (2000). *Storytelling in Organizations: Facts, Fictions, and Fantasies*. Oxford: Oxford University Press.

Grosz, E. (2004). *The Nick of Time: Politics, Evolution, and the Untimely*. Durham: Duke University Press.

Hawking, S. (2011). *A Brief History of Time: From the Big Bang to Black Holes*. London: Bantam Books.

Heidegger, M. (1996). *Being and Time* (J. Stambaugh, Trans.). Albany, NY: State University of New York Press.

Hernes, T. (2014). *A Process Theory of Organization*. Oxford: Oxford University Press.

Jones, J. M., & Brown, W. T. (2005). Any time is Trinidad time! Cultural variations in the value and function of time. In A. Strathman & J. Joireman (Eds.), *Understanding Behavior in the Context of Time: Theory, Research and Application* (pp. 305–323). Hillsdale, NJ: Lawrence Erlbaum.

Leonardi, P. M. (2013). Theoretical foundations for the study of sociomateriality. *Information and Organization, 23*(1), 59–76.

Levine, R. V. (2006). *A Geography of Time: The Temporal Misadventures of a Social Psychologist or How Every Culture Keeps Time Just a Little Bit Differently*. Oxford: Oneworld Publications.

Marx, K. (1930). *Kapital* (4th ed.). London: Dent.

Muzzetto, L. (2006). Time and meaning in Alfred Schütz. *Time & Society, 15*(1), 5–31.

Penrose, R. (2011). *What Came Before the Big Bang? Cycles of Time*. London: Vintage Books.

Rose, M. (1978). *Industrial Behaviour: Theoretical Developments Since Taylor*. Harmondsworth: Penguin.

Schütz, A. (1962). Scheler's theory of intersubjectivity and the general thesis of the alter ego. In A. Schütz (Ed.), *Collected Papers* (pp. 150–179). The Hague: Martinus Nijhoff.

Schütz, A. (1972). *Phenomenology of the Social World*. Evanston, IL: Northwestern University Press.

Shutz, A. (1982). *Life Forms and Meaning Structure*. Boston: Routledge & Keegan Paul.

Wajcman, J. (2008). Life in the fast lane? Towards a sociology of technology and time. *The British Journal of Sociology, 59*(1), 59–77.

Wajcman, J. (2015). *Pressed for Time: The Acceleration of Life in Digital Capitalism*. London: University of Chicago Press.

Weick, K. E. (1995). *Sensemaking in Organizations*. Thousand Oaks, CA: Sage.

Weick, K. E., Sutcliffe, K., & Obstfeld, D. (2005). Organizing and the process of sensemaking. *Organization Science, 16*(4), 409–421.

Wiebe, E. (2010). Temporal sensemaking: Managers' use of time to frame organizational change. In T. Hernes & S. Maitlis (Eds.), *Process, Sensemaking and Organizing* (pp. 213–241). Oxford: Oxford University Press.

Willmott, H. (1995). The odd couple? Re-engineering business processes, managing human resources. *New Technology, Work and Employment, 10*(2), 89–98.

Zimbardo, P., & Boyd, J. (1999). Putting time in perspective: A valid, reliable individual-differences metric. *Journal of Personality and Social Psychology, 77*(6), 1271–1288.

Zimbardo, P., & Boyd, J. (2010). *The Time Paradox: Using the New Psychology of Time to Your Advantage*. London: Rider, Ebury Publishing.

Author Index

Subject Index

For Product Safety Concerns and Information please contact our EU
representative GPSR@taylorandfrancis.com
Taylor & Francis Verlag GmbH, Kaufingerstraße 24, 80331 München, Germany

www.ingramcontent.com/pod-product-compliance
Ingram Content Group UK Ltd.
Pitfield, Milton Keynes, MK11 3LW, UK
UKHW021607240425
457818UK00018B/426